GREGORY OF NAZIANZUS

Rhetor and Philosopher

D1259680

GREGORY
OF NAZIANZUS

Rhetor and Philosopher

———————

Rosemary Radford Ruether

Academic
RENEWAL PRESS
w w w . a r p r e s s . c o m

GREGORY OF NAZIANZUS

First Academic Renewal Press Edition 2003
Copyright © 2003 by
Academic Renewal Press

Library Of Congress Cataloging In Publication Data pending

ISBN 0-7880-9914-0   PRINTED IN U.S.A.

CONTENTS

INTRODUCTION

GREGORY OF NAZIANZUS, the least well known of the three Cappadocian Fathers, particularly in books written in English, is especially interesting as an exemplar of the fourth-century conflict between Christianity and classical culture. This study of Gregory as rhetor and philosopher discusses the roots of this conflict in the ancient rivalry between rhetoric and philosophy, and describes it in its transmuted form in Gregory's writings, where it is treated both biographically and systematically; biographically as a tension in Gregory's personal life, and systematically as two modalities of thought which form his mind and underlie his writings.

The clash between rhetoric and philosophy found its classical *locus* in Plato's criticism of the fifth-century sophists, and the terms of this original dispute continue to determine the relation of rhetoric and philosophy even when the conflict becomes transformed in the fourth-century Fathers into a broader *Kulturkampf*. As Werner Jaeger has shown, the fifth-century sophists were educators rather than speculative philosophers.[1] Their bold pedagogical claim was that they could teach *politikē aretē*, that they could impart the art of political leadership. Their *politikē technē*, as Protagoras calls it in Plato's dialogue,[2] was based on a new rationalization of prose style and argumentation. Although they did not originate either of these arts,[3] they did make formative contributions to the development of rhetoric with its analysis of tropes, figures of speech and thought, organization, and *topoi*, as well as to logic with its systematization of the types and methods of disputation.

[1] *Paideia* (New York, 1943) i. 286, 291.
[2] *Prt.* 315 C, 319 A.
[3] Gorgias' name was particularly associated with the development of prose rhythm and rhetorical figures; see C. A. Robertson, *The Gorgianic Figures in Early Greek Prose* (Baltimore, 1903). According to Aristotle, scientific rhetoric was first developed by the Sicilians Tisias and Corax (Cicero, *Brut.* 46), but Gorgias' rhetoric was most directly dependent on his teacher, Empedocles of Agrigentum: see H. I. Marrou, *A History of Education in Antiquity* (New York, 1956) 53 and notes. Protagoras' name was linked with eristic, which he developed from Eleatic dialectic (Marrou 51).

In addition to these formal tools of sophistic, the sophists also claimed to offer a liberal education, and to produce leaders of men able to speak and act in all situations. This claim was typified by Hippias of Elis, who declared his mastery not only of all knowledge, but even of all arts and crafts.[1] Thus, from the outset, sophistic wished to be more than a set of techniques for successful litigation. It aspired to be a universal *paideia* embracing the whole man.[2]

It was Plato who issued the fundamental challenge to these new educators of Greece, and his dialogues, especially *Gorgias* and *Protagoras*, remain the essential source for the philosophic refutation of the pedagogical claims of rhetoric. Plato's polemic against sophistic is closely linked to his metaphysical dualism of being and appearance. This ontological dualism gives rise to the epistemological dualism of knowledge (*epistēmē*) and opinion (*doxa*). True knowledge is obtained through dialectic, and requires a rigorous *askēsis* of mental and moral purification, leading finally to an intuitive grasp of the Ideas which transcends discursive reason.[3] Sophistic, on the other hand, is a vulgar trading on the opinions of the mob. The sophistic teachers lack any basis for their teaching in the true perception of knowledge, but they gather up the notions of the masses and from these fashion a pseudo-art of power and political advantage. They have no *technē*, but only a 'knack' of argumentation. Sophistry and rhetoric are analogous to pastry-making and cosmetics, for they are counterfeits of the true arts of the soul, statesmanship and justice, as pastry-making and cosmetics are the counterfeits of the bodily arts of medicine and gymnastic.[4]

Isocrates undertook the defence of rhetorical *paideia* against these criticisms. In his teaching rhetoric assumes the proportions of a universal culture, comprising all the arts of civilization.[5] The word 'sophist' originally meant simply 'wise man', and, as

---

[1] Plato, *Hippias Minor* 368 B, C.   [2] Marrou, op. cit. 54–7.

[3] In the *Seventh Letter* Plato particularly discusses the deficiencies of all discursive language in expressing truth, since all language belongs to the world of appearance and partakes of the distorting defects of the image. True knowledge requires *katharsis* or purification, by which the soul becomes akin to truth, without which truth cannot implant itself in the soul. Then, after a long process of dialectical discourse between teacher and pupil, the mind is suddenly illuminated by the spark of intuitive understanding (343 A–344 B).

[4] *Gorgias* 462 B.

[5] See particularly his 'hymn to Logos' as the creatrix of culture in *Nicocles* 5–9.

such, was the common designation for the pre-Socratic thinkers.[1]
Plato developed the polemical use of the word, and, in his
Against the Sophists, Isocrates turns this pejorative usage against
Plato himself, using 'sophist' for the dialecticians, i.e. Socratics,
while 'philosophy' is reserved for the rhetorical culture of
Isocrates' school.[2]

For Isocrates the orator is the successor of the poet and the
rhapsode as the prophet of *politikē aretē*. Isocrates rejects Plato's
epistemological antithesis of rhetoric and dialectic. Absolute
knowledge of the type Plato claimed as the goal of dialectic is
beyond the capacities of mortal men. In pursuing such knowledge the 'disputers' pursue a phantom and their results are useless to the community.[3] Opinion is the highest knowledge
available to men, and rhetorical training is practical and valu-
able in the *polis* precisely because it is based on *doxa*. Rhetorical
knowledge is empirical in nature. It is derived from the study of
history and politics as they actually operate, and thereby the
teacher of *politikē aretē* draws the practical insights which are
genuinely useful to the guidance of human conduct. Not baseless
opinion but 'right opinion', empirically deduced and verified;
this is Isocrates' answer to Plato's attack on the epistemological
basis of rhetorical culture.[4]

Actually Isocrates rather than Plato became the educator of
the ancient world, although Plato was to exact an account-
ing at the end. In Marrou's words, 'it was from Isocrates that,
"as from a Trojan horse",[5] there emerged all those teachers
and men of culture, noble idealists, simple moralists, lovers of
fine phrases, all those fluent, voluble speakers, to whom classical

---

[1] The words 'rhetor' and 'sophist' have a complicated history. By the fifth century B.C. 'sophist' tended to become restricted to the travelling teacher, while
'rhetor' had the broad sense of 'statesman'. In Hellenistic times the two words
acquired the limited sense of school teachers. The Second Sophistic orators revived
the broader meaning of 'sophist' as a thinker imparting an encyclopedic education
and claimed to be the descendants of the old sophists. Yet by Libanius' time the two
words had become very restricted, and often meant no more than two professorial
levels within the schools, the 'sophist' being a master rhetorician, and the 'rhetor'
his assistant who taught *technai*; see J. W. H. Walden, *The Universities of Ancient
Greece* (New York, 1910) 75 and n. 1, 271 and n. 1.
[2] See also *Antid.* 270. At this time 'philosophy' still meant 'culture' in general,
making Isocrates' claim to teach 'philosophy' more explicable; see F. Blass, *Die
Attische Beredsamkeit* (Leipzig, 1892) 28.
[3] *Hel.* 5; also *Soph.* 17.   [4] Jaeger, *Paideia* iii. 46–70.
[5] Cic. *De Or.* ii. 94.

antiquity owed both the qualities and defects of its main cultural tradition'.[1] Isocrates not only formulated rhetoric's ideals, he also set what was to prove its foremost theme, the glorification of Hellenism.[2] When he called for the unification of Greece for the conquest of the barbarians, he was setting both a political and a cultural programme. The political programme, realized by Alexander, was to be absorbed into the greater achievement of Rome, while the cultural programme provided the common culture upon which Rome was able to build a world empire.

The vehicle by which Hellenic culture became the universal medium of a far-flung empire was rhetoric. With the disappearance of the free city state, much of the opportunity for political oratory was lost, and rhetoric retired to the classroom, where its task became that of transmitting a literary tradition. It was at this time that the educational system took shape that was to be standard for the rest of the classical world, adopted almost unchanged by the Roman conquerors.[3] This system of education consisted of the primary school, which taught reading and writing, and the secondary school, which concentrated on reading, recitation, and *explication de texte* of the classic authors. The *grammaticus* assumed some of the preparatory work for the study of rhetoric, and we have several examples of *progymnasmata* which give us a vivid picture of the literary stock-in-trade of the schoolboy of antiquity.[4]

The school of the rhetor was the crown of this literary education. Here the student practised declamation in written or oral form. He studied the *technai* or rhetorical handbooks,[5] collections

[1] Marrou, op. cit. 79.
[2] See Jaeger, 'Political Culture and the Panhellenic Ideal', *Paideia* iii. 71–83.
[3] Marrou, op. cit. 150–76 and 265–92.
[4] Hermogenes' *Progymnasmata* from the second century A.D. and Aphthonius' work from the fourth century A.D., for example. Both works are found in H. Rabe, *Rhetores Graeci*, and a translation of Aphthonius by Ray Nadeau appears in *Speech Monographs* 19 (1952), 264 ff. The standard exercises were: a fable, a tale, a *chreia*, a proverb, a refutation, a confirmation, a commonplace, an encomium, an invective, a comparison, a characterization, an ecphrasis, a thesis, and a proposal for a law, arranged in increasing order of difficulty with rules and topics for the development of each exercise. Aphthonius' work is the more useful, as he furnishes illustrative examples. This system of exercises originated about the second century B.C.; see Barwick, *Hermes* 63 (1928), 283.
[5] Typical of such handbooks are Anaximenes' *Rhetorica ad Alexandrum* (fourth century B.C.) and the Latin treatise, *Rhetorica ad Herennium* (first century B.C.).

of commonplaces, and model introductions and conclusions.[1]
He also studied and did imitations of model speeches and
stylists of the past, as well as the orations of the rhetor himself.
Finally the student gave his own declamations, and so en-
amoured were the ancients of this exercise that grown men continued to declaim before audiences into old age, and crowds
of the educated public attended upon the open orations of
renowned rhetors.[2]

It was here in the school system that we have the tap-root
of classicism; that is, the transmission of a canon of authors
from Homer to the Attic writers of the fourth century, whose
works were seen as the incarnation of the Hellenic heritage. This
standardization of the classic authors, whose works were taught
to generation after generation of students, is the key to that
uniformity of cultural and intellectual formation of all peoples
brought within the orbit of Hellenistic culture. Only in the context of this school system can we understand how men of Sardes,
Gaza, Gaul, Egypt, and Africa could write and think in much
the same way and all share with the same cultural heritage.

During the last century of the Roman Republic, rhetoric once
more enjoyed a direct role in law and politics, and in Cicero's
De Oratore, *Orator*, and *Brutus* the Isocratean ideal of the philosophic orator is revived and translated into Roman terms. But
rhetoric once more became the province of the schoolmaster
with the fading of republican institutions. This loss of direct
contact with the forum is often seen by historians of rhetoric as
the cause of the sterility and pedantry of imperial oratory.[3] The

Cicero's *De Inventione* treats only the first topic of the *technē*, the gathering and organization of ideas and arguments. Quintilian's *Institutio Oratoria* is a highly
elaborated *technē* enlarged into a philosophy of the ideal orator.

[1] Gorgias and the other early sophists composed such books of commonplaces;
see G. Kennedy, *The Art of Persuasion in Greece* (Princeton, 1963) 54 ff. The handbook of the Roman Valerius Maximus (first century A.D.), *Facta ac Dicta Memora-
bilia*, is an example of 'quotable quotes' for the orator. For a collection of model
introductions for deliberative speeches see A. Rupprecht, 'Die demosthenische
Prooemiumsammlung', *Philologus* 82 (1927), 365 ff.

[2] The letters of the younger Pliny are full of such pursuits and give us a picture
of the gentleman of the second century A.D. who continued to study the poets and
orators and do literary exercises and imitations long after his formal schooldays
were over; see, for example, *Ep.* 7, 9. In *Ep.* 7, 17 Pliny defends his passion for
public recitation of his own speeches as a means of perfecting his style.

[3] This is Tacitus' argument in *Dialogus*, repeated in numerous modern writers,
e.g. D. L. Clark, *Rhetoric in Greco-Roman Education* (New York, 1957) 258–9.

rhetorical schools appear to provide an enormously long and intensive training with limited utility. We would mistake its purpose, therefore, if we did not realize that its essential function was that of a leisure culture, rather than a vocational training. It was in this cultural role that rhetoric enjoyed a renaissance in the second and fourth centuries of the Empire. This movement, known as Second Sophistic, is marked more by the position which the sophist occupied in society than by any new stylistic developments.[1] The history of Second Sophistic falls into two periods: first, from the mid first to the early third centuries with such representatives as Dio Chrysostom, Nicostratus, Polemo, Herodes Atticus, the Philostrati, and Aelius Aristides; and the second, from about 330 to 390 A.D., with Libanius, Themistius, Eunapius, Prohaeresius, and Himerius, as well as their Christian offspring, Basil the Great, Gregory of Nazianzus, Gregory of Nyssa, and John Chrysostom.

The Greek cities of Asia Minor had a continuous tradition of rhetorical schools going back to the early Hellenistic period. These schools were, in large part, the source of the revival. The cultivation of eloquence was also favoured by the general prosperity of the second century and the survival of Greek city-state institutions, which gave the orator some opportunity for public activity. However, the sophists were essentially professors of literary style, and imperial sophistic did not revive the full Isocratean ideal of rhetoric as a universal culture so much as put forth a strictly rhetorical education as sufficient for all occasions and careers.[2] The key to this revival was imperial patronage of

[1] The stylistic ancestry of Second Sophistic, whether 'Attic' or 'Asian', has been much debated. Rohde, *Der griechische Roman*, ch. 3, and again in 'Die Asianische Rhetorik und die Zweite Sophistik', *Rh. Mus.* 41 (1886), 170 ff., saw it as a continuation of Asianism, while Kaibel, 'Dionysios von Halicarnassus und die Sophistik', *Hermes* 20 (1885), 497 ff., argued for its 'Attic' character. A. Boulanger, *Aelius Aristide et la sophistique dans la province d'Asie au IIᵉ siècle de notre ère* sums up the arguments on this subject, and shows that, far from representing a single style, the mantle of Second Sophistic covered an assemblage of all the styles since the time of Gorgias and Thrasymachus. All 'atticize' in the sense that they write a strict literary language provided by a canon of authors, but among these there are many tendencies to choose between. All imperial sophists exhibit 'asian' or mannerist traits as well; all are virtuosos of language who are addicted to artificial modes of expression and enhance their language with poetic words, excessive use of tropes and figures, and rhythms that tend to fall over into metre.

[2] See E. Rohde's article in *Rheinisches Museum* (above, n. 1). Rohde in this article replied to Kaibel who, in his 'Dionysios von Halicarnassus und die

schools and teachers. It now became one of the emperor's chief
concerns to oversee the national education and the maintenance
of the cultural traditions as an essential pillar of imperial
strength and coherence. To that end the Flavian and Antonine
emperors issued a series of edicts establishing public chairs of
sophistic and grammar in all cities and towns of any size.[1]

Rhetoric thus continued its ancient task of teaching *politikē
aretē*. If the orator was no longer the statesman, he still celebrated
the statesman, and in its very cultural role rhetoric possessed a
prime political significance. In his provocative book, *Christianity
and Classical Culture*, C. N. Cochrane traces the search for an in-
tegrating ideal of society which would hold the Empire together
as a coherent civilization, a search which led to the Constan-
tinian compromise with Christianity and finally to Theodosius'
full capitulation.[2] But, remarkably enough, Cochrane pays
almost no attention to sophistic. Yet sophistic may well be seen
as the only other alternative to Christianity as a unifying
Weltanschauung for the tottering Empire. It was as such that
sophistic was the object of such imperial solicitude. With Constantine the Empire turned to the Church for added strength,
but tried not to choose between the two cultures. Yet the two
were unable to live side by side, for each was a complete creed
which demanded the devotion of the whole man. Thus, under
the Emperor Julian, the 'Hellenes'[3] staged their counter-
reformation. When orthodoxy triumphed under Theodosius,
imperial patronage was quickly withdrawn from the schools,
and the adherents of the old ways soon found themselves a pro-
scribed sect.

When Gregory of Nazianzus was a student in Athens, sophistry was in its last florescence. His return to Cappadocia coincided
with Julian's effort to turn back the clock, while Gregory's
episcopacy in Constantinople was climaxed by Theodosius'
triumphant establishment of orthodoxy as the official creed of
the Empire. Thus Gregory's life paralleled the decisive transitional period between the Roman and the Byzantine empires.

Sophistik' had argued that Second Sophistic did revive the Isocratean ideal of
the philosophic orator.   [1] Walden, *Universities* 89 ff.
    [2] See especially chs. 5 and 8.
    [3] Under imperial sophistic 'Hellene' became a technical term for the students of
rhetoric in the schools, so closely was Hellenism linked with rhetoric; see Philostr.
VS 571 and 613.

For a brief period during his lifetime Christians and Classicists
stood on equal terms, each arguing their own case.[1]

In this confrontation the rivals restated in a new form and
context the old dispute between rhetoric and philosophy.[2] The
relationship between these ancient foes constituted a continual
dialectical tension throughout classical culture. This dialectic
was one of constant mutual assimilation and yet constant diastasis. Rhetoric could shrink into a narrow set of stylistic tricks,
and it could open into a broad humanism of general culture and
political virtue. Philosophy could be understood as the teaching
of a set of doctrines of the traditional philosophic schools; it
could move into close assimilation with rhetorical humanism
until, in figures like Dio Chrysostom and Themistius, it is difficult
to draw the line between philosopher and sophist, or it could
separate out into a radical ascetic moralism and mysticism
which defined itself sharply against the whole humanistic tradition represented by rhetoric. It was this latter strain in the philosophic tradition that led into the version of the *bios philosophikos*
which fourth-century Christians had come to identify with
Christianity.

The story of this process of mutual assimilation and conflict
between rhetoric and philosophy is one that embraces the
whole of ancient civilization, and only a brief elucidation can
be attempted here. Rhetoric and philosophy after Plato and
Isocrates continued as two rival school traditions each disputing
with the other (and among themselves) for the mastery of the
educational system.[3] Since each type of education saw itself as

[1] Themistius is an example of this brief moment of equality. He enjoyed the
favours of the Christian emperors, Constantius II, Jovian, Valens, and even
Theodosius, and in the court at Constantinople used his position to plead continually for toleration for the old religion and ways. In his orations we find the cul-
minative defence of the old culture. Philosophy and rhetoric are merged into an
ideal of general culture, and this, imparted through the traditional Hellenic
education, Themistius argued, would be the best *paideia* for uplifting and unifying
the Empire. See Glanville Downey, 'Education and Public Problems', *T.A.P.A.* 86
(1955), 291–307.

[2] Jaeger has summarized this dispute as the fundamental conflict between the
anthropocentric and the theocentric view of man, and, as such, Christianity and
humanism restate the old conflict between the Protagorean view that 'man is the
measure' and the Platonic view that 'God is the measure' (*Leg.* 716 c); see *Humanism and Theology* (Marquette, 1943) 38 ff.

[3] For the most complete account of this pedagogical rivalry, see 'Sophistik,
Rhetorik, Philosophie, in ihrem Kampf um die Jugendbildung' in the Introduction
to H. von Arnim's *Leben und Werke des Dio von Prusa* (Berlin, 1898) 1–114.

a total *paideia*, neither could define itself as a specialty, but each claimed the best of the other as merely a branch of its own discipline. In the *Republic* Plato had subsumed the traditional Hellenic education in a purified form as *propaedeia* for philosophy, and, in Plato's old age, Aristotle taught rhetoric in the Academy.[1] For the Stoics rhetoric was an integral part of logic, the first of the three branches of philosophy.[2] The Cynics alone spurned rhetoric altogether, for even Epicureanism, which was normally uninterested in rhetoric, made its contribution in the work of Philodemus. The Peripatetics, following Aristotle, always had considerable interest in rhetoric and literary criticism,[3] while the eclectic Academy of Cicero's time made rhetoric and rules of style and disputation an integral part of its teaching.[4]

The rhetoricians, in turn, borrowed philosophic themes, particularly in the fields of ethics and psychology, and included them as a part of *inventio*, and the *thetika*, or discourse on philosophic themes, became a regular part of the orator's repertoire.[5] In a celebrated debate with the rhetor Hermagoras, Posidonius tried to hold the line against this encroachment, and insisted that rhetors could debate only specific cases (hypotheses), while general ideas (theses) were the domain of the philosopher.[6] But rhetoric was not to be so limited, and the thesis became one of the standard exercises of the *progymnasmata*.[7] A certain amount of philosophy came to be considered a part of the *enkuklios paideia* and was included in the syllabuses of the *ephēbeia*.[8] Moreover, sophistic culture was such an all-pervading ethos that the teaching of philosophy in the philosophic schools took colour from it.

[1] For the tradition of Aristotle's teaching of rhetoric in the Academy, see Jaeger, *Paideia* iii. 147 and 320, n. 108.

[2] The other two being physics and ethics.

[3] For Peripatetic contributions to rhetoric and literary criticism in the Hellenistic period, see G. Kennedy, *The Art of Persuasion in Greece* 273–90.

[4] *De Or.* iii. 80; Kennedy (op. cit. 321–30) has an excellent section on the dispute between philosophers and rhetoricians in the generation prior to Cicero as the source of the arguments about rhetoric and philosophy and the ideal orator in *De Oratore*. In this period it was actually the philosophic schools that taught rhetoric as an eloquence springing from a broad culture, while the rhetoricians tended to take a narrow technical view of their art.

[5] See Walden, *Universities* 72 n., 223 n.

[6] For the argument about theses between philosophers and rhetors, see H. von Arnim, *Dio von Prusa* 93–6.

[7] Above, p. 4, n. 4.   [8] Marrou, *Education in Antiquity* 108, 211.

The philosopher expounded the works of his tradition as the rhetors did their canon of authors, and he even declaimed to the public as did the rhetors.[1]

Despite these tendencies of assimilation, philosophy continued to imply a break with the standard aesthetic education and a conversion to another way of life. It is significant that the conversion to philosophy was often seen as a conversion from rhetoric. One need only mention the case of Marcus Aurelius, whose conversion to philosophy was simultaneously a conversion from rhetoric, much to the chagrin of his teacher, Fronto, who had laboured so hard to make a brilliant orator of his promising student.[2]

The philosopher's conversion was symbolized by the *tribōn*, the coarse, dark cloak later adopted by the Christian monk. In Cynicism the rejection of normal social *mores* was developed in its most radical form. The sage became the philosophic outcast. Freeing himself from all dependence on the social and economic system, he strove for *autarkeia* or self-sufficiency. His boldness of speech (*parrhēsia*) and shamelessness (*anaideia*) testified to his freedom from the shams of society and to his life according to nature (*physis*). In his *askēsis* the Cynic inured himself to hardship, so that, having reduced his wants to the bare necessities, he might never desire what he could not obtain.

In Stoicism and Cynicism, the goal of conversion and asceticism is freedom. The external world is seen as an impersonal order beyond human control. Freedom is found in detachment (*apatheia*). Man cannot control destiny, but he can control his relation to destiny. By loosening the bonds of either hope or fear which tie him to the course of events, he can be free and tranquil within.

Although the Stoic sage might continue to operate on the political stage, the gospel of salvation through *apatheia* implied non-involvement and withdrawal from the political community

---

[1] Marrou, *Education in Antiquity* 208, 212.

[2] For many years the correspondence of the prince and his teacher was filled with rhetorical shop-talk. Letters 108 (Naber 75) and 175 (Naber 113) signal Marcus' break with rhetoric. In his *Meditations* the Emperor dismisses rhetoric with the words 'I owe it to Rusticus [his Stoic preceptor] that I formed the idea of the need for moral reformation, and that I was not devoted to literary ambition or to write treatises on philosophical subjects or make rhetorical exhortations . . . and that I kept away from rhetoric and poetry and frippery of speech' (i. 7).

as well.[1] Hellenic thought had assumed that life in the *polis* was the essential arena of human fulfilment. A philosophy of conversion and detachment of the individual from the community, therefore, struck at the heart of the old understanding of *aretē*. The antithesis between philosophic salvation and political action was already expressed in Plato, although he struggled all his life to find a synthesis between the two. Yet, even for Plato, the reconciliation of philosophy and political action fled into the ideal community of the philosopher's imagination, and in the real world of fourth-century politics the contemplative man was fast becoming the apolitical man.[2] In the *Theaetetus* philosophy is defined as the life that flees the agora and the dicastery, which is ignorant of and indifferent to all political matters, and which, in solitude, contemplates the eternal cosmos.[3]

These two tendencies of antipathy towards aesthetic culture and apathy towards political action, when reinforced by ethical and metaphysical dualism, give later Greek philosophy an increasingly ascetic and mystical cast. Man is seen as an antithetical diarchy of soul and body; his true ruling principle being his soul, and his body an alien and hostile encasement.[4] This anthropological dualism corresponds to the ontological dualism of matter and spirit, sensible and intelligible, visible and invisible. In the eclectic philosophy of the Empire as well as in the developing Christian theology, this dualism has become standard. Thus Stoicism, originally based on the pre-Socratic hylozoism of Heraclitus, by the time of Seneca, Epictetus, and Marcus Aurelius has come to speak a dualistic and even otherworldly language.[5]

The original mythological expression of this anthropological dualism is found in the idea of the soul's previous existence in the celestial regions, its fall into matter through some mistake or

[1] Epictetus' discourse 'on those who have spent their energies on advancement in Rome' (i. 10) is typical of the tendency to despise the life of political action and contrast it with that of philosophic tranquillity, which alone is of real value.

[2] See W. Jaeger, 'On the Origin and Cycle of the Philosophic Life', *Aristotle* (Oxford, 1948) 426–61; also R. Joly, *Le Thème philosophique des genres de vie dans l'antiquité classique* (Bruxelles, 1956) 69–105.   [3] *Theaetetus* 173.

[4] For the classical pun on the words *sōma* and *sēma*, expressing the equation of the body with the tomb, see Philolaus, frg. 14 (Diels); also Plato, *Crat.* 400 B, C.

[5] See, for example, Seneca's *Epistle* 102. 26, where he draws a sharp contrast between body and soul, and expresses a longing for the liberation of the soul from the bonds of the body, praising death as the beginning of true life.

fault, and its return through the heavenly spheres at death to its true home.[1] Death then becomes the entrance to true life, the discarding of the unnatural body, and a return to the soul's proper disincarnate state. This myth had already travelled to Greece in the sixth century, and, in the form of Orphism, influenced Plato's myth of the soul.[2] This saga of the soul and the *Weltanschauung* which it implied arose with new vigour under the Empire, and found its most radical expression in gnosticism, where the dualism between the sensible and the intelligible, the material and the spiritual, became a complete alienation.[3]

For the Platonist the sensible was opposed to the intelligible only in a relative way. Appearance was still appearance of the intelligible. The cosmos still reflected the divine; it is the image of the intelligible universe and can itself be spoken of as a visible god. Gnosticism split apart the foundation of classical cosmos piety. This world does not proceed from true being. It is not the creation of God, but it is the result of some error or fault, and is ruled by evil and daemonic forces.[4] Only man's inner core of being, his spirit, contains sparks of the world of 'light', the world of true being. These sparks are the remnants of truth entrapped in the daemonic cosmos which struggle to be released and return to their transcendental home. Not only man's body but his psyche as well are the work of the alien principle, and salvation is to be found in the negation of these along with the rest of 'this world'.

Asceticism in the sense of 'mortification' becomes the way of salvation. Already, in Plato's *Phaedo*, philosophy had been

[1] The origin of this myth of the soul probably is to be found in Chaldean astral religion; see F. Cumont, *Afterlife in Roman Paganism* (New York, 1956) 95.

[2] Plato's teachings on the pre-existence and incarnation of the soul are in *Phaedrus* 247–9 and *Timaeus* 41–2. In the former, incarnation is seen as a fall due to pre-incarnational fault, while, in the latter, it is seen as a natural pedagogy by which the soul 'that lives well during his appointed time, returns and dwells in his native star and there has a blessed and congenial existence'.

[3] According to Hans Jonas, gnosticism, far from being 'radical Hellenism', as Harnack had said, arose from the submerged oriental intelligentsia of the eastern Empire, and, in its acosmism, represented a fundamental assault upon the Hellenic world view; *The Gnostic Religion* (Boston, 1958) 21–7, and 241–4.

[4] It was from gnosticism that Hellenistic Judaism and Christianity learned to use words like 'demon' and 'Demiurge' (which in Hellenic philosophy meant divine agents) for agents of evil. In the gnostic re-evaluation, *ho kosmos* becomes 'this world'; i.e. this alien world that imprisons us and keeps us from our true home. In speaking of the devil as 'the Prince of this world', Christianity reflected the gnostic acosmism; cf. the Gospel of John 12. 31, 16. 11.

described as the 'practice of dying', and the philosopher's *askēsis* defined as the separation of the soul from the body and all material things in anticipation and preparation for the final separation of the soul from its alien encumbrance.[1] Yet Plato was too much a Hellene to be oblivious to the beauty of the outward form, and for him the visible form remained a stepping-stone to the invisible form. But in gnosticism these teachings are carried through to a full re-evaluation of classical concepts of *aretē*. Virtue can no longer consist in the perfection of man's natural powers. These are the instruments of the evil one. Nature can no longer set any guides to morality. All the norms of *physis* and *nomos*, nature and convention, also belong to the alien power. The result is either an extreme antinomian and libertine ethic or else extreme asceticism. Both are ways of repudiating man's allegiance to nature; in the one case through abuse, and in the other through non-use of natural faculties.

Both Christianity and Hellenism rejected gnostic acosmism. To Christianity, it was incompatible with Biblical creationism, and, to the classical philosopher, it affronted his sense of the cosmos as an emanation from and imitation of the divine, intelligible world.[2] Yet the gnostic world view permeated late antique thought, both Christian and pagan. The doctrine of man as a sojourner in an alien universe whose true home is 'above', whose life in this world should be one of mortification in preparation for death and the return of the soul from whence it came, all this was common property for both Christian and Platonist.

The great Hellenistic metropolis of Alexandria was the melting-pot for all current religious and philosophic ideas. There the religious traditions of the old oriental world, of Judaism, Christianity, and Greek philosophy met and mingled. Philo, Origen, and Plotinus represent the Jewish, Christian, and Platonic versions of this Graeco-oriental synthesis. For Philo, Scripture has become an allegory of Platonic mystical philosophy,[3] and the Old Testament so many symbolic stories of the

---

[1] *Phaedo* 64; also *Phaedrus* 66.
[2] It was Plotinus who stated the Platonist's rejection of gnostic acosmism; *Enn.* 2. 9.
[3] In *De Vita Contemplativa* Philo describes the Therapeutae studying Scripture as an allegory of philosophy, and says that the words of the text act as a 'reminder' leading them from the outer and visible to the inward and hidden truths of the soul (78, also 29).

flight of the soul from the body, the passions, and the material
world, its ascetic purification and discipline, and finally its mystical illumination and experience of the divine.[1]

Origen, building upon Philo, brought together Platonic and
gnostic thought with the Old and New Testaments to create
Christianity's first systematic theology. In his *De Principiis* the
world is seen as a vast pedagogical drama in which the *logikai*,
or spiritual beings of the original creation, having fallen into
materiality through abuse of free will, struggle to overcome the
effects of the fall and return to their pristine state of incor-
poreality and perfect adherence to God.[2]

Along with this rise of syncretic ascetical and mystical philosophy in the eastern Empire, one finds the rise of communities
devoted to living some version of this 'philosophy'. In his *De
Vita Contemplativa* Philo describes such a community of Egyptian
Jews in the first century A.D. He declares that such groups
devoted to ascetic practices, contemplation, and communal
worship were not uncommon in his time, especially in Egypt.[3]
Gnostics also had their ascetic communities, and probably
similar groups stood behind the eclectic philosophic treatises of
the *Corpus Hermeticum*.[4] By the end of the third century Christian
monasticism began as a distinct movement. Ascetic tendencies
had existed within Christianity from the beginning, but it was
only when the ascetic separated himself from the local church
and lived a life apart, either singly or in groups, that one can
speak of monasticism. The first such anchorites and cenobites
appear among the *fellahin* of Egypt, a group virtually untouched
by Greek ideas. Their asceticism was not that of philosophical
dualism, but welled up from popular daemonology.[5] The old
hermit of the Antonian type might live many years in the desert

[1] For a discussion of the 'Philonic mystery' see E. Goodenough, *By Light, Light;
the Gospel of Mystic Judaism* (New Haven, 1935), esp. 235–65.

[2] Jaeger has a brief but illuminating discussion of Origen's adaptation of
classical *paideia*: *Early Christianity and Greek Paideia* (Cambridge, Mars., 1961) 46–67.

[3] *De Vita Contemplativa* 21.

[4] A. D. Nock and A. J. Festugière, *Corpus Hermeticum* (Paris, 1945) i. 1–53.

[5] Basic sources for this non-hellenized monasticism are Athanasius' *Vita Antonii*
and the *Apophthegmata Patrum*, compiled in Greek about the fifth century, but based
on an oral Coptic tradition: see J. Quasten, *Patrology* (Utrecht, 1960) iii. 187. Here
the monk's *askēsis* is the battle with the daemons rather than the battle against the
body, although it was not hard to fuse the one into the other, especially with
the gnosticizing tendency to see the body as the work of the daemons and hence
the seat of their influence.

in solitude, but when his reputation as an adept went abroad, novices flocked to him and settled around his cave, looking to him as their spiritual master. In this way a loose organization grew up, based on the personal relationship of the novice and his *Abba*. These forms of monastic life were regularized in the formal cenobite community by Pachomius, who created the first 'rule'. However, eremitism did not die out but continued to flourish in Eastern Christianity and even to be looked upon as the more strictly 'contemplative' life in contrast to the more 'practical' communal monasticism.[1]

This primitive Christian monasticism was unspeculative and even anti-cultural, but, as the movement spread to the hellenized Christians of Egypt, its meaning was inevitably interpreted along the lines of the syncretic platonizing theology that had already developed. The Cappadocians were the disciples of these Origenist monks of Egypt and the Near East. Basil particularly studied Egyptian and Palestinian monastic life closely and transmitted it to the Church as a whole in a form that it could integrate with its own developing theology. Basil, as theologian and *nomothetēs*, and Gregory of Nyssa, as mystical philosopher, therefore, bequeathed to the Christian tradition in a matured form both the speculative and the social framework for the expression of '*nostra philosophia*'. In their hands the fusion of Christianity with monasticism and Platonic spirituality becomes complete. For them it is axiomatic to describe Christianity in terms of monastic life, and, in turn, to describe monastic life in a language derived from Alexandrian Platonism. Thus, by their time, the equation of Christian with monk and monk with philosopher was widely accepted.[2]

Fourth-century Christianity thus assumed both the dress and

---

[1] Thus Gregory can speak of the hermit as living the theoretic life as opposed to the practical life of the cenobite (see below, p. 139). Interestingly enough, Philo uses the same terminology for the Therapeutae as a community devoted to *theoria* or contemplation as opposed to the *praktikos* or active life of Essenes (*V. Contemp.* 1).

[2] Gregory of Nazianzus and Gregory of Nyssa habitually refer to the ascetic life as the 'philosophic life' and the monk as the 'philosopher'. The same terminology is found in Basil, even though he often eschews philosophic for Biblical language. Thus, at the opening of his second *sermo asceticus* (*P.G.* 31. 891), he says, 'it therefore behooves those undertaking the ascetical life to enter upon the way of philosophy, stripped of all worldly and material things, in the same manner as they who enter the bath take off all their clothing.' The same equation of philosopher and ascetic is found in other contemporary Christian writers, for example Eusebius, *H.E.* 6. 3. 9–12, and *Dem. Ev.* 3. 6, and Sozomen 6. 33.

the language of the Greek philosopher. It was in this form that men like Gregory of Nazianzus understood the conflict between their classical education and their conversion to 'philosophy'. Yet Christianity no sooner absorbed philosophy's old hostility to rhetoric than it too renewed the process of mutual assimilation. If Gregory of Nazianzus stands for the Christian who abjures his rhetorical education in the name of the higher life of 'philosophy', he also stands for that fourth-century phenomenon, the Christian rhetor, the creator of a renaissance of letters within the Church. In this study I wish to examine both sides of this dialectic, both the diastasis between Christianity and classicism and the synthesis which was taking place.

In the first chapter I shall examine this dialectic in a biographical context. The university of Athens and Gregory's education there will be described. His rejection of rhetoric for philosophy, and yet the ambivalence throughout his life *vis-à-vis* the two cultures, as well as the two modes of life, the active and the contemplative, will then be discussed to show how this tension acted as a central existential problem.

In the second chapter Gregory's use of rhetorical techniques will be spelled out in detail. The purpose of this chapter is not primarily philological, but rather to show, through a wide sampling, the extensive influence which rhetorical culture exerted on Gregory's style of expression and thought.

In the third chapter I shall extract from Gregory's writing and systematize as much as possible exactly what he means by philosophy and the philosophic life. Having examined his use of both rhetoric and the philosophic life, we discover a striking conflict between his actual indebtedness to classical sources and his conscious attitudes towards Greek rhetoric and philosophy. This conflict points to a basic tension in fourth-century Christianity, a tension between the extent of the influence of classical culture upon its linguistic and mental ethos, and the ability of the Christian world adequately to recognize and accept this fact. Even today the Christian Church has not been able fully to assimilate the fact of its hellenization into a satisfactory understanding of its own identity and purpose. In Gregory of Nazianzus we are able to see the Christian Church at the moment when the fact of hellenization and its conscious attitudes towards this fact first begin to crystallize into explicit form. This problem of Gregory's attitudes towards ancient rhetoric and philosophy will furnish the material for Chapter IV. The chapter will conclude with a summation of the relationship of fourth-century Christianity to classical culture as explored in this study.

The Greek text of Gregory's writing which has been used is, in all cases, Migne, *Patrologiae graecae* which is still the most recent text of his entire *corpus*. Greek words will be transliterated wherever possible and longer passages cited in Greek only when this is essential to see the original phrasing of an idea. Other quotations will be given in English. For translations I have used the twenty-four English versions of the orations found in Wace and Scaff, *Nicene and Post-Nicene Fathers*. In addition to this, *Orations* 4 and 5, Gregory's two invectives against the Emperor Julian, are translated by G. W. King in the Bohn Classical Library volume entitled *Julian the Apostate*, which also contains Libanius' encomium on Julian. For quotations or paraphrases of the other nineteen orations, I have made my own translation. For the translation of the letters, Father Denis Meehan, O.S.B. (St. Andrew's Priory, Valyermo, California) has an unpublished manuscript of *Epistles* 1–101, which I have used, and, under his supervision, I have made a translation of *Epistles* 102–244. The *Carmen de vita sua*, Gregory's long autobiographical poem, which is crucial for an understanding of his life and intellectual development, has also been translated by Father Meehan, and his translation provided the English version for the quotations from this work. Abbreviations of classical authors follow the form found in the *Oxford Classical Dictionary*, and abbreviations of classical journals follow the form found in Marouzeau's *Dix Années* (1914–24).

I

THE CONFLICT OF CULTURES IN GREGORY'S LIFE

GREGORY was born in Arianzus,[1] a village which was a part of the ancestral estates of his family, near Nazianzus in south-west Cappadocia. The date of his birth can be established as about 329–30.[2] His family belonged to the wealthy land-holding class of the province. Though they were Christians, and from an area removed from the centre of Hellenistic culture, they seem to have belonged to the hellenized upper class which formed a pan-imperial aristocracy. Although their outlook as Christians modified their relationship to the cultural environment somewhat, they seem to have felt no fundamental estrangement from the contemporary world, either as a political or as a cultural system. The sons of the family, Gregory and his younger brother, Caesarius, were sent, as a matter of course, for their education to the great centres of ancient learning.

Education and Travels

Gregory received his elementary education at Nazianzus,[3] and his secondary schooling in Caesarea, the capital of

---

[1] For the ancient testimonia on Gregory's birthplace, see *P.G.* 35. 148 A; 790 and 934.

[2] There is some dispute about the time of Gregory's birth. Suidas (*Lexicon*, tom. i, p. 196; see *P.G.* 35. 308 c) says that he lived about ninety years and died in the twenty-third year of Theodosius' reign, which would place his birth at about A.D. 301. But this contradicts internal evidence of Gregory's writing, which places Gregory's departure from Athens at about A.D. 359, at the age of thirty: see Paul Gallay, *La Vie de S. Grégoire de Nazianze* (Paris, 1943) 27–9. Some Catholic scholars in the nineteenth century objected to this dating because it placed Gregory's birth after his father's episcopal ordination, but this objection seems to have been based on a mistaken notion of the universality of episcopal celibacy in the Church at this time. For a discussion of this question, see Karl Ullmann, *Gregory of Nazianzus* (London, 1851), Appendix I.

[3] Though we have little mention of Nazianzus in ancient times, in Gregory's day it was apparently a flourishing city. Ullmann (op. cit. 307–8) quotes from

Cappadocia.[1] It was here that Gregory first met Basil, who was also studying in Caesarea.[2] Having completed this phase of his education, Gregory embarked on advanced training in rhetoric and philosophy, and for this it was necessary to travel to more distant lands to seek out the famous teachers of the day. He went first to the important centre of Christian education in Palestinian Caesarea. There Origen, Pamphilus, and Eusebius had worked and taught. The school was famous for its library and had some reputation in rhetoric. Jerome tells us that Gregory studied there under the rhetorician Thespesius.[3] From Caesarea, Gregory went to Alexandria, where Christian and classical education had mingled since the days of Pantaenus and Clement. He may possibly have met Athanasius at this time.[4] Gregory's studies in Palestine and in Alexandria undoubtedly helped to shape his predilection for Platonism and for Origenist theology and exegesis. His stay in these centres was probably only two or three years, and about 350 he departed for Athens,[5] the city which, despite its faded glory, was still the most renowned university in the Empire. Here in Athens, which he calls 'the home of letters',[6] Gregory was to spend some ten years studying rhetoric and philosophy.

His teachers in rhetoric were the pagan Himerius and the Christian Prohaeresius. There is also a tradition that he studied under Libanius, but no confirmation of this can be gained from Gregory's own life and writings.[7] It was customary for students

the diary of Paul Lucas, an eighteenth-century traveller: 'This traveler points out as the locality of ancient Nazianzum, the place called . . . Hadeschi Bertas . . . where a noble library of manuscripts and a seat of learning are still said to exist. The appearance of extensive ruins proves that a considerable city once stood on the identical spot. This city was Nazianzum.'

[1] Gregor. Presbyter, 'Vita Gregor. Nazianz.', *P.G.* 35. 248; see also *Or.* 43. 13: *P.G.* 36. 512.

[2] In *Oration* 43. 14: *P.G.* 36. 513, Gregory indicates that he knew Basil before their studies in Athens.

[3] Jerome, *De Vir. Ill.*, cap. 113.

[4] Gregory speaks of Athanasius with great personal affection (*Or.* 21). Athanasius returned to Alexandria in 350, and Gregory's stay there may have been prolonged to that date.

[5] Gallay, *Vie* 36 and n., estimates this date from hints in Gregory's poems that indicate that he was about twenty when he arrived in Athens.

[6] *Or.* 43. 14; *P.G.* 36. 513 A.

[7] Socrates (4. 26) and Sozomen (16. 16) tell us that Gregory and Basil were students of Himerius and Prohaeresius at Athens and then of Libanius in Antioch. Neither one can be satisfactorily linked with Libanius or Antioch. However, Basil

to attach themselves to sophists from their regions, and Prohaeresius, as an Armenian, commanded most of the students from Asia Minor.[1] It was probably for this reason rather than for his religion that the two Cappadocians attached themselves to this sophist. There seems to have been no strong feeling among Christians that they must study with Christian teachers, and it was customary for Christians to study with pagan sophists, since most of the sophists were pagan at this time. Prohaeresius, as a Christian, would teach the same classical curriculum in the same way as his pagan counterpart. Indeed, if Eunapius, a pagan and great admirer of Prohaeresius' eloquence, had not told us that Prohaeresius was a Christian, we would have had no reason to suspect it, for in every other way he was typical of the contemporary sophist.[2]

One of the notable features of fourth-century education was the intense rivalry and animosity among sophists. The chairs of sophistry carried not only a salary paid by the Emperor or the city,[3] but also immunities from taxation and services to the government, privileges greatly to be prized in this period. Whenever an appointment to a chair was to take place, cabals, intrigue, and even violence between rivals were commonplace. Eunapius' account of how Prohaeresius succeeded to the Athenian chair of sophistry (which probably also made its holder head of the university)[4] illustrates this state of affairs. Julian had been the head of the university in the thirties, and Prohaeresius was his favourite and most gifted pupil. When Julian died in 363 he bequeathed his home to Prohaeresius, a simply furnished dwelling which Eunapius describes as 'breathing

---

was at Constantinople at the same time as Libanius and has an extensive correspondence with him, and he may have heard Libanius there. Since Gregory was so often linked with Basil in life and letters and Libanius did most of his teaching in Antioch, the tradition may have arisen through an extension of these facts.

[1] Thus Eunapius says 'to Prohaeresius were sent the students from the whole of Pontus and the neighbouring regions—for the people there admired the man as a treasure that was their own—and not from Pontus only, but from all Bithynia as well, the Hellespont, and the parts above Lydia, stretching through what is now called Asia, to Caria and Lycia and ending at Pamphylia and the Taurus' (Eunap. VS. 487–8).

[2] Eunap. VS 493: ἐδόκει γὰρ εἶναι χριστιανός.

[3] See Walden, Universities 171, on the financing of official chairs of rhetoric.

[4] There were probably three official chairs of sophistry at Athens in the fourth century, and, of these, one held the superior position and made its occupant head of the school. See Walden 142, and n. 3.

the atmosphere of the Muses',[1] and intended that his student should succeed him. However, the power of appointment lay in the hands of a local council,[2] who made their choice after a rhetorical contest. Many claimants came forward and six were chosen to give display declamations. The whole Roman world was divided over the contestants, but Prohaeresius' five rivals banded together, and, bribing the proconsul, drove Julian's protégé out of the city. After wandering as an exile in dire poverty for some time, Prohaeresius earned the favour of the new proconsul, and, with the Emperor's permission, re-entered the city. The proconsul then called the other sophists together and brought Prohaeresius forward to vindicate his claim as king of eloquence. Eunapius' description of this event gives us a vivid picture of the atmosphere of the sophistic school; the jealousy of the rivals, the pomp and hauteur of the great sophist, the fickle enthusiasm of the crowds.

Then Prohaeresius, gracefully saying a few words of introduction from his chair, and touching on the merits of extempore speech, arose with confidence when he came to the main part of his task, and, as the proconsul was about to propose a theme, raised his eyes and looked around the room. Seeing the enemy faction in great force and his own small and retiring, he naturally for a moment lost heart. But, as his spirit began to boil within him and he grew hot for the fray, he cast his eyes over the crowd, and, seeing in the far end of the room two men wrapped in their cloaks, whom he recognized as past-masters of the art of sophistry and the chief offenders against himself, he raised his voice and shouted, 'Aha! behold my gallant friends! command these, proconsul, to propound the theme.'

The two sophists attempted to hide in the crowd, but the proconsul had them brought forward and urged them to propound the theme. Putting their heads together, they came up with the most unlikely topic they could think of (unfortunately, we are not told what it was). Prohaeresius then demanded shorthand writers to take down his speech, and after requesting silence from the crowd:

Prohaeresius began to speak fluently, and with a sonorous ring at the end of each period, while the audience, which perforce kept a Pythagorean silence, in their amazed admiration broke through

1 *VS* 483.   2 Walden, op cit. 135.

their restraint and overflowed into murmurs and sighs. As the speech grew more vehement and the orator soared to heights which the mind of man could not describe or conceive of, he passed on to the second part of the speech and completed the exposition of the theme. But then, suddenly leaping in the air like one inspired, he abandoned the remaining part, left it undeveloped, and turned the flood of his eloquence to defend the contrary hypothesis. The scribes could hardly keep pace with him, the audience could hardly endure to keep silence, while the mighty stream of words flowed on. Then, turning his face toward the scribes, he said: 'Observe carefully whether I remember all the arguments that I used earlier.' And, without faltering over a single word, he began to declaim the same speech for the second time. At this the proconsul did not observe his own rules, nor did the audience observe the threats of the magistrate, for all who were present licked the sophist's breast as though he were the statue of some god; some kissed his feet, some his hands, others declared him to be a god, or the very model of Hermes, the god of eloquence. His rivals lay racked with envy, but even so some of them did not fail to praise him. The proconsul, with his bodyguard and officers, escorted him from the lecture-room. After that no one dared oppose Prohaeresius, but all, as if struck by lightning, acknowledged his superiority.[1]

Not only did the sophists contend among themselves, but each sophist gathered around himself a *phratria* of students with fierce devotion to their master. Clashes between followers of rival sophists took place frequently, and bands of students waited for newcomers and impressed them into the service of their teacher. After a student had been enlisted, he was conducted through an initiation. Gregory of Nazianzus describes these activities in his oration on Basil, and his account is corroborated by Libanius' account of his student days in Athens.[2]

Most of the young men at Athens are mad after rhetorical skill. . . . They are just like men devoted to horses and exhibitions, as we see at the horse races. They leap, they shout, raise clouds of dust. . . . This is how the students feel in regard to their tutors and their rivals, in their eagerness to increase their own numbers and thereby enrich them. The matter is absolutely silly and absurd. Cities, roads, harbours, mountain tops, coast lines are seized upon—in short, every

---

[1] Eunap. *VS* 489–90.

[2] See Walden, *Universities* 303–5, for translations of sections from Libanius' letters and orations describing student press-gangs and initiatory hazing.

part of Attica, or the rest of Greece, with most of the inhabitants; for even these they have divided among rival parties.

Whenever a newcomer arrives and falls into the hands of those who seize upon him, either by force or willingly, they observe this Attic law of combined jest and earnest. He is first conducted to the house of one of those who were the first to receive him, or of his friends or kinsmen, or countrymen or of those who are eminent in debating power, and purveyors of arguments, and therefore especially honoured among them; and their reward consists in the gain of adherents. He is next subjected to the raillery of any one who so desires, with the intention, I suppose, of checking the conceit of the newcomers, and reducing them to subjection at once. The raillery is of a more insolent or argumentative kind, according to the boorishness or refinement of the railer; and the performance, which seems very fearful and brutal to those who do not know it, is to those who have experienced it, very pleasant and humorous, for its threats are feigned rather than real. Next he is conducted in procession through the market-place to the bath. The procession is formed by those who are charged with it in the young man's honour, who arrange themselves in two ranks separated by an interval and precede him to the bath. But then when they have approached it, they shout and leap wildly, as if possessed, shouting that they must not advance, but stay, since the bath will not admit them; and, at the same time frighten the youth by furiously knocking at the doors; then, allowing him to enter, they now present him with his freedom and, after the bath, receive him as an equal and one of themselves.[1]

In Olympiodorus' account of these same events, we learn that after the bath the student is then presented with his crimson gown, the distinctive garb of those engaged in sophistic studies.[2] Sometimes these rites were omitted as a mark of deference to a special student. For example, when Basil arrived some time after Gregory, being then some twenty-five years old and having already won renown in rhetoric and other studies in Caesarea and Constantinople, Gregory persuaded the students to suspend the usual indignities as a mark of respect for his friend.[3] However, Basil did not evade hazing altogether, for a group of Armenian students, jealous of his reputation, came up to him and began to put questions to him in an effort to get the better of him

[1] *Or.* 43. 15–16.
[2] See Photius, *Bibl.*, cod. 80, p. 60; also *Schol. in Greg. Naz.*: *P.G.* 36. 906 A.
[3] *Or.* 43. 16.

in public debate. Gregory, anxious to defend the reputation of Athens, and fearful that these *habitués* would be too quickly put down by the novice, at first took the side of Basil's antagonists. But then, perceiving their malicious intent, he took Basil's side, and the newcomer was able to vindicate his syllogistic prowess.[1]

In Gregory's description of their schooldays, he details the various academic fields in which Basil was proficient: rhetoric, grammar, mathematics, and philosophy, in its three branches, physics, ethics, and dialectic, as well as music and medicine. But it is doubtful whether we should take this as the curriculum of their studies at Athens. It was a commonplace of the encomium to exaggerate the person's academic accomplishments and dilate on his mastery of all branches of learning. Music and mathematics as well as grammar were secondary-school subjects. The mathematical branches of the seven liberal arts continued to hold their place in educational theory, but in practice they were taught in a very rudimentary way, and 'grammar' or literary studies usurped most of the curriculum.[2] If Basil actually studied these subjects on a more advanced level, his education would have been quite exceptional. Ancient education generally lacked technical or professional training. The one exception was medicine, which had its own schools and taught from a developed tradition.[3] Basil may have studied this subject in Constantinople, where Gregory's brother Caesarius also went to study and later to practise medicine. However, given the ordinary traditions of higher education, we can be reasonably sure that Gregory's and Basil's studies in Athens were primarily in the field of rhetoric with some, but by no means equal, attention to philosophy.

The state of the schools of philosophy in the mid fourth century is uncertain. Marcus Aurelius had established one and perhaps two official chairs in philosophy for each school,[4] but during the third century many of the salaried chairs of philosophy were dropped and never restored. Philosophy did not enjoy the patronage that sophistry could command, and the philosopher often found immunities and even fees denied to him on the ground that a true philosopher should not be concerned with such things.[5] Ironically, in this one area, the philosopher

[1] *Or.* 73. 17. [2] Marrou, *Education in Antiquity* 177.
[3] Ibid. 191–3. [4] Walden, *Universities* 92 and n. 2. [5] Ibid. 171, 189.

was taken at his word. By the mid fourth century the Stoic and Epicurean schools most probably had ceased to exist at Athens, and Peripatetic studies were generally taken over by Academics. Thus, of the four schools, the only one which certainly survived as an independent institution in Gregory's time was the Academy. Whether he studied there is another question.

Athenian Academics at this time were probably Neoplatonists with the theurgistic interests developed by the Pergamene school.[1] There was a strong coterie of such philosophers in Athens at the time Julian visited the city in A.D. 355 who were much interested in the revival of ancient pagan rites. Gregory was aware of this group, and his remark that Athens was the city most given over to idolatry while he was there[2] probably refers to this antiquarian neo-paganism. If so, Gregory probably would have avoided tutelage under such philosophers. This group was to confirm the young Julian in his return to the pagan religion and initiate him into the ancient rites, and would play a prominent part in his attempt to re-establish the old ways. Such a group in Athens in the fifties would have been enthusiastically hostile to Christianity, and Gregory's attitude towards it is probably indicated by his remark that 'we, our minds being closed up and fortified against this, suffered no injury'.[3]

On the other hand, the student of rhetoric commonly mastered certain general material in philosophy. Plato and Aristotle were studied among the classics as stylists,[4] and the introductory course in philosophy was considered part of the rounded education, enriching the sophist's store of themes and commonplaces. This introductory course in philosophy started with the general history of philosophy, beginning with the Milesian Physicists—Thales, Anaximander, and Anaximenes—much as students of ancient philosophy begin today. Indeed it was from this ordinary introduction to philosophy, developed in the ancient

---

[1] E. Zeller, *Outlines of the History of Greek Philosophy* (London, 1955) 303–6.

[2] *Or.* 43. 21: 'Athens was richer . . . in those evil riches—idols—than the rest of Greece, and it is hard to avoid being carried along with their devotees and adherents.' Julian's initiation into Neoplatonic theurgy dates particularly from his years in Nicomedia, under the tutelage of the philosophers Maximus, Edesius, Chrysanthius, and Eusebius, and he came to Athens with the express purpose of consulting the leaders of the cult there; see G. Negri, *Julian the Apostate* (London, 1905) ii. 41, 47–9.

[3] *Or.* 43. 21: *P.G.* 36. 524 C.

[4] Walden, *Universities* 211.

educational system, that we derive the 'doxographical tradition' which provides our fragmentary knowledge of the lost
ancient philosophers.[1] After this survey, the student would be
expected to learn the doctrines of the four major schools. These
subjects were studied from handbooks and summaries. The
introductions to Platonism written by Apuleius and Albinus[2]
give us an idea of the nature of these handbooks.

If the student was seriously interested in philosophy, he
might then become an adherent of a particular school, don the
philosopher's robes, study the classics of the school in detail,
and attend upon the lectures of a philosopher, who, in the
best tradition, would become his 'spiritual director'.[3] Gregory
probably did not study philosophy on this more intimate level.
Study of his references to philosophy in the letters and orations
seems to indicate that his training in this field remained on
the more elementary level. He refers to many philosophers—
Empedocles, Epictetus, Anaxarchus, Cleambrotus, Pythagoras,
Chrysippus, Xenocrates, Diogenes the Cynic, Epicurus, Crates,
Socrates, Zeno, Antisthenes, Cleanthes, Anaxagoras, Heraclitus,
Sextus Empiricus, Pyrrho of Elis, Empedotimus, Aristaeus, as
well as Plato and Aristotle,[4] but, with the exception of the last
two, his remarks are anecdotal. They consist either of traditional *chreiai* or *apophthegmata* handed down about the different
philosophers, or general remarks about the doctrines of the four
schools which were imparted by handbooks. Thus his knowledge
seems to correspond to the introductory instruction in philosophy described by Marrou.[5] Only in the case of Plato and
Aristotle does Gregory make the kind of references that imply
closer study, and this too we might expect, given the sophist's
use of the two as a part of the canon of Attic authors. No names
of philosophers under whom Gregory studied have come down
to us. The evidence points then to the conclusion that Gregory's
knowledge of the Greek philosophical tradition was antiquarian,
not a living contact with the Neoplatonism taught in the existing
schools. Furthermore, Gregory seems ignorant of Neoplatonic

[1] Marrou, *Ancient Education* 208.
[2] Translations of these two works can be found in Bohn Classical Library's
edition of Plato, G. Bruges, trans. (London, 1855), vol. 6.
[3] See Samuel Dill, *Roman Society from Nero to Marcus Aurelius* (New York, 1956)
286-333, on the Philosophic Director.
[4] See Appendix I.   [5] See above, p. 9, n. 8.

writings, of Plotinus in particular. If we conclude that he did not know Neoplatonic thinkers or writings directly, this helps to explain why Gregory, who inherited his Neoplatonism from Origen, can so readily assume these ideas to be Christian.[1] In this he differs from Augustine, who had studied Plotinian writings in Latin translation and thus was more aware of Neoplatonic doctrines in their original setting distinct from Christianity than Gregory seems to have been.

Gregory and Basil, who had already been acquainted during their schooldays in Caesarea,[2] became the closest companions in Athens. Gregory tells us that:

In studies, in lodging, in discussion I had him as companion. We made a team, if I may boast a little, that was celebrated throughout Greece. We had all things in common, as it were a single soul bound together our two distinct bodies.[3]

The two young Cappadocians kept away from the rowdy life of the students, and confined themselves to serious pursuits. Gregory says they knew only two routes: the one leading to the church, the other to the classroom.[4] Yet they were not alone in this austere pursuit of knowledge and virtue, but were surrounded by a group of fellow spirits whom Gregory calls a 'far from ignoble band [phratria]'.[5] Many of these school companions were to be lifelong friends.[6] Here in the seat of Greek letters Basil and Gregory first worked out their plans to lead 'the philosophic life'. From an early letter from Gregory to Basil, written soon after Gregory's return to Cappadocia, it seems that they planned to form a monastic community together.[7] Basil, the more rigorous and austere of the two, probably was the originator of the plan, while Gregory was the eager follower whose ardent idealism was captivated by the vision of the philosophic life.[8]

[1] See below, Chapter IV, pp. 172-4.
[2] In Or. 43. 13, Gregory calls Caesarea the mistress of their common studies, and, in the following section (14), says that Athens brought him to know Basil perfectly, although he had not been unknown to him before.
[3] Carm. de vita sua, ll. 226-30: P.G. 37. 1045. See also Or. 43. 20: P.G. 36. 521.
[4] Or. 43. 21.   [5] Or. 43. 22: P.G. 36. 525 A.
[6] For example, Sophronius (Ep. 93); Eusebius, Celsius, and Julian (see Or. 19). All four became leaders in the Church or the imperial administration. See Gallay, Vie 59.
[7] Ep. 1: P.G. 37. 21.
[8] Basil was clearly the leader of the phratria, and Gregory is always happy to

Basil departed from Athens a year or two before Gregory and began his tours of the monastic communities of Palestine and Egypt, which were to serve as models for his own monastic rule. Gregory seems to have planned to go with him, but crowds of students surrounded him upon Basil's departure and prevailed upon him to stay on as a lecturer in rhetoric.[1] Basil apparently slipped away without telling Gregory. There may have been some misunderstanding, and Gregory expected Basil to wait for him. His dismay at discovering his friend's departure is still vivid in his mind as he recalls this event almost twenty-five years later.[2] Finally Gregory tore himself away from his beloved Athens and about 358–9 joined his brother Caesarius, who was returning from his medical studies in Constantinople, for the journey home to Cappadocia.[3]

Return to Cappadocia; The Problem of Decision between Modes of Life

After such an extended period of study, Gregory was expected to be a local luminary and give a display of his skills.

When I arrived home, to satisfy the inordinate desire of some people who kept importuning me, I gave a display of eloquence. It was, so to speak, a debt I owed, because personally I place no value upon vapid applause or upon those stupid and intricate conceits which are the delight of sophists when a crowd of youths confronts them.[4]

He also taught rhetoric for a while or at least did some private tutoring.[5] However, he had already determined to renounce the career of a rhetor in favour of the philosophic life.

In the beginning of the *Carmen de vita sua*, Gregory tells us that the purpose of his pursuit of rhetoric for those many years was to create a Christian eloquence, to 'turn bastard letters to the service of those that are genuine'.[6] Whether this is the wisdom of

speak of Basil as his preceptor. But Gregory was probably more personable, while Basil's arrogance and *froideur* made him less popular with his fellows. See *Or.* 43. 17–18, 22.

[1] *Carm. de vita sua*, ll. 245–64: *P.G.* 37. 1046–7.   [2] *Or.* 43. 24.
[3] *Or.* 7. 8: *P.G.* 35. 763 B.
[4] *Carm. de vita sua*, ll. 265–74: *P.G.* 37. 1048.
[5] His letter to Evagrius, written in 359 (see Gallay, *Vie* 254), seems to indicate that he was instructing E.'s son in rhetoric; *Ep.* 3: *P.G.* 37. 24 B.
[6] *Carm. de vita sua*, ll. 113–14: *P.G.* 37. 1037.

hindsight, or actually represents a position articulated upon Gregory's departure for Athens is impossible to tell, although the former is more likely. However, a few years later in the same poem, Gregory tells us that upon his return home he decided to renounce the labour of letters 'like people who abandon their property to be grazed by sheep or cast the treasure they have amassed to the bottom of the sea'.[1] These two statements well represent the classic tension between rhetoric and philosophy which Gregory experienced in his personal moment of decision. On the one hand, there was the feeling that the two were incompatible; that one must abandon the one to cultivate the other; on the other hand, the urge to create a synthesis.

Soon after his return to Cappadocia Gregory was baptized, and, as was frequently the case in the fourth century, this embrace of full Christian status signalled his intention to turn from 'the world' to the ascetic life. But, despite his plans with Basil in Athens and his profession that he had returned to Cappadocia to seek the contemplative life,[2] Gregory displayed an uncertainty about his course of action. He seemed reluctant to commit himself for any extended period to the kind of life that Basil was living. In 361 Basil wrote to him, urging Gregory to join him in his newly founded hermitage in Pontus. Gregory replied, begging off because of his duty to his parents.[3] Later that year he joined Basil for a while, and it was probably at this time that they prepared the celebrated *Philocalia*, a collection of excerpts from the works of Origen.[4] Later that year he returned to Nazianzus. In his letters to Basil he chooses to assume a jocular tone and describes their monastic haven as a 'mouse hole' and a 'thoughtery' and dubs the contemplatives 'poor sunless Cimmerians from Pontus'.[5] Gregory wrote this letter in parody

[1] *Carm de vita sua*, ll. 270–3: *P.G.* 37. 1048 A.

[2] Gregory described his decision to leave Athens in these words: 'my native land was beckoning ... to live the philosophic life there seemed a noble ideal'; *Carm. de vita sua*, ll. 260, 261: *P.G.* 37. 1047.

[3] 'I must confess it. I have gone back on my promise to be with you and live the philosophic life with you as I had promised as far back as our Athenian days. ... One duty clashed with another; duty to care for my parents overrode the law of friendship.' *Ep.* 1: *P.G.* 37. 21.

[4] J. A. Robinson, *The Philocalia of Origen, edited by Gregory of Nazianzus and Basil the Great* (Cambridge, 1893).

[5] *Ep.* 4: *P.G.* 37. 25 A, B: μυωξίαν ... φροντιστηρίου ... καὶ τὸν ποθούμενον ἥλιον ὃν ὡς διὰ κάπνης αὐγάζεσθε ὦ Ποντικοὶ Κιμμέριοι. ...

of Basil's own glowing account of the beauties of his hermitage,[1]
and followed it with a second, joking about their labours together and displaying the same light-hearted refusal to take the
whole thing completely seriously.

Since you accept my chaff with equanimity, I shall give you the
next instalment. I shall take my prelude from Homer: 'Come now,
change thy theme and sing of the adornment within', the roofless and
doorless shelter, the fireless and smokeless hearth, the walls fire-
dried (lest the blobs of mud fall on one)—condemned indeed we were
like Tantalus, thirsty in the midst of water; that pitiable and starve-
ling banquet to which I was invited from Cappadocia, in hopes not
indeed of lotus-eater penury, but of the table of Alcinous; I, another
unfortunate ship-wrecked mariner. Yes, I remember the bread and
the broth (so-called). I shan't forget it—the way my teeth slid
around the morsels, and then had to recover themselves as if they
were being dragged out of a swamp. You, indeed, with grandilo-
quence induced by the discomforts you suffered yourself, will insist
on dramatizing these matters on a noble plane; but, if your good
mother, great and generous nurse of beggars that she is, hadn't
proved a true port in a storm and rescued us from it all, we should
have been corpses long ago, martyrs to our Pontic faith, more to be
pitied than praised. And how could I omit the gardens (bless the
mark) which hadn't a vegetable? And the Augean mess we cleared
out of the house to put on the gardens? When we dragged the cart
piled high with soil, I all bent over, and you insatiable—Oh, earth,
sun, air and virtue! (I shall dramatize a little too, in the tragic mode)—
and all, mind you, not to dam the Hellespont, but to level a rocky
patch.[2]

In a following letter, indeed, Gregory goes on to praise their
Pontic sojourn in more appreciative tones:

. . . 'Who will restore to me the state of those former days', in which
it was my delight to suffer hardship with you? For hardship voluntarily undertaken is better than involuntary joy. Who will give me
back the psalmody and the vigils, the journeys to God through the
medium of prayer, that life which wrested one (as it were) from the

[1] See Basil's letters, *Ep.* 14.
[2] *Ep.* 5: *P.G.* 37. 28–9. Such letters give us a picture of the youthful high-
spirited Gregory as he was in his thirties after his return from Athens. They warn us
that Gregory's picture of his piety and serious-minded youth in his *Carmen de vita
sua*, written in his fifties, has undergone some later schematizing and should be
balanced against these early letters.

body and material things? Who will restore that close-knit brotherly intimacy of souls, amongst men who were uplifted and made holy by your influence? Who will restore that friendly rivalry and ardour for virtue, which we had made secure by written regulations and canons? Who will restore that loving study of the divine oracles, and the light that we found therein, under the guidance of the Spirit? Or, to speak of less important and of menial tasks, the bringing of wood and the quarrying of stone, the planting and the ditches for irrigation? And the plane tree, a golden tree more precious than that of Xerxes, for it was no monarch enervated by luxury that came to sit there, but a monk worn out by toil? It was I that planted it, Apollo that watered it (meaning your excellent self) but God who gave the increase. . . . Yes it is very easy to yearn for those things; but it is not easy to regain them. Be mindful of me; let me have the benefit of your inspiration and your help in the quest for virtue; preserve by your prayers such progress as we have made in that quest, lest it be dissipated gradually like a shadow at the close of day. You mean more to me than the air I breathe, my only life is to be with you, and when I am not with you, to hold you in my heart.[1]

Such a letter breathes the spirit of Gregory's youthful idealism and his affectionate nature. Yet though the monastic period had meant much to him, his previous joking indicates a certain ambivalence. He exclaims 'who will restore those former days?',[2] and yet he seemed in no great haste to return, and his protestation at the outset of this letter that 'in all that I have written to you about our sojourn in Pontus, I was, of course, joking, not serious' suggests that this more eulogistic vein was inspired by a mild rebuke from Basil, who thought that Gregory should treat such matters with greater seriousness. Gregory was to return several times to Pontus, but never for long, and the following year Basil himself returned and took up clerical duties in Caesarea. In 364-5 Basil had a falling out with his bishop and returned to Pontus, and Gregory probably was with him during part of that time.[3] Pontus was also the scene of his brief flights from clerical office in 362 and possibly again in 370, when Basil wished to consecrate him a bishop.

[1] *Ep.* 6: *P.G.* 37. 29, 32.
[2] The quotation is from Job 29. 2.
[3] *Oration* 43. 29: *P.G.* 36. 536 B: the phrase φυγὰς ἐνθένδε σὺν ἡμῖν πρὸς τὸν Πόντον μεταχωρεῖ indicates that Gregory at least initially shared this exile with Basil.

This state of ambiguity about his commitment to the solitary life received a rude blow at the end of that year, however; for at Christmas 361, his father, deciding that Gregory should use his talents in more active service of the Church, forcibly ordained him during the liturgical services. In that period, when there was a sharp cleavage between the monk and the priest, ordination meant a commitment to the 'active life', the life of service of the world. Gregory seems to have regarded such a commitment on virtually the same plane as any other worldly career, as a burden of external affairs and duties and a formidable obstacle to that life of *hésychia* and contemplation to which he was tending. Thus, before Gregory could make up his mind to give himself completely to the solitary life, Gregory the Elder had pre-empted the decision and abruptly bound him to another way of life.

Stung to the core by what, years afterwards, Gregory still spoke of as an 'act of tyranny',[1] he fled to the monastery in Pontus. There, oscillating between his feelings of duty and filial responsibility on the one hand, and his attraction for the solitary life on the other, Gregory was forced to make some decision about the future course of his life. Shortly before Easter of 362 the former feelings prevailed, and he decided to return and take up his duties as a presbyter under his father in Nazianzus. We have the Easter sermon which he preached in that year and a long address, which was probably circulated in pamphlet form, in which Gregory explains to the people of Nazianzus the reasons for his unseemly flight. He includes among these his surprise at the suddenness of his ordination, his longing for the solitary life, thus so unexpectedly interrupted, and, perhaps to dramatize his situation on a somewhat more noble and unselfish plane, his feelings of unworthiness for the sacerdotal office.[2]

However, the issue between the active and the contemplative life was by no means solved by this return, but was to remain a fundamental tension throughout Gregory's life, and the pattern of flight and return was to become a characteristic motif of his

---

[1] *Carm. de vita sua*, l. 345: P.G. 37. 1053: ἤλγησα τῇ τυραννίδι.

[2] *Oration* 2: P.G. 35. 407–514: in this oration Gregory especially develops the theme of the contemplative life and the great responsibility of the director of souls, who must purify his own spirit in order to be fit to lead others along this road to God. His remarks became a classic exposition of the ideal of the priesthood, and John Chrysostom modelled his treatise *De Sacerdotio* on this sermon.

career. In so far as he solved the problem, it was by trying to gain the better part of both modes of life, by contributing a certain share of his energies to the work of letters and the Christian ministry, while trying to live the life of contemplation and keep some of the monastic routine of prayer, vigils, and fasting within the semi-seclusion of his home. Such a solution was almost inevitable for Gregory, for the ability to see the good in many ways of thought and the desire for the mean rather than the extreme were so characteristic of his temperament. In the section of the poem on his life when he discusses his ordination, he speaks very clearly of his hesitation between these two modes of life and suggests the solution that was to guide him for the remainder of his life.

My mind was, in fact, in the throes of an intense turmoil, because I was in search of the nobler among noble pursuits. I had long previously made up my mind to reject the flesh completely, and now the idea pleased me more. But as I surveyed the actual paths to holiness it was not easy to discern the better path, or the serene one. As often happens in the practical domain, for different reasons this course or that seemed good or bad. . . . Finally, after hesitating considerably between the two courses, I came to this solution for conflicting desires and brought my mental turmoil to a reasonable calm. I kept noticing that those people who are attracted by an active life do good to some of the people they encounter, but they do themselves no good and are harassed by anxieties that wreck their serenity. On the other hand, those that stay detached are somehow more stable and turn with quiet mind to God. But their charity is narrow; they are useful only to themselves; the life they live is unsocial and harsh. I decided upon a middle way between the life without ties and the life of mixing, one which would combine the serenity of the former with the practical use of the latter. . . . Part of my philosophy was this: not just to seem concerned about the higher life, but to be rather than to seem a friend of God. Consequently I took the view that people living the active life too deserve our love. They receive their measure of honour from God because they lead people by means of the divine mysteries.[1] Still, however much I seemed involved with people, I was possessed by a greater longing for the monastic life, which I regarded as a matter of disposing of one's character, not one's body.[2]

[1] Gregory here is speaking of his father and by implication all pastors, whose ministry Gregory equates with 'the active life'.
[2] Carm. de vita sua, ll. 280–329: P.G. 37. 1048–52.

Dispute with Basil

Just as Gregory was working out this synthesis of the *bios praktikos* and the *bios theōrētikos*, the life of service to people and the detached life of contemplation, he received another more severe challenge to his scheme of life, and that from the quarter whence he least expected it, from the one man who he thought was most in sympathy with his longing for 'detachment'. In Caesarea Basil had become more and more indispensable and was bishop in all but name.[1] In 370, when Eusebius died, Basil felt that he alone could administer the Church in its hour of crisis, and he set about to secure his own election as Eusebius' successor. Gregory was now virtual bishop of Nazianzus, his father being very sickly and aged, and Basil counted on his support in the episcopal election. Knowing Gregory's aversion to ecclesiastical politicking, he apparently tried to bring him to Caesarea on grounds of illness. It is difficult to know if he really meant to deceive his friend, but Gregory thought he had been treated in bad faith.

With a council pending concerning the question of a bishop, you have invited me to Caesarea, and what a specious and persuasive pretext you invented. You were ill, forsooth, at death's door, yearning to see me and make your adieux. What your object was I cannot guess, or how my presence was going to achieve it. I was, of course, heart-broken and was for hurrying off. There is nothing I prize higher than your life, and no blow that could be so severe as your death. I shed floods of tears and groaned in lamentation, finding it impossible for the first time in my life to be resigned. I had every detail of your funeral arranged. However, when I noticed the bishops gathering into the city, my haste received a check. I began to wonder. I wondered first of all at your insufficient realization of what was fitting in this matter and at your failure to guard against popular gossip, which is so swift to denigrate the purest of intentions. In the second place it surprised me that you should not consider a similar line of conduct suitable for both of us, to whom life, learning, everything is in common, in that God set his seal on our association from the beginning. Thirdly, (this too I must say) I was surprised that you should consider such elections the business of pious men, and not, as they are, the business of power-mongers, who are concerned with popular favour.

Consequently I am turning tail and beating a retreat. Do you, if

[1] See *Or.* 43. 33: *P.G.* 36. 540–1.

you please, decide too to shun public disturbance and malicious minds. Whenever the business is finished with and the opportunity presents itself, I shall see Your Reverence and administer further, more severe reproofs.[1]

Although Gregory's father tore himself from his sick-bed and journeyed to Caesarea to vote for Basil,[2] and Gregory himself wrote several letters urging the bishops and people of Caesarea to elect Basil,[3] he refused to attend the synod in person, and relations between the two friends remained strained for some months. As is often the case with over-sensitive people, Gregory probably exaggerated the rift and was slow to be mollified. Basil, for his part, was annoyed and felt that Gregory was allowing his foolish pride to interfere with an office of friendship and responsibility to the Church.[4] By the turn of the year, however, the dispute was healing over, and we have a warm letter from Gregory urging Basil to stand firm against the attacks of the Arians,[5] and offering to be at his side if he felt the need of support or advice.

This was only the prelude to a more serious break. In 371 Valens, from financial motives, divided Cappadocia into two provinces and made Tyana the capital of Cappadocia Secunda. Anthimus, the bishop of Tyana, argued that the ecclesiastical division should follow the civil, and claimed the churches of Cappadocia Secunda as his jurisdiction. There seems to have been no question of heresy, since Anthimus apparently belonged to the orthodox faith,[6] so the dispute was purely one of ecclesiastical prerogative. Basil, in order to assert his episcopal claims over the disputed territory, proceeded to institute a number of new bishoprics and place his own partisans in these positions.

[1] Ep. 40: P.G. 37. 81, 84.   [2] Or. 18. 36: P.G. 35. 1033 B, C.
[3] Ep. 41 (to the people of Caesarea); Ep. 42 (to Eusebius of Samosata); Ep. 43 (open letter to the bishops at the synod).
[4] See Epistles 45 and 46.   [5] Ep. 47: P.G. 37. 96, 97.
[6] Several modern authorities have assumed that Anthimus was an Arian, possibly because it seemed derogatory to Basil that he be engaged in a dispute that was solely one of ecclesiastical jurisdiction. However, there is no good evidence to support this assertion. Furthermore, Gregory would have mentioned the fact, and would never have tried to mediate for Anthimus, nor would Basil have later been reconciled to him, if he had been a member of a heterodox party. Gregory, moreover, specifically says that dogma, and concern for the salvation of souls, were only pretexts and the real issue was ambition and avarice. For the bibliography on this issue, see Ullmann, Gregory of Nazianzus 121 and n.

Gregory, and Basil's brother Gregory, were drawn into the plan, and were assigned to the bishoprics of Sasima and Nyssa respectively.

Gregory was deeply offended by this action on Basil's part. The town of Sasima was most disagreeably situated. It was scarcely a town at all, but a kind of staging-post in a melancholy, waterless tract of countryside. Gregory, in his poem on his life, expresses his distaste for this vile little backwater in no uncertain terms.

Midway along the high road through Cappadocia, where the road divides into three, there is a stopping-place. It is without water or vegetation, not quite civilized, a thoroughly deplorable and cramped little village. There is dust all around the place, the din of wagons, laments, groans, tax-officials, implements of torture, public stocks. The population consists of casuals and vagrants. Such was my church of Sasima. He who was surrounded by fifty chorepiscopi (Basil) was so magnanimous as to make me incumbent there. The whole idea was to get the better of a violent intruder by founding a new see. And amongst his warrior friends, I held first place. Oh yes, I was a doughty fighter once, wounds that are blessed being no great disaster, because, added to the features I've already enumerated, that particular see couldn't be held without bloodshed. It was a no man's land between two rival bishops. A division of our native province gave occasion for the outbreak of a fearful brawl. The pretext was souls, but in fact, it was desire for control; control, I hesitate to say, of taxes and contributions which have the whole world in a state of miserable commotion.[1]

That Gregory saw no motive but greed and pride in this action is evident from the concluding sentences of this passage, and, never one to mince words or hide his feelings, he wrote Basil an angry letter accusing him of being haughty, overbearing, and inflated by episcopal power.

Are you going to put an end to this railing—I am unfriendly, boorish, untutored—I don't deserve to be alive—all because I was courageous enough to realize how I have been put upon? This is my sole offence, and you yourself should admit it, for I am unaware of having behaved badly towards you in any matter, great or small, and I hope I never shall.

In this matter, however, I do realize that I have been put upon.

[1] *Carm. de vita sua*, ll. 439–62: *P.G.* 37. 1059–61.

The realization came too late, but it came and I blame this matter of a bishopric, which has suddenly given you airs. I am tired of having to answer for your mistakes, of defending you to people who are under no illusions about the change in our relationship. Indeed the most ridiculous aspect of the situation is precisely this, that I am at the same time wronged and put in the wrong. All sorts of things are being said by all sorts of people, according to the temperament of the individual and his indignation on my behalf. The most charitable people say this: that you have shown yourself haughty and over-bearing—when you had no further need of me, you have thrown me aside like a cheap and worthless piece of property, or like the sup-ports under an arch which are removed and ignored when the build-ing is completed. Well, I shall let such people alone and let them say what they please—no one will keep tongues from wagging.

You can go on paying me out false coin in the shape of hollow-sounding hopes, which you have invented to counter your critics, suggesting that your real object in affronting me was to do me honour, I being a hypersensitive individual and very easily hurt. For my part I shall make my own position clear, and you have no right to be angry about it. I repeat what I said when the matter was first mooted, and I am not so stricken as a result of what has occurred or so disturbed emotionally as to have lost my power of reasoning, and to be incapable of realizing what I said. I am not going to take arms at this stage or become a student of military tactics, seeing that I did not do so before, when everyone was raging about under arms and the time seemed more opportune. . . . Bare-handed as I am, and a peace-loving man, I am not going to engage the war-lord Anthimus, even though he be a rather ancient warrior. . . . I am somewhat sus-ceptible to wounds.

Fight him yourself, if you like (necessity often makes a warrior of a weak man), or look for someone to fight him, when he mounts guard at the pass, like the famous Amalech barring the road to Israel, and seizes your mules. But above all leave me in peace. What is the point of joining battle about livestock and poultry, as if the issue were souls and ecclesiastical canons? Above all when they belong to some-one else? Why try to detach the magnificent city of Sasima from the metropolis, and lay bare the secrets of your policy which you ought to keep private?

Play the man then and wax strong and drag everything in to aggrandize yourself, as rivers draw in the winter torrents. Disregard friendship, disregard our association in the pursuit of what is noble and godly, and never consider the sort of impression you are likely to make in this line of action. I have gained one thing from our friendship; I have learned never to trust friends, or to prefer anything to God.[1]

Basil, however, was not to be put off by these outraged pro-testations, and shortly arrived in Nazianzus to consecrate Gregory a bishop. Gregory's father joined forces with the young bishop of Caesarea, and together they prevailed upon the reluctant Gregory to accept his consecration. As Gregory put it, in an oration delivered upon this occasion: 'Once more in the rite of consecration, has the Holy Spirit been poured out upon me, and once more I enter upon my calling sad and downcast.'[2]

Although elevated to episcopal station, Gregory continued to tarry in Nazianzus and seems to have had no intention of actually occupying the throne of Sasima. Basil wrote him severe reproofs and urged him to take up his responsibilities, but Gregory only replied in tones of injured dignity:

You censure me for lethargy and sloth, because I have not taken possession of your precious Sasima, because I don't behave like a bishop, because I refuse to arm you two against one another as if I were a bone between two dogs. Well, for me the highest activity is to be free of activity. Lest you be in any doubt about my ideals, so highly do I prize the withdrawn life that I look upon myself as an example to everyone of high-minded devotion to it, and I think that, if everyone had followed my example, troubles would not have fallen upon Churches, and the faith would not be swept away as it is today to become the weapon of any and everyone in private brawls.[3]

While he was thus sulking at Nazianzus, Basil's rival, the 'ancient warrior' Anthimus, arrived there and attempted to persuade Gregory to come over to his side. Gregory refused to accede to Anthimus, but attempted instead to conciliate the two rivals. But his efforts seem only to have further complicated the issue and brought down censures upon his head from both sides. In baffled, angry tones he wrote Basil the following letter:

What a coltish and mettlesome spirit you display in your letter. To be sure this is no wonder, your recent elevation makes you want to show me the great dignity you have received, and thus add to your stature, like those portrait-painters who concern themselves with handsome subjects.

[1] *Ep.* 48: *P.G.* 37. 97, 100.   [2] *Or.* 9. 1: *P.G.* 35. 820.
[3] *Ep.* 49: *P.G.* 37. 101.

For my part I take the view that a letter is not the proper medium in which to set forth the full narrative of my procedure in this affair from beginning to end, with details concerning the bishops and the letter which offended you. It is matter for a history rather than an explanatory letter. However, I shall give you a summary account.

The estimable Anthimus called here with some bishops, ostensibly to visit my father, but his real object being to deal with this affair, as he actually did. He expended much effort in canvassing many topics—the dioceses, Sasima, Limnae, my own consecration. He was conciliatory one moment, demanding the next; he threatened, he pleaded, he abused, and he praised. He sketched his boundaries, and pointed out that I ought to acknowledge him alone, the new metropolis being the more important one. 'Why include our city in your territory?' said I. 'We constitute a church ourselves, we are indeed a mother church by tradition.' Finally he went away baffled, having wasted much breath, and accusing me of Basilism, like another Demosthenes. I cannot think that there is any evidence in this of my wronging you.

Then that letter of mine, consider the evidence it provides of disrespect on the part of the sender. A formal summons to synod was served upon me. I protested that the matter was an outrage. They (Anthimus and company) rejoined by asking me to invite you to a meeting and discuss the whole matter. This I undertook to do, in order to avoid a contretemps like the former one, and I left everything in your hands—you might summon them if you wished, and you could determine the time and the place. Thus it was a gesture, not of disrespect, but of respect, and since I have done you no wrong let me tell you the rest of the story. If you really need to learn from me, I shall read you the actual letter of Anthimus. When, in spite of my protests and threats, he occupied Limnae, he wrote to me in outrageous and insulting terms, like a man chanting a victory paean over a fallen foe. It doesn't make sense—that I should be involved in a clash with him on your account, and at the same time give offence to you on the score of being conciliatory.

You ought, my dear Sir, to have acquainted yourself with these facts before you proceeded to write in such terms, because you were writing to a priest, if for no other reason. If, however, you are so given to ambition and display, that you must hold converse with me from a pedestal—the metropolitan to the incumbent of a tiny see, or rather a seeless incumbent—even I have some pride to oppose that. There is no course easier for any man, and perhaps it is the more reasonable course.[1]

[1] *Ep.* 50: *P.G.* 37. 101, 104.

Having delivered himself of this missive, Gregory decided that he had no more to contribute to the situation and resolved to retire from the whole affair and go off to a hermitage where he could live the kind of life which he desired.[1] Betaking himself to a lonely mountain range, he lived in solitude for some months. But his father continued to besiege him there with earnest entreaties to take up his duties in Sasima. When Gregory showed himself firm in his refusal to have any part in the affair, the elder Gregory begged his son at least to return to Nazianzus and act as his own assistant bishop. Gregory finally acceded to this demand, but only on the condition that he would remain there as long as his father lived, and then he would be free to return to the solitary life. On this basis the son was reconciled to his father, although he remained at enmity with Basil.

In assessing the import of this Cappadocian tragi-comedy, it would be a mistake to judge it merely as evidence of pride on Gregory's part. It is clear that he was offended by the meanness of the see of Sasima, but this was only an additional insult to the essential injury. The real explanation for Gregory's reaction to this whole affair lies in the nature of Gregory's relationship to Basil. Sasima, to Gregory, was a symbol of Basil's betrayal both of their friendship and of the ideals upon which their friendship had been built. To renounce the world and all its attachment and live the life of philosophic contemplation had been the substance of their youthful ideals, and in this Gregory had always looked upon Basil as his preceptor and guide. Now he saw Basil as a complete traitor to this ideal, concerned only with ignominious power struggles and so completely oblivious of their previous plan of life as to be willing to drag his friend into the same pit. One might easily condemn Gregory for having an extremely impractical turn of mind and being blind to the very good reasons which Basil may have had for wishing to keep the disputed territory under his jurisdiction, but this would be to miss the point. To turn away from all such concerns and involvements was the very core of the philosophic ideal for Gregory, and the basis for his feeling of betrayal. The fact that Basil saw the matter in a different light indicated that all their conversations about *apatheia* and the philosophic life were only so many

[1] *Carm. de vita sua*, ll. 486–525: *P.G.* 37. 1062–5.

fine words, and that when a real situation presented itself he was as 'worldly' as anyone else. Thus one can scarcely understand Gregory's reaction without understanding the ideal of life which possessed him, and one cannot condemn his reaction without at the same time setting this ideal at naught. Gregory expresses his feelings on the matter in remarks in which the ascetic mingles with the aesthete.

In God's name where did the proper course of action lie for me? Acquiescence? Patient endurance of assaults by scoundrels? Blows at all hours? Suffocation by dust? Not to have a place to rest my ageing bones? Always being driven forcibly from my house? Not having bread to break with a guest? Penniless with a penniless flock for my portion, unable to discover anywhere a corrective for the evils with which cities are filled? Feeding upon thorns with never a rose to cull? Always a harvest of trouble without a single redeeming feature? Offer this sort of thing, if you please, to people with more wisdom than I can muster, and request another sort of generosity from me. Athens, our studies together, our sharing of roof and hearth, the single spirit animating two people, the marvel of Greece, the troth we pledged that we would cast aside absolutely the world and live the common life for God, placing our words in the service of the one wise Word? This was the outcome of it all! Everything was shattered, abandoned on the ground; the old high hopes were gone with the wind.[1]

But it was not long before Gregory was to have another chance to seek the life of solitude. In 374, shortly over a year after his return from this second flight, Gregory's father died, followed shortly by his mother, and he now felt freed from further episcopal duties. His fellow bishops and the people of Nazianzus felt differently, however. Unsympathetic to his need for *hēsychia*, they demanded that he continue to minister to the church. Gregory made some efforts to persuade the bishops to find a successor, declaring that the see had never been formally allotted to him, and that he wished to devote himself to the contemplative life. Failing to convince them, he finally fled to Seleucia, where he lived in retirement for some four years in the convent of St. Thecla.[2]

---

[1] Ibid., ll. 464–84: *P.G.* 37. 1061–2.
[2] Ibid., ll. 525–9: *P.G.* 37. 1067.

Constantinople: The Blossoming of the Christian Orator

Early in 379 there came a call from the orthodox community in Constantinople to come there and lead the flock. The capital was then in the hands of the Arians, and Gregory's decision to accept this plea catapulted him into the most intense period of activity in his life. Thus we are presented with the paradox of a man who had fought continually for his solitude and freedom from ecclesiastical responsibility, and who, having achieved it, surrendered it voluntarily to shoulder one of the most difficult tasks in the Eastern Church. The truth, perhaps, is that, although in theory Gregory longed for the solitary life, in practice he could not long stay away from people.

Gregory's two years in Constantinople were to see the blossoming of his powers as a Christian orator, and, indeed, his reputation in eloquence was probably a primary reason for his being invited there.[1] In his *Poem on his Life* Gregory constantly rebuts the charge that he came to the city seeking ecclesiastical power. It is certainly true that he had little taste for pomp and prestige as such, but we perhaps do him no injustice if we suggest that he was not unattracted by the thought of defending orthodox doctrine before the cultured audience of the metropolis, who could appreciate his rhetorical powers. Here was an arena truly worthy of his skill and training. Half of his orations date from this crowded period.[2] The most important are his five theological orations, in which he attempted to delineate the orthodox doctrine of the Trinity. These orations became the standard of orthodoxy for later generations, and were introduced as such in the records of later Church councils.[3] For this, he, with St. John the Evangelist, became honoured in the Eastern Church by the title of 'Theologos', as the ones who, above all, gave the correct understanding to the nature of the Deity.

His time in Constantinople was a tumultuous one. Shortly after his arrival, during the baptismal ceremonies on Holy Saturday night, an unruly mob of Arians, including women and city rabble, and led on by monks, forced their way into the

[1] See Gallay, *Vie* 135; also *Carm. adv. Episcopos*, ll. 81 ff.: *P.G.* 37. 1172.
[2] See Appendix II for the chronology of Gregory's orations.
[3] See E. R. Hardy, *Christology of the Later Fathers* (London, 1954) 26 ff.

church and scattered the congregation.[1] His friendship with Maximus, the Cynic, was to turn out disastrously. Maximus, who was in the confidence of Peter, bishop of Alexandria, ingratiated himself with Gregory, and then, at the propitious moment, tried to seize the church and have himself consecrated bishop of Constantinople.[2] He was expelled from the city, but Gregory emerged much shaken by the event, and he was revealed as the provincial simpleton amid the intrigues of the great city. However, in spite of these events Gregory's firm leadership, magnanimity towards estranged Christians, and brilliant preaching attracted many to the little Church of the Anastasis where the orthodox were housed, and Gregory succeeded in unifying and strengthening the scattered fold, as well as enticing many members of other congregations into his church to hear his sermons. In describing these events in his autobiographical poem, Gregory composes a little tract on the principles of Christian oratory and persuasion.

In those days was there anyone so steadfast (in heresy) as not to bend an ear to my teaching? Some were influenced by the force of what I had to say; others became tractable because of the way in which I said it, for I chose my language very carefully, avoiding controversy or ridicule. I spoke in sorrow, did not lash out, did not, like some people, capitalize on easy and smooth opportunities, for power and persuasion have nothing in common. Nor did I try to conceal bad reasoning with bluff—this is a very tricky performance, squirting up ink from the depths like a cuttle-fish and routing one's critics by a smoke-screen. On the contrary, I was gentle and suave in my preaching, regarding myself as the proponent of a doctrine that is sympathetic and mild and smites no one. . . . Another principle of my training is this, not to make the mistake of regarding facile and dubious eloquence as the only road to piety. Not to be hail-fellow-well-met in theatres, on the piazzas, at parties, amidst laughter and singing, before my own tongue was purged of unseemly language. Not to pour forth wantonly the mysteries of doctrine into profane ears alien to Christ, making fun of things that are studied only with effort. On the contrary, I should fulfil the commandments as perfectly as possible by ministering to the poor, exercising hospitality, tending the sick, persevering in . . . mortifications. . . . There are

---

[1] These events are described in *Epp.* 77 and 78.

[2] The Maximus incident is described at length in *Carm. de vita sua*, ll. 745–1055: *P.G.* 37. 1080–101. Also of importance are his eulogy on Maximus (*Or.* 25) and his subsequent denunciation of Maximus (*Or.* 26).

many ways of salvation that one must tread, not that way only which depends on eloquence. The language of even a simple faith suffices. ... If you are full of anxiety and desirous of eloquence and put out if you do not produce a copious flow ... speak, but speak with fear, not always, not everything, not before everybody nor everywhere. ... Everything has its opportune moment, as one of the sages said. The territories of the Mysians and the Phrygians are far apart; so too are my brand of eloquence and that of the seculars (sophists). Their speeches are made for display before gatherings of young men on fictitious topics, where results or lack of results don't matter much. There is nothing more insubstantial than a shadow. But in my case, where the aim is to speak the truth, it is a matter of grave concern how the speech turns out. The way is beset by pitfalls and to tumble off is obviously to fall to the gates of hell. Consequently one must be exceedingly careful to use language wisely on the one hand and to listen to it wisely on the other. And there are times when both one and the other should be avoided; the prudent yardstick of fear should be used. Listening, of course, is less dangerous than speaking, and less dangerous still is the absenting of oneself altogether. There is no point in deadening one's mind with a drug or in approaching the breath of a mad dog.[1] So I learned from the oracles of scripture in which, before my mind was formed, I was brought up. And so as pastor of citizens and visitors I was by that time a prosperous husbandman, even though my harvest was not completely assembled.[2]

At this time Gregory's position in Constantinople was still unofficial. He laboured there purely on his own initiative and at the wish of his congregation. In the autumn of 380 Theodosius began to apply himself more zealously to the establishment of the Nicene creed in the Empire. He had been brought up in that faith, but, after the custom of the day, had postponed his baptism. In 380 he was taken ill in Thessalonica and was baptized by the orthodox bishop Acholius.[3] Imbued with a new fervour by this event he issued an edict declaring the Nicene faith to be the established and catholic creed, and anathematized the Arians.[4] He then hastened to Constantinople to set the Church's house in order in the capital city. Demophilus, the Arian bishop was expelled,[5] and the churches of the metropolis were vacated

---

[1] This apparently refers to the really incorrigible heretic or pagan with whom it is useless for the evangelist to argue.

[2] *Carm. de vita sua*, ll. 1190–262: *P.G.* 37. 1110–16.

[3] Sozomen 7. 4.   [4] *Cod. Theod.*, lib. xvi, tit. i, 1, 2.

[5] Socrates 5. 7 describes Demophilus assembling his followers outside the walls

for the orthodox. Then Gregory and his congregation were escorted in triumph from the Church of the Anastasis to the central church of the city, then the Church of the Apostles.[1] During
the installation the congregation raised the shout that Gregory
be enthroned as bishop. Gregory silenced the crowd, declaring
that another time would be more appropriate for such issues.[2]

His attitude toward the episcopate of the city displayed his
usual state of vacillation. He was not closed to the idea of
accepting it, if he were really wanted, but he wished to make
clear that he had no personal ambitions for it, and was certainly
not going to enter into ecclesiastical politics in order to get
it. Again Gregory demonstrated his violent aversion to factions
in the Church. Such disputes offended his sense of the proper
milieu of the Christian community, and he was determined to
have nothing to do with them, even if everyone else in the
Church was given over to such wrangling. In a sermon given in
the Church of the Apostles before the Emperor and his retinue,
he defended himself against the charge of seeking the episcopate.
He must indeed be ashamed, he said, if at his age, bowed down
by infirmity, he cherished such views. It would be strange if he
were now to be reproached for lusting after the wife of another
(i.e. Constantinople) when he never wished for his own (i.e.
Sasima). His only reason for coming to Constantinople was to
sustain the orthodox faith, which was then in a tottering condition.[3]

Theodosius followed up his actions on arrival in the capital
with several edicts intended to confirm the orthodox position.
To complete this work he determined to convene a council of
the Eastern Church in order to define more exactly the rule of
faith, and clarify various disciplinary matters, especially the
throne of Constantinople itself. This council, assembled in the

of the city, saying 'if they persecute you in one city flee ye to another. Since now the
emperor shuts us out of the churches, be it known to you that tomorrow we shall
meet outside the city [for worship]'; compare with Sozomen 7. 5.

[1] Tillemont and the Benedictine editors assume that it was the Church of St.
Sophia that was given to Gregory, but St. Sophia was not the cathedral church
until Justinian's time, and the references in Gregory's farewell speech (*Or.* 42. 26)
indicate that it was from the Church of the Apostles that he was taking leave. See
G. Downey, 'The Builder of the Original Church of the Apostles at Constantinople', *D.O.P.* (1951) 53–80.

[2] *Carm. de vita sua*, ll. 1375–95: *P.G.* 37. 1123–5.

[3] *Or.* 36. 6: *P.G.* 37. 272–3.

spring of 381, was attended by 150 Eastern bishops, the most significant among them being Meletius of Antioch, Helladius of Caesarea, Gregory of Nyssa (Basil's brother), Amphilochius of Iconium (Gregory of Nazianzus' first cousin), Diodorus of Tarsus, and Cyril of Jerusalem.[1]

Meletius of Antioch arrived somewhat earlier than the other bishops for the express purpose of seeing that Gregory was appointed bishop and to set aside the spurious election of Maximus.[2] After this was accomplished, Meletius died, and Gregory succeeded him as president of the council. He took this occasion to try to heal the ancient Antiochene schism.[3] Throwing away previous party ties, he gave his support to Paulinus, hoping that now that Meletius was dead, the orthodox community might unite around the remaining bishop. Gregory declared his willingness to forgo his own position, if only he could effect the unification of the Antiochene church.[4] But his effort to play the peacemaker was of little avail. Scarcely had he finished his address when the partisans of Meletius rose in opposition, 'screaming like jackdaws' and fell upon him 'like a swarm of wasps'.[5] One Flavianus was elected Meletius' successor, and the schism was renewed rather than healed.

The sittings of the council grew more and more stormy, and Gregory, in disgust, was glad to have the excuse of illness to absent himself for a few days. Seeing that he could do no good, he renewed his determination to withdraw altogether, but he was restrained by the pleas of his devoted congregation. As he was vacillating over his course of action, the Macedonian and Egyptian delegations arrived, much disgruntled over the decrees that had been passed against them in their absence,[6] and

[1] Socrates 5. 8; Sozomen 7. 7; Theodoret 5. 7. 8. See N. Q. King, 'The 150 Holy Fathers of the Council of Constantinople in 381 A.D.', S.P. 1 (1955), 635–41.

[2] Socrates, ibid. See also Canons 2 and 4 of the council, Mansi, tom. 3. 559.

[3] The immediate origin of the schism went back to the reign of Constantius II when Meletius was elected by the Arians. He then turned his support to the orthodox and was banished. Paulinus took over the orthodox community in his absence. Meletius returned during Julian's reign, but the conservative wing of the orthodox refused to recognize him, and thus there arose two orthodox communities in Antioch, Meletius being favoured by the Asians, while Rome and Alexandria recognized Paulinus.

[4] Carm. de vita sua, ll. 1590–680: P.G. 37. 1140–6.

[5] Ibid., l. 1680. P.G. 37. 1146.

[6] Canon 2 (Mansi, tom. 3. 559) was particularly directed against the meddling of Alexandria in the ordinations of other dioceses.

bent on stirring up trouble. They immediately contested Gregory's election, citing the fifteenth canon of the Nicene council that 'no bishop, presbyter, or deacon could transfer from one city to another'.[1] Ironically, the see of Sasima, which Gregory had never accepted, was now used to bar him from the throne of Constantinople.

With this new dissension Gregory made up his mind to depart. He describes, with some humour, how he sat in the council, listening to the harangues against him, feeling all the while like a fettered horse that was plunging in his stable, straining to break loose and gallop to pasture and freedom.[2] At the appropriate moment he rose and silenced the noisy assembly with the words:

My lords, God has brought you together so that you may determine something that He would wish. As for my own affairs, let them take second place; for, in the business of such an important assembly, it is really trivial what the outcome be (of his own affairs), even though my elevation has been in vain. You should elevate your minds to a higher consideration. You are actually met together; then, even though it be the eleventh hour, decided eventually to be together. How long can we go on being a laughing-stock? People regard us as insensitive creatures devoid of any feelings except combat. Please join hands with a good will in a gesture of fellowship. I am become Jonas the prophet. I am giving myself as victim for the safety of the ship, even though it will be a case of the innocent encountering the waves. Take me then, on the issue of the lot, and cast me forth. The hospitable whale will welcome me in the depths. From now on begin to be of one mind, and then make your way towards everything in due order. Let this place be known as the place of openness, and I will then have played not an ignoble part. If you persist with me, I shall have a single criticism—that you are making a contest over thrones. If you take the view that I suggest, nothing will be difficult. When I was enthroned it was without enthusiasm, and now I take my leave with a will. My state of health suggests this course too. I have only one death to die and this is in the hands of God. But, O My Trinity, you are all I care for! What tongue will you have, trained for your defence? an independent one I hope and full of zeal! Fare you well, my lords, and be mindful of my labours.[3]

[1] Theodoret 5. 8.
[2] Carm. de vita sua, ll. 1818–22: P.G. 37. 1156–7.
[3] Ibid., ll. 1828–55: P.G. 37. 1157–9.

Gregory then proceeded to the Emperor and wrung from him a reluctant confirmation of his resignation.[1] After bidding adieu to his congregation in a last noteworthy address,[2] Gregory turned his back for ever on the great capital of the East and returned to Cappadocia.

Closing Years in Nazianzus

Gregory returned to his homeland with the evident intention of entering into semi-monastic retreat on his family estates at Arianzus. He wished above all to be his own master, to be free of ecclesiastical affairs with their quarrels and trials, but such leisure was not to be easily acquired. When he had abruptly quit the church at Nazianzus six years before, he had hoped thereby to force the bishops to appoint a successor, but no action was taken. He no sooner returned than the old matter rose up again to engulf him. The bishops intended to see to it that he took up the ministry at Nazianzus, and a movement to that effect was already under way when another council was convened in Constantinople in 382. The Emperor and several of Gregory's friends tried to get him to return for this synod, but Gregory was adamant in his determination to have nothing further to do with Church councils. In a letter to Procopius he frankly declares his views on the subject.

If the truth be told my attitude toward all gatherings of bishops is to avoid them. I have never seen a good outcome to any synod, or a synod that produced deliverance from evils rather than addition to them. You must not think me tiresome when I write in this vein, but rivalries and manœuvres always prevail over reason, and in trying to decide between others it is easier to get accused of wickedness oneself than to deal with their wickedness. Consequently I have withdrawn to myself. I consider retirement to be the only means of saving my soul.[3]

Gregory was actually quite anxious about the outcome of the synod, despite his determination not to attend. He was particularly concerned by the criticism that might be levelled at himself, and the accompanying insistence that he take charge of the Nazianzene church. Although the Alexandrian clergy had used

[1] *Carm. de vita sua*, ll. 1871–905: *P.G.* 37. 1160–1. [2] *Supremum Vale, Or.* 42.
[3] *Ep.* 130: *P.G.* 37. 225. See also *Ep.* 131 to Olympius.

his consecration to Sasima to disqualify him from Constantinople, nobody seems to have taken this seriously. The consensus was that he had been appointed to Nazianzus by his father, and it was this church that he should administer. In the summer of 382 Gregory wrote a series of letters to acquaintances in Constantinople, requesting that they promote harmony in the synod and keep an eye on his personal fortunes.[1] But the bishops continued to insist that he take charge of his native church, and finally, in the autumn of 382, his health somewhat improved, Gregory acceded, but he wrote to Bosphorius of Colonia, the leader of his critics, with a very ill grace.

I am such an old-fashioned and futile person that I actually thought that you owed me an apology on previous scores. But you go on criticizing me, continually finding additional things to wrangle about, thinking up insult to pile on injury. Why you do so I can't imagine; you must either hate me, or you're seeking to curry favour with others by insulting me. However, I shall leave these things to be known and judged by God. Nothing escapes Him, as the Holy Scripture says, however much we distort the face of truth in order to make a good show before the multitude.

But I have good news for Your Reverence. I have given in, and in so far as God gives me the power, I shall not hesitate to undertake the care of the church, this being the matter that engages you, especially now that the crisis urges because of the expected assault of the enemy,[2] as your own letter indicates. This miserable body, for as long as it and my strength lasts, I shall devote to God. I don't want to go on being bothered by condemnations like this on your part, by having the clergy rail at me and heap all sorts of reproaches on me for ignoring the business of the church. Furthermore, I don't want you to exhaust yourself in upbraiding me. If, as you yourself say and the actual state of affairs demonstrates, you hesitate to take care of the church yourself, I shall do so with the help of your prayers. It is better I suppose to die surrounded by anxieties like that than by the sort I have now, since one is going to be miserable anyway, God having so shaped one's life.[3]

For over a year Gregory administered the church at Nazianzus, but his career was a stormy one, marked by battles with the

---

[1] See *Epp.* 132, 133, 135, and 136 to Saturninus, Victorinus, Sophronius, and Modarius respectively. All four men were either military or civil officials, not ecclesiastics.

[2] This refers to the Apollinarians, who were growing into a powerful rival community.   [3] *Ep.* 138.

Apollinarians and periodic illnesses. The local clergy also treated him despitefully, criticizing him for his former neglect of the church, and then ignoring his present position by conducting an ordination without him.[1]

By the end of 383 Gregory's health was such that he felt incompetent to cope with the duties of the church and the contending factions that were disrupting the community. Writing to Theodore of Tyana, he renewed his plea for a successor.[2] He was successful this time, and soon after wrote to Gregory of Nyssa to tell him that his cousin Eulalius was to take over the Nazianzene church. Rumour had it that Eulalius had been appointed against Gregory's wishes, so he wanted to make clear that he himself had requested this successor. Ironically, he then remarks that the appointment of a successor in the lifetime of an incumbent was not contrary to the canons, because he had never been appointed to Nazianzus, but only to Sasima![3]

As for Bosphorius, who originally forced Gregory to take responsibility for Nazianzus, he favours him only with the following note:

Twice already I have been tripped up and deceived by you in this matter; you know what I mean. If you were right, may it carry an odour of sweetness before the Lord; if wrong, may the Lord forgive you. It is only proper that I speak about you in such terms, because we are commanded to be patient even when wronged. However, just as you are the master of your own mind, so am I of mine. The tiresome Gregory will tire you no longer. I propose to take refuge in God, Who alone is pure and guileless. I shall withdraw into myself— that is my prescription for myself. According to the proverb, only fools stumble twice over the same stone.[4]

The last five years of Gregory's life were spent in peaceful retirement on his family estates in Arianzus. He passed his time there in religious devotions, in reading and composition of poetry, and in correspondence with friends. Almost a third of his extant letters date from this period, and probably a considerable amount of his poetry, although much of it is undatable.

---

[1] See *Ep.* 139 where Gregory writes to the newly elected bishop of Tyana, Theodore, to protest against these indignities and explain his own by now rather complicated episcopal history.

[2] *Ep.* 152; see also *Ep.* 183 to Theodore of Mopsuestia, explaining his withdrawal.

[3] *Ep.* 182.

[4] *Ep.* 153: *P.G.* 37. 260.

Having surrendered his pulpit, Gregory composed no more orations, but we have numerous short meditative poems as well as longer didactic poems on theological and ascetic themes. The purpose of this didactic poetry, such as his epic on the Trinity written in stately hexameters,[1] may have been similar to the reworking of Biblical books in classical genres undertaken by the Apollinarii, to create an *ersatz* Christian literature to replace the study of the classics for Christian youth.[2]

Gregory had a coterie of friends who were interested in the practice of philosophy, and he communicated with them on this subject in numerous letters.[3] He had a relationship with the monks of Lamis, and on the occasion of the death of one of the brethren wrote them a letter indicating the proper 'philosophic' spirit to adopt on such an occasion.[4] His hesitancy in giving such advice suggests that his role as an adviser was an informal one. He did act as spiritual adviser for several individuals. The young priest Sacerdos and his sister Thecla were close friends, and he often wrote them letters of advice and counsel in the spiritual life.[5] When he felt that a friend had a capacity for the 'higher life', he did not hesitate to try to lure him from his 'worldly' concerns. We have some interesting letters written to the rhetor Eudoxius, his great-nephew Nicobulus' teacher, in which he tried, apparently unsuccessfully,[6] to convert him from sophistry to philosophy.

To what end do we preen ourselves about trivialities, earth-bound things, diverting ourselves with the youngsters and their fictions, elated by applause? Let us get away from these, be men, throw away the dreams, pass by the empty shadows, let others have the joys of this life and its greater pains. Let envy, time, and fortune engage other people, sway them this way and that, make playthings of them. That instability and unevenness that go, they say, with the human lot; thrones, power, wealth, success, failure—a plague upon them. A plague upon bubble reputation, cheap and contemptible, which brings more discredit in elation than when a man chooses to laugh at

---

[1] *Poemata Dogmatica*: *P.G.* 37. 397–522. See Appendix II on the dating of Gregory's works.

[2] Cf. C. E. Raven, *Apollinarianism* (Cambridge, Mass. 1923) 131–76.

[3] See, for example, the letters to Timotheus (164–6); Celeusius (112–14); Palladius (110, 119); Pansophius (228–9); Ablabius (233); Adamantius (235), and Epiphanius (239).

[4] *Ep.* 238; also *Ep.* 116 in which he tells of a visit to the monastery.

[5] *Epp.* 212–15, 222–3.   [6] *Epp.* 179, 180.

the puerilities and theatricalities of this great stage of ours. Let us take a firm grip on doctrine and choose before all things God, the only lasting value we have. . . . The reward of virtue is to become God,[1] to be suffused with that purest light which we behold in the triune unity, the rays of which but lightly touch us now. Journey towards that goal, go forward, take wing in thought, grasp at eternal life, cease not to hope until you reach the blessed and longed-for height.[2]

Yet the pursuit of the philosophic life need not exclude *belles lettres*. In one letter to his close friend Philagrius we see how the counsels of philosophy can merge effortlessly into the pursuit of culture, and indeed philosophy itself is dressed in explicitly Platonic terms.

. . . by despising the body and everything that is of it—all that is impermanent, turbulent, or destructible—one may become totally concerned with higher values, living in future hope rather than in the present, making this life, in Plato's phrase, a rehearsal for death, and again in his phrase, delivering the soul in so far as one can from the tomb of the body.[3] My dear friend, if you take this philosophic way, you will find it of immense benefit to yourself, you will make me feel easier in your regard, and you will teach many people how a philosopher should bear adversity. . . . Of the books you asked me for, I have found one, and I have the pleasure of sending it—the Demosthenes, I mean. The other I have lost. I have not got the *Iliad* you want.[4]

Gregory characteristically runs down cultural interests whenever he feels that a person is exclusively concerned with such pursuits and has not yet turned his mind to 'higher things'. On one occasion a young man teaching literature wrote asking him for some books, and Gregory, feigning lack of interest in such childish pursuits, declared that he had not looked at the books for years and that the young man could have whatever moths and rust had not consumed. But he does not quite succeed in concealing his own former zeal for such things:

---

[1] Such a phrase, *Theon genesthai*, to become God, or to become divine, is characteristic of Eastern Christianity in contrast with the West. Here the goal of Christian life is seen as 'divinization'.

[2] *Ep.* 178: *P.G.* 37. 292–3.

[3] These phrases are from *Phaedo* and *Cratylus* respectively; see above, p. 13, n. 1, and p. 11, n. 4.

[4] *Ep.* 31: *P.G.* 37. 68–69.

It would have been better if you had requested holy books instead of these; they would, I'm sure, be more suitable and profitable for you. But since the wrong side has won and I can't change you around, here are the books you ask, as many of them as have survived the moths and smoke. That is where they were stored, like the sailor's rudder when the time of voyaging is over. However, seeing that people like Cynaegeirus and Callimachus and the trophies at Marathon and Salamis do mean a lot to you,[1] and you think they make you and the youngsters happy, throw yourself into the sophist's work right heartily and courageously without any hesitation or misgivings. I am allowing myself this much badinage, even though it is not very appropriate for one in my way of life. An old habit I suppose. Here they are for you and may you make good use of them.[2]

In spite of these protestations Gregory continued to take a keen interest in the rhetorical education of the young. We have some interesting letters to rhetoricians and sophists recommending young men to their care and encouraging them in their progress.[3] His particular protégé was his great-nephew Nicobulus, the grandson of his sister Gorgonia. Gregory had an affectionate relationship with this family,[4] and in his old age became a second father to the younger Nicobulus. He watched over his education with the keenest concern and wrote a number of letters to his teachers inquiring after the progress of his studies.[5] Nicobulus, like his great-uncle, was a devotee of rhetoric, and upon completion of his studies in Caesarea wished to continue his education in Athens. His parents were reluctant to let him embark on such a trip, but Gregory, perhaps reliving his own youthful pursuit of culture, wrote a poem to the father to persuade him to consent to the journey.[6] He then provided introductory letters to several celebrated sophists in Athens, and even intervened when two teachers became engaged in a quarrel over their right to act as Nicobulus' tutor.[7] Gregory and Nicobulus corresponded on the subject of *belles lettres*, and on one

[1] This refers to the *suasoriae* of the schools, which commonly took historical themes drawn from the Hellenic period; see Philostratus, *VS* 538.

[2] *Ep.* 235: *P.G.* 37. 377.   [3] For example, *Epp.* 234–6, 189.

[4] See *Ep.* 12, in which Gregory lightly admonishes the elder Nicobulus for making fun of his wife's *petite* stature.

[5] See *Epp.* 174–7, 187.

[6] *Nicobuli filii ad patrem*; *P.G.* 37. 1505–1521.

[7] *Epp.* 188, 190–2, concerning a dispute between the sophists Eustochius and Stagirus.

occasion Gregory wrote him two letters explaining the principles of good epistolary style.[1] It is probable that Nicobulus is responsible for the collection of Gregory's letters, for we have one letter in which his great-uncle responds to a request to make such a collection and send it to him.[2]

Amid such peaceful and elevating pursuits, Gregory died about 389/90. He illustrates perhaps better than anyone else the problems of the cultured Christian caught between two ideals of life. On the theoretical level he never really succeeded in reconciling the two. Yet on the practical level, through the dialectic of his own life, he succeeded in creating a rich interpenetration of the life of culture and the life of contemplation.

[1] *Epp.* 52 and 54.
[2] *Ep.* 51; in a second letter (*Ep.* 53) Gregory says that he is prefixing a collection of Basil's letters to his own.

II

GREGORY OF NAZIANZUS AS RHETOR

IN the first chapter on Gregory's life we have seen his extensive training in rhetoric and his brief activity as a rhetor after his return from Athens. We also saw his lifelong interest in the problems of style and contact with the world of sophistic. In this chapter we shall examine the influence of rhetoric on Gregory's style and thought. This subject has already been treated in an excellent work by M. Guignet,[1] and much of the material here will simply use new examples to reinforce his conclusion that not only Gregory's language but also his habits of thought are much under the influence of sophistic education.

The purpose of this study will not be to amass large numbers of examples of each rhetorical figure, as is the case with studies which aim at furnishing material for philological analyses in depth.[2] I hope to discuss the material synthetically rather than analytically, to give a glimpse of the cumulative effect of rhetorical style in the total context. Since my interest in style is focused on the formative influence of sophistic on Gregory's mentality, most of the chapter will be directed towards figures of thought, imagery, and laws of genre rather than figures of speech, for it is in these that the influence of rhetoric on the psychology of the Christian writer is most clearly revealed. I shall continually try to show points of synthesis where Christian and sophistic ideas and images have been combined. It is this amalgamation of the two traditions, sometimes in a

---

[1] Marcel Guignet, *S. Grégoire de Nazianze, orateur et épistolier* (Paris, 1911). This work is a companion piece to that of L. Méredier, *L'Influence de la second sophistique sur l'œuvre de Grégoire de Nysse* (Paris, 1906). Both follow the same methodology and were inspired by A. Puech, who, in 1900, called for greater attention to the influence of late Greek rhetoric on the Christian Fathers.

[2] Several American works of this type exist on Second Sophistic and the Christian Fathers: T. E. Ameringer, *The Stylistic Influence of Second Sophistic on the Panegyrical Sermons of St. John Chrysostom* (Washington, 1911); J. M. Campbell, *The Influence of Second Sophistic on the Style of the Sermons of Basil the Great* (Washington, 1922).

paradoxical manner, that makes the study of Gregory as a rhetor particularly interesting.

We should be on our guard against the tendency of writers on this subject to say that a certain Father is 'sophistic' chiefly when he is saying something trite and shallow.[1] It is true that when we see passages where the writer is straining after effect, pressing into service figures of speech and thought and rhythmic devices for the sake of a rather insubstantial idea, we can well mark these as 'sophistic' in the pejorative sense of the term. But sophistic is basically an instrument of expression, and these techniques of style—questions, exclamations, imagery, oxymoron, methods of vivacity and verisimilitude—can just as well be used to say important things. This is precisely the reason why sophistic training in the hands of the fourth-century Christians often gives the impression of greater power than among contemporary pagans, simply because the Christians have more significant things to say, as well as having all the refinements and resources of style with which to say them.

The organization and cataloguing of figures in this chapter will follow the methods used in Guignet's and Méredier's works. Much of the type of material discussed in the two French works has been reclassified here under the simplified headings of figures of speech, figures of thought, imagery, and laws of genre.

The discussion of figures of speech is prefaced by some general notes on vocabulary and syntax in order to show the relation of Gregory of Nazianzus' language to the language of Second Sophistic. By figures of speech one means figures of sound and structure. Figures such as parison, isokolon, anaphora, rhyming devices like homoioteleuton and homoioptoton, alliteration, and puns; all these go together to show how the ancient orator balanced sound against sound, phrase against phrase, and finally structured the period into an artistic whole. Here certain figures such as puns, which Quintilian classed as a trope, seemed to fit most naturally under sounding devices.[2]

---

[1] See H. Hubbell's review of T. E. Ameringer's work (above p. 55, n. 2); *C.W.* 16 (1922), 95 ff.

[2] Quint. *Inst.* 8. 6. 1–4. Here Quintilian notes that the genera and species of tropes had been interminably disputed among grammarians and philosophers, and he takes the word to mean all forms of substitution, both in single words and thoughts, and in structures of composition. This leads to rather diverse kinds of material classed under a single heading, and this author has found it more useful

Under figures of thought one includes all manner of conceits and artful patterns of thinking, such as rhetorical question, exclamation, apostrophe, invocation, impersonation, and personification. Certain techniques of argumentation, such as *communicatio* and *paraleipsis, dialectikon*, irony, and paradox all fit most naturally under this heading. The third section will be devoted to imagery in general: simile, metaphor, allegory, and typology, as well as *ecphrasis* (which Quintilian took as a figure of speech, but which is so closely linked with metaphor in its usage that it will be discussed in the same context).

Although the method of the chapter draws from the ancient *technai*, especially Quintilian, as well as the organization of the two French works, it does not rigidly follow the categories established by any of these sources. Rather there is an attempt to adapt these rules to the features of Gregory's style, omitting many minor figures for which examples could be found, but which would not add anything significant to the discussion, and focusing at length on typical features, such as metaphor. The governing principle is synthetic rather than disjunctive analysis; that is, not to list a multitude of single features discussed in relative isolation, but to gather these features into larger configurations in order to expose that which is most characteristic and significant about Gregory's style.

Vocabulary and Syntax

An examination of Gregory of Nazianzus' vocabulary and syntax reveals conclusions similar to Méredier's findings on Gregory of Nyssa. Gregory's language is a combination of classical Attic, *koine*, poetic words, and neologisms. Gregory is not a rigid Atticist like Libanius, but neither by any stretch of the imagination does he write a 'popular' language. Rather his language is an artificial literary creation founded basically on the classical canon, but also drawing on the *koine* of the Bible, which, though considered barbarous by an Atticist, for a Christian had the authority of God's Word. In Gallay's discussion of Gregory's language and style,[1] it is clear that Gregory employs

to adapt the traditional third type of *ornatio*, confining it to a discussion of imagery rather than tropes.

[1] Paul Gallay, *Langue et style de Saint Grégoire de Nazianze* (Paris, 1933) 74–80. Guignet did not attempt a chapter on Gregory's vocabulary and syntax.

both archaisms and a wealth of poetic words, characteristics which were generally true of Second Sophistic. Gregory is an eclectic and creates a rich language of his own, but at the same time he has a sure artistic taste that usually forbids banalities. He always remains close to classical usage, and as A. Puech says, he employs 'un vocabulaire et une syntax d'une pureté remarquable pour le temps'.[1] In addition to poetic words, which Gregory uses in accordance with the general customs of Second Sophistic, and words from the *koine* which he draws from Scripture and uses in the context of scriptural reference, Gregory also has two other traits of vocabulary: theological neologisms and Byzantine *politesse*. In the process of defining theological doctrines and distinguishing orthodox understanding of the Trinity or the incarnation from heretical interpretations, interpretations which were often founded on scriptural usages, Christians often had to construct new terms to cover ideas which simply did not exist before in the language. Thus, to distinguish the orthodox doctrine of the incarnation as a joining of the godhead to a complete human nature, we find the neologism ἐνανθρώπησις to distinguish the correct understanding of Christ's incarnation from the doctrine of the Apollinarians, who used the text of John, ὁ λόγος σὰρξ ἐγένετο, to prove that the *Logos* was incarnated just in a human body and not in a complete human nature.[2] One also finds, particularly in the letters to dignitaries, the usages of Byzantine *politesse*, where such titles of address would be employed as: ἡ σὴ τιμιότης,[3] ἡ σὴ εὐλάβεια,[4] ἡ σὴ ἀγαθότης,[5] ἡ σὴ μεγαλόνοια,[6] ἡ σὴ καλοκαγαθία,[7] ἡ σὴ εὐγένεια,[8] ἡ σὴ θεοσέβεια,[9] ἡ σὴ καθαρότης,[10] ἡ σὴ ὁσιότης,[11] ἡ σὴ σεμνοπρέπεια,[12] ἡ σὴ λογιότης.[13] From this blending of literary sources—classical prose, the Attic historians, orators, and sophists of the first and second school, both ancient and modern poets, Scripture, and theological language—Gregory creates

[1] A. Puech, *Histoire de la littérature grecque chrétienne*, t. 3, 369.
[2] *Ep.* 102 (to Cledonius), P.G. 37. 197 B. See Lampe's *Patristic Greek Lexicon* for the development of this word, which seems to have originated with Athanasius in the context of the Arian controversy.
[3] 37. 32 A.   [4] 37. 49 C.   [5] 37. 205 C.
[6] 37. 228 A.   [7] 37. 296 B.   [8] 37. 334 A.
[9] 37. 305 C.   [10] 37. 249 C.   [11] 37. 120 B.
[12] 37. 88 B.
[13] 37. 317 B. See also L. Dineen, *Titles of Address in Christian Greek Epistolography to 527 A.D.* (Washington, 1929).

a rich synthesis of great variety and colour. Guignet contrasts Gregory's language with that of Nyssen,[1] showing that where Nyssen takes over sophistic usages in a pedantic manner so that they dominate and oppress his style, Nazianzen is the artistic genius who can weld these elements into an original creation:

Il importe de savoir que, en dernière analyse, et par-dessus les multiples rapprochements signalés, il y a, entre l'évêque de Nysse, d'une part, et notre Grégoire, de l'autre, la distance d'un esprit scolaire, méticuleux, assez impersonnel, à une nature d'élite, fine, mobile, essentiellement intelligente et originale.

Figures of Language

In studying the general formation of Gregory's language, symmetry is the overriding characteristic. Balance and symmetry are the guiding principles in the parison of words, the equilibrium of kommata and kola, and the balancing of periods. Every word, every phrase, is complemented by or played against another word or phrase. The second overriding characteristic is prolixity. This, like the concern for symmetry, was also characteristic of Second Sophistic. An idea is never stated in just one way. It is stated in numerous different ways. One does not just use one metaphor or example; one uses numerous metaphors or examples. One aims at virtually overwhelming the listener with the richness of thought, the myriad images and nuances of language which tumble out in rapid succession. Like all good sophists, Gregory does not use just one style but is the master of numerous styles suited to the genre he is using. His epistolary style is altogether different from that which he employs in his orations. In the letters, in accordance with correct rhetorical usage, he employs a much simpler language, without elaborate metaphors or elaborate sentences. In the orations his style varies considerably, from a speech in the panegyric mode where many rhetorical devices such as exclamations, hyperbole, and metaphors of a more secular nature are used to the strictly theological orations where these are employed more sparingly. Gregory is the master of both the *logos politikos* and the *logos aphelēs*. As Guignet remarks,[2] 'C'est ce que fit Grégoire, qui montre une égale virtuosité dans la structure savante d'une

---

[1] Guignet, *S. Grégoire* 10.   [2] Ibid. 85.

longue période et dans l'accolement de kôla antithétiques ou successifs.' In the formal presentation of a theme Gregory can roll forth a flowing and majestic periodic style, where each kolon is integrated into an organic whole, but he more often prefers the loose or kommatic style.[1] This kind of clipped and broken style seems to be better suited to his poetic and intuitive way of presenting religious themes, so that a prolixity of images and ideas follow each other in rapid succession to give the impression of a 'danse éperdue'.[2]

Gregory makes constant use of the Gorgianic figures. Parison or isokolon, anaphora, homoioteleuton or homoioptoton are such a predominant feature of his oratorical style that Norden speaks of his rhythmic and musical flow of phrases as the 'signature of his style'.[3]

Anaphora or the repetition of the same word at the beginning of successive phrases is very common in Gregory. The following is a typical example:

Χριστὸν ἐπισκεψώμεθα, Χριστὸν θεραπεύσωμεν,
Χριστὸν θρέψωμεν, Χριστὸν ἐνδύσωμεν,
Χριστὸν συναγάγωμεν, Χριστὸν τιμήσωμεν.[4]

As is frequently the case with such sequences in Gregory's work, the rhythmic effect is reinforced by homoioteleuton, or rhyming endings.

Another use of anaphora in Gregory is to produce a didactic effect by reiterating the same word over and over:

Τοῦτο ἡμῖν ὁ παιδαγωγὸς βούλεται νόμος·
τοῦτο οἱ μέσοι Χριστοῦ καὶ νόμου προφῆται·
τοῦτο ὁ τοῦ πνευματικοῦ νόμου τελειωτὴς καὶ τὸ τέλος Χριστός·
τοῦτο ἡ κενωθεῖσα θεότης·
τοῦτο ἡ προσληφθεῖσα σάρξ·
τοῦτο ἡ καινὴ μῖξις, Θεὸς καὶ ἄνθρωπος.[5]

In this sequence we see the careful styling of structure, sound, and sense which is very typical of Gregory. In the first three members we have a reiteration of the word *nomos* used in

---

[1] In the poetic features of his style, Gregory probably shows the influence of his training under Himerius, who was pre-eminently the poet-orator. See Burgess, *Epideictic Literature* 181 ff.; also Gallay, *Vie* 55.

[2] Guignet, *S. Grégoire* 85.   [3] E. Norden, *Antike Kunstprosa* 2. 565.

[4] *Or.* 14. 39: *P.G.* 35. 909 B.   [5] *Or.* 2. 23: *P.G.* 35. 432 B.

successive senses, and climaxing with the paronomasia νόμου τελειωτὴς καὶ τὸ τέλος Χριστός. The second three members then form a kind of thesis, antithesis, and synthesis representing the incarnation: θεότης ... σάρξ ... μῖξις.

Another type of anaphora in Gregory is the reiterated rhetorical question. The following example also illustrates another typical habit of mind in Gregory; the tendency to try to gather up several aspects of an idea and integrate them into a single structural pattern:

τίς σοφὸς καὶ συνήσει ταῦτα;
τίς παραδραμεῖται τὰ παρατρέχοντα;
τίς προσθήσεται τοῖς ἐπιμένουσι;
τίς περὶ τῶν παρόντων, ὡς ἀπιόντων διανοηθήσεται;
τίς περὶ τῶν ἐλπιζομένων, ὡς ἱσταμένων;
τίς διαιρήσει τὰ ὄντα καὶ τὰ φαινόμενα
    καὶ τοῖς μὲν ἕψεται τῶν δὲ ὑπερόψεται;
τίς γραφὴν καὶ ἀλήθειαν;
τίς τὴν κάτω σκηνὴν καὶ τὴν ἄνω πόλιν;
τίς παροικίαν καὶ κατοικίαν;
τίς σκότος ἀπὸ τοῦ φωτός;
τίς ἰλὺν βυθοῦ καὶ ἁγίαν γῆν;
τίς σάρκα καὶ πνεῦμα;
τίς θεὸν καὶ κοσμοκράτορα;
τίς θανάτου σκιὰν καὶ ζωὴν τὴν αἰώνιον;
τίς τοῖς παροῦσι τὸ μέλλον ὠνήσεται;
τίς τῷ ῥέοντι πλούτῳ τὸν μὴ λυόμενον;
τίς τοῖς ὁρωμένοις τὰ μὴ βλεπόμενα;[1]

In this passage we see a series of skilfully matched antitheses, a figure which was very expressive of the dualistic structure of Christian thought. Gregory also displays his virtuosity of language by the use of rapid antitheses which employ the pun (parēchēsis) such as παροικίαν καὶ κατοικίαν and σκότος, φωτός or a clever chiasmus ἰλὺν βυθοῦ καὶ ἁγίαν γῆν· Another notable use of anaphora occurs in Oration 40, On Baptism, where Gregory creates a remarkable effect by repeating the word φῶς at the beginning of nine successive kola,[2] or in a passage in Oration 34 where he addresses the Egyptian sailors who have come to visit

[1] Or. 14. 21: P.G. 35. 884 C.   [2] P.G. 36. 364 D–85 B.

his church by starting successive sentences with the phrase λαὸς ἐμός· ἐμὸν γάρ.[1]

In this phrase we also observe another procedure of style, the repetition of the last word of one kolon at the beginning of the next. This figure is called anastrophe. This device is also useful to create emphasis, as in the following examples:

> Ἐπεὶ δὲ κεφάλαιον ἑορτῆς μνήμη Θεοῦ,
> Θεοῦ μνημονεύσωμεν.[2]
>
> καὶ λυθῇ τὸ κατάκριμα τῆς σαρκός,
> σαρκὶ τοῦ θανάτου θανατωθέντος.[3]

This second example also makes use of polyptoton, or the use of the same word in different inflexions. One of Gregory's most elaborate uses of polyptoton occurs in this passage:

> μεταληπτόν, οὐ μεταληπτικόν·
> τελειοῦν, οὐ τελειούμενον·
> πληροῦν, οὐ πληρούμενον·
> ἁγιάζον, οὐχ ἁγιαζόμενον·
> θεοῦν, οὐ θεούμενον· . . .
> ἀόρατον, ἄχρονον, ἀχώρητον, ἀναλλοίωτον,
> ἄποιον, ἄποσον, ἀνείδεον, ἀναφές,
> αὐτοκίνητον, ἀεικίνητον, αὐτεξούσιον, αὐτοδύναμον . . .
> ζωὴ καὶ ζωοποιόν,
> φῶς καὶ χορηγὸν φωτός,
> αὐτοαγαθὸν καὶ πηγὴ ἀγαθότητος. . . .[4]

This passage is on the working of the Holy Spirit, and it is an excellent example of what might be called Gregory's 'hymnic' style. Here we observe that the two sets of phrases using polyptoton are broken up by a *tour de force* of twelve words in alliteration. In another interesting passage he creates a complex rhythmic pattern by using both anaphora and alliteration:

> Χθὲς συνεσταυρούμην Χριστῷ, σήμερον συνδοξάζομαι·
> Χθὲς συνενεκρούμην, συζωοποιοῦμαι σήμερον·
> Χθὲς συνεθαπτόμην, σήμερον συνεγείρομαι·[5]

[1] *P.G.* 36. 245 B–D; see also 312 A.   [2] *Or.* 39. 10: *P.G.* 36. 345 B.
[3] *Or.* 39. 13: *P.G.* 36. 349 B.
[4] *Or.* 41. 9: *P.G.* 36. 441 B; see also *Or.* 31. 29: *P.G.* 36. 165 C, where a similar series in polyptoton occurs.   [5] *Or.* 1. 4: *P.G.* 35. 397 B.

In this passage we also observe a kind of continuation of anastrophe where a kolon is begun with a word, a succeeding kolon
ends with the same word, and then a third begins with the word.
This was called *klimax*. A variation of *klimax* is found when
several words are repeated in succession, as in the following
example where we have an A, B, A, C, B, C pattern.

> οὔκουν διάστασις, ἵνα μὴ λύσις·
> οὐδὲ μάχη, ἵνα μὴ διάστασις·
> οὐδὲ σύνθεσις, ἵνα μὴ μάχη·
> διὰ τοῦτο οὐδὲ σῶμα, ἵνα μὴ σύνθεσις·[1]

Gregory is fond of all kinds of rhyming devices such as a series
like the following:

> Χάρισμα, βάπτισμα, χρῖσμα φώτισμα. . . .[2]

The rhyming series is very characteristic of his style, and he is
particularly fond of stringing out a series of mysteries of faith
in a rhyming sequence, as in the following example, where he
lists the mysteries of the life of Christ:

> περιτεμνόμενος, βαπτιζόμενος,
> μαρτυρούμενος ἄνωθεν, πειραζόμενος,
> λιθαζόμενος δι’ ἡμᾶς . . . . προδιδόμενος,
> προσηλούμενος, θαπτόμενος,
> ἀνιστάμενος, ἀνερχόμενος·[3]

The above example also makes use of asyndeton, or the series
without connectives. This is also a favourite technique of
Gregory's which makes for a kind of 'drum beat' effect. In his
oration *On Baptism* he makes use of another such series, repeating the word φώτισμα[4] and then evoking a whole series of
synonymous phrases:

> τὸ φώτισμα, σαρκὸς ἀπόθεσις,
> Πνεύματος ἀκολούθησις,

[1] In *Or*. 40. 5: *P.G.* 36. 364 B, Gregory also uses this striking example of *klimax*
in which a progressive structure of language expresses an ascending progress of
thought:
> ὅσον ἂν καθαιρώμεθα, φανταζόμενον·
> καὶ ὅσον ἂν φαντασθῶμεν, ἀγαπώμενον·
> καὶ ὅσον ἂν ἀγαπήσωμεν, αὖθις νοούμενον·

[2] *Or*. 40. 4: *P.G.* 36. 361 D. [3] *Or*. 41. 5: *P.G.* 36. 436 B, C.
[4] φώτισμα is the word commonly used for baptism.

Λόγου κοινωνία,
πλάσματος ἐπανόρθωσις,
κατακλυσμὸς ἁμαρτίας,
φωτὸς μετουσία,
σκότοις κατάλυσις·
τὸ φώτισμα, ὄχημα πρὸς Θεόν,
συνεκδημία Χριστοῦ,
ἔρεισμα πίστεως,
νοῦ τελείωσις,
κλεὶς οὐρανῶν βασιλείας,
ζωῆς ἤμειψις,
δουλείας ἀναίρεσις,
δεσμῶν ἔκλυσις,
συνθέσεως μεταποίησις·
τὸ φώτισμα ....[1]

The rhyming effect is reinforced by homoioteleuton and assonance such as φωτός ... σκότοις and Χριστοῦ ... πίστεως.

The same effect could be produced by polysyndeton, or the
repetition of connectives:

Δεινὸν ὀφθαλμοῖς ἁλῶναι,
καὶ γλώσσῃ τρωθῆναι,
καὶ ἀκοῇ δελεασθῆναι,
καὶ διὰ θυμοῦ ζέσαντος ἐμπρησθῆναι,
καὶ γεύσει κατενεχθῆναι,
καὶ ἁφῇ μαλακισθῆναι,
καὶ τοῖς ὅπλοις τῆς σωτηρίας,
ὅπλοις θανάτου χρήσασθαι.[2]

One can see in this passage, as in so many others, how carefully
Gregory works out the rhythmic effect of his kommata: an
opening phrase, then a pair of phrases, then another pair,
broken by a longer phrase, the five ending in the same sound,
and the whole group ending in a *sententia* with its rapid antithetical play on the word ὅπλοις.

Gregory makes considerable use of word-play and puns. The
pun becomes particularly clever when two words which sound
alike are used antithetically, such as:

[1] *Or.* 40. 3: *P.G.* 36. 361 B.
[2] *Or.* 25. 19: *P.G.* 35. 1192 C.

οὐδὲ τὴν ὑλακήν,
ἀλλὰ τὴν φυλακὴν τοῦ καλοῦ[1]

φιλοχρύσους . . . φιλοχρίστους[2]
φιλοχρυσότατος . . . μισοχριστότατος[3]
φιλοσοφία καὶ φιλοπονία[4]
φιλόσοφος . . . φιλόδοξος[5]
φιλεόρτοις . . . φιλοθέοις[6]
φιλοσοφία . . . κενοδοξία.[7]

In addition to these simpler plays on words, one also finds the more elaborate pun. In the second theological oration against the Eunomians (*Or.* 28) Gregory refutes their arguments concerning the incarnation by saying 'this argument concerning the body [of Christ] is shown to have no body [i.e. no substance]'.[8] In his oration on baptism he indulges in some particularly egregious puns:

Βαπτισθῶμεν σήμερον,
ἵνα μὴ αὔριον βιασθῶμεν . . .
μηδὲ γενώμεθα Χριστοκάπηλοι καὶ Χριστέμποροι.[9]

In the next paragraph he makes a bold play on the two meanings of the word βαπτίζω, to be baptized (i.e. to be saved) and to be drowned (i.e. lost):

Βαπτισθῶμεν σήμερον . . .
ἵνα μὴ αὐτάνδρῳ τῇ νηὶ βαπτισθῶμεν,
καὶ τὸ χάρισμα ναυαγήσωμεν, . . .[10]

Gregory's fertile imagination then goes on to conjure up the death-bed scene of the unbaptized man with the Christian and the legacy hunter both contending for his last favours:

. . . μάχη βαπτιστοῦ καὶ χρηματιστοῦ,
τοῦ μέν, ὅπως ἐφοδιάσῃ φιλονεικοῦντος,
τοῦ δέ, ὅπως γραφῇ κληρονόμος, . . .[11]

These figures of redundancy and assonance are, of course, used as a part of the larger structure of the sentence. In the composition of the period Gregory makes constant use of the Gorgianic

[1] *P.G.* 35. 1200 B.   [2] Ibid. 1105 B.   [3] *P.G.* 36. 536 D.
[4] Ibid. 528 B.   [5] Ibid. 536 D.   [6] Ibid. 345 B.
[7] *P.G.* 35. 416 A; also 35. 1137 A.   [8] *P.G.* 36. 36 A.
[9] *Or.* 40. 11: *P.G.* 36. 372 B.   [10] Ibid. 372 C.   [11] Ibid. 373 A.

826619   F

figures; that is, the parallelism of kommata and kola, a parallelism of words, sounds, and grammatical composition. When parallelism includes not only the structure, but also the number of syllables in successive phrases, this is called perfect parison or isokolon. Gregory makes frequent use of this device, although always with care not to overdo it but to introduce a certain asymmetry to prevent monotony. In the following example of isokolon, we also notice the common Gregorian use of homoioteleuton:

> Ἰουδαῖοι σκανδαλιζέσθωσαν,
> Ἕλληνες διαγελάτωσαν,
> αἱρετικοὶ γλωσσαλγείτωσαν, ...[1]

In another example of almost perfect parison, the figures of anaphora, homoioteleuton, and assonance reinforce the parallelism:

> τὴν τῶν δαιμόνων καθαίρεσιν,
> τὴν τῶν νόσων κατάλυσιν,
> τὴν τοῦ μέλλοντος πρόγνωσιν.[2]

Another striking example of anaphora, homoioteleuton, and perfect parison:

> πάλιν τὸ σκότος λύεται,
> πάλιν τὸ φῶς ὑφίσταται,
> πάλιν Αἴγυπτος σκότῳ κολάζεται,
> πάλιν Ἰσραὴλ στύλῳ φωτίζεται.[3]

In this example of parison we notice a contrast of sense, darkness against light, Egypt against the promised land. This device of antithetical parison, which combined parallelism of structure and contrast of meaning, was a favourite with the sophists, but in the hands of Christian orators it found very skilful use as an expression of the basic dualism and antitheses of Christian theology; this world against the next world, the flesh against the spirit, the Old Creation against the New Creation.

Like all sophists Gregory is consistently pleonastic. An idea is seldom stated simply but is repeated in numerous versions.

---

[1] Or. 38. 2: P.G. 36. 313 B, C.   [2] Or. 25. 18: P.G. 35. 1192 A.
[3] Or. 38. 2: P.G. 36. 313 A.

Thus in contrasting the pagan with the Christian, or the earthly with the heavenly way of celebrating a festival, Gregory writes:

Τοιγαροῦν ἑορτάζωμεν,
μὴ πανηγυρικῶς, ἀλλὰ θεϊκῶς,
μὴ κοσμικῶς, ἀλλ᾽ ὑπερκοσμίως,
μὴ τὰ ἡμέτερα, ἀλλὰ τὰ τοῦ ἡμετέρου,
μᾶλλον δὲ τὰ τοῦ Δεσπότου·
μὴ τὰ τῆς ἀσθενείας, ἀλλὰ τὰ τῆς ἰατρείας·
μὴ τὰ τῆς πλάσεως, ἀλλὰ τὰ τῆς ἀναπλάσεως.[1]

Another set of neat antitheses contrasts the orthodox with the heretical mode of disputation:

δογματικῶς, ἀλλ᾽ οὐκ ἀντιλογικῶς·
ἁλιευτικῶς, ἀλλ᾽ οὐκ Ἀριστοτελικῶς·
πνευματικῶς, ἀλλ᾽ οὐ κακοπραγμονικῶς·
ἐκκλησιαστικῶς, ἀλλ᾽ οὐκ ἀγοραίως·
ὠφελίμως, ἀλλ᾽ οὐκ ἐπιδεικτικῶς.[2]

Another common sophistic device, also useful for Christian didacticism, is the series of antitheses deduced one from the other which grow more and more complicated as the thought progresses:

τοὺς μὲν ἔπαινος ὤνησε, τοὺς δὲ ψόγος,
ἀμφότερα μετὰ τοῦ καιροῦ·
ἢ τοὐναντίον ἔβλαψεν ἔξω τοῦ καιροῦ καὶ τοῦ λόγου.
Τοὺς μὲν παράκλησις κατορθοῖ·
τοὺς δὲ ἐπιτίμησις·
καὶ αὕτη, τοὺς μὲν ἐν τῷ κοινῷ διελεγχομένους,
τοὺς δὲ κρύβδην νουθετουμένους.
Φιλοῦσι γὰρ οἱ μὲν καταφρονεῖν τῶν ἰδίᾳ νουθετημάτων,
πλήθους καταγνώσει σωφρονιζόμενοι.
οἱ δὲ πρὸς τὴν ἐλευθερίαν τῶν ἐλέγχων ἀναισχυντεῖν,
τῷ τῆς ἐπιτιμήσεως μυστηρίῳ παιδαγωγούμενοι . . . .[3]

Antitheses have many sources in Gregory. A major source, as we have noted, is the basic dualism of Christian thought, which finds expression in such antitheses as the exposition of the nature of man in *Oration* 38 on the *Theophania*, where Gregory

[1] *Or.* 38. 4: *P.G.* 36. 316 A, B.   [2] *Or.* 23. 12: *P.G.* 35. 1164 C, D.
[3] *Or.* 2. 31: *P.G.* 35. 440 A, B.

68   GREGORY OF NAZIANZUS AS RHETOR

discusses man's dual nature, standing partly in the visible, partly in the invisible creation.[1] This dualism also shows up in Gregory's discussion of the Christian life, in antitheses of speech and silence[2] or the contemplative versus the active life.[3] Many antitheses can be put down mainly as sophistic *jeux d'esprit* or commonplaces such as the following:

καὶ θεραπεύεται μὲν τὸ ὑψηλόν,
ἀτιμάζεται δὲ τὸ θεῷ ταπεινούμενον.[4]

Another major use of antithesis in Gregory is in the work of theological definition, where a point is explained by contrasting it with its opposite. For example, in clarifying orthodox trinitarian doctrine, Gregory expounds the proper formulation of three persons in one substance by contrasting it with its opposites; Sabellianism, on the one hand, which unifies both persons and substance, and Arianism, on the other, which divides the substance as well as the persons. The following example shows Gregory's penchant for word-play even in the midst of the most solemn theological definitions:

μήτε οὕτως ἀλλήλων ἀπήρτηται,
ὡς φύσει τέμνεσθαι·
μήτε οὕτως ἐστένωται,
ὡς εἰς ἓν πρόσωπον περιγράφεσθαι·
τὸ μὲν γὰρ τῆς Ἀρειανῆς μανίας,
τὸ δὲ τῆς Σαβελλιανικῆς ἀθείας ἐστίν·
ἀλλ' ἔστη, τῶν μὲν πάντη διαιρετῶν ἑνικωτέρα,
τῶν δὲ τελείως μοναδικῶν ἀφθονωτέρα.[5]

Our author found this particular didactic antithesis so effective that he used it again and again.[6]

Gregory, as we noted before, is the master of both the *logos politikos* and the *logos apheles*, the closely reasoned and integrally structured periodic style and the loose style where phrases are strung together without much use of subordination and often with omission of connectives. In Guignet's chapter on the

[1] *Or.* 38. 11: *P.G.* 36. 324 A.   [2] *Or.* 12. 1: *P.G.* 35. 844 A, B.
[3] *Or.* 12. 4: *P.G.* 35. 848 B, also 848 C.   [4] *P.G.* 35. 520 A.
[5] *Or.* 34. 8: *P.G.* 36. 249 A.
[6] For example, *Or.* 21. 13: *P.G.* 35. 1095 C; *Or.* 43. 30: *P.G.* 36. 537 A; *Or.* 38. 15: *P.G.* 36. 329 A.

Gregorian period, he analyses Gregory's use of the first style.[1]
I will, therefore, confine my analysis to an example of Gregory's
use of the loose style, which he prefers and uses more frequently.
In the loose style the period is still structured into an organic
whole, but not so much by grammatical structure as by groupings of kola and kommata, by parison and antithesis and by
rhythmic and euphonic devices, as in the following example:[2]

> 3 { τὸ δὲ εὐσεβὲς μὴ ἐν τῷ πολλάκις περὶ θεοῦ λαλεῖν,
> ἀλλ' ἐν τῷ τὰ πλείω σιγᾶν εἶναι τιθέμενοι·
> γλῶσσα γὰρ ὄλισθος ἀνθρώποις μὴ λόγῳ κυβερνωμένη·
>
> 2 { καὶ ἀκινδυνοτέραν ἀκοὴν ἀεὶ λόγου νομίζοντες,
> ὥστε τι μανθάνειν ἥδιον, ἢ διδάσκειν περὶ θεοῦ·
>
> 3 { τὴν μὲν ἀκριβεστέραν τούτων ἐξέτασιν τοῖς οἰκονόμοις
> τοῦ λόγου παραχωροῦντες·
> αὐτοὶ δὲ λόγῳ μὲν εὐσεβοῦντες ὀλίγα,
> ἔργῳ δὲ πλείονα,
> καὶ τῇ τηρήσει τῶν νόμων μᾶλλον ἢ τῷ θαυμάζειν
> τὸν νομοθέτην τὸ περὶ αὐτὸν φίλτρον ἐπιδεικνύμενοι·
>
> 2 φεύγοντες κακίαν, διώκοντες ἀρετήν,
> 2 πνεύματι ζῶντες, πνεύματι στοιχοῦντες·
> 2 { τούτῳ τὴν γνῶσιν ἕλκοντες,
> ἐποικοδομοῦντες τῷ θεμελίῳ τῆς πίστεως,
> 3 μὴ ξύλον, μηδὲ χόρτον, μηδὲ καλάμην,
> 2 { ὕλην ἀσθενῆ καὶ ῥαδίως δαπανωμένην,
> ἡνίκα ἂν πυρὶ κρίνηται τὰ ἡμέτερα ἢ καθαίρηται·
> 3 ἀλλὰ χρυσὸν ἄργυρον, λίθους τιμίους,
> τὰ μένοντα καὶ ἱστάμενα.

The first group contains an antithesis of thought rounded out by
a concluding commonplace. This group of three kommata is
followed by a comparison in perfect syllabic parison. Alliteration is also used (ἀκινδυνοτέραν ἀκοὴν ἀεί). This comparison
is followed by another group of three phrases, consisting of a
general statement played against two statements each of which
contains an antithesis. This group is followed by three pairs of
kommata. The first is a rhymed pair in perfect syllabic parison.

---

[1] Guignet, S. Grégoire 82–106.
[2] Or. 3. 7: P.G. 35. 524 A, B. The breakdown of this period into groupings
follows not so much the strict grammatical sequences of kommata and kola as it
does the groupings of sound and sense as the phrases would strike the ear in oral
delivery.

The figures of anaphora and homoioteleuton are found in the second pair. The pattern is varied in the third pair by ending the first komma and beginning the second with the same form (ἕλκοντες, ἐποικοδομοῦντες). The first two of these pairs are antithetical in thought, the third contains complementary ideas. Then a series of three negative phrases in asyndeton which progress in crescendo (three, four, five syllables); then another pair of complementary phrases. An assonance is set up by concluding the previous komma, and starting and concluding the succeeding komma, by -λάμην, ὕλην, -μένην. Then another series of positive statements in asyndeton which contrast with the three negative statements, and a concluding rhythmic clausula with the pleonastic pair μένοντα καὶ ἱστάμενα which parallels the previous pleonasm κρίνηται . . . ἢ καθαίρηται. In addition to this pairing of word against word, sound against sound, komma against komma, the whole period forms a geometric structure of 3, 2, 3; 2, 2, 2; 3, 2, 3 including the concluding clausula. In addition to these figures of language one notes in such a sentence the general prolixity of thought characteristic of Second Sophistic. One is never content to state an idea simply; one must contrast it with its opposite. One cannot just make one antithesis, but must present it in several variations. It was this kind of highly stylized patterning of thought, words, and phrases that marked the master of sophistic style that Gregory was. Only when we realize that the sophist or sophistic preacher spoke to an audience trained to catch all the nuances of such word and sound patterns can we understand the great excitement created by a great orator whose flow of language was an art form in itself.

Figures of Thought

Gregory makes constant use of the common figures of thought, particularly rhetorical question and exclamation. Exaggeration was the characteristic of sophistic style, and Gregory uses these techniques so frequently that we must speak of his style as consistently hyperbolic and exclamatory. The rhetorical question could serve a number of functions in sophistic prose. One could use it as a technique for opening the exposition of a subject, or continuing the enumeration of the details of a subject which threatens to become tedious in its prolixity. One could use it as a mode of hyperbole or as a part of the diatribe question-and-answer method of argumentation. In Gregory's eulogy on his brother, for example, he uses a rhetorical question as a way of opening an exposition of the virtues of Caesarius. He pretends to be overwhelmed by the subject and uncertain where to begin. This pretence of not knowing where to begin was a figure much developed in court rhetoric (*diaporesis*), but it could be put to skilful use in the encomiastic speech.

Which of his qualities shall I place first and foremost, or which can I omit with least injury to my description? Who was more faithful to his teacher than he? Who was more kindly to his classmates? Who more carefully avoided the society and companionship of the depraved? Who attached himself more closely to that of the most excellent and, among others, of the most esteemed and illustrious of his countrymen?

After some amplification of this material, Gregory continues the exclamatory question style:

What branch of learning did he not master, or rather, in what branch of learning did he not surpass those who made it their sole study? Whom did he allow even to approach him, not only of his own time and age, but even of his elders who had devoted many more years to study?[1]

The encomium by its nature tended to exaggeration and extreme prolixity. The orator attempted virtually to sweep his audience away in the apparently endless enumeration of virtues and marvels. Since the orator must be verbose but never tedious, the rhetorical question was useful in picking up the thread of the exposition and launching into a new series of *aretai*. Thus after a long exposition of the beauty and modesty of his sister, Gregory, in his encomium on Gorgonia, launches into a new series of eulogies with the words

Enough of such topics. Of her prudence and piety no adequate account can be given. . . . What could be keener than the intellect of her who was recognized as the common adviser, not only by those of her family . . . but even of all men about, who treated her counsels and advice as a law not to be broken? What were more sagacious than her words? What more prudent than her silence? Who had

[1] *Or.* 7. 6: *P.G.* 35. 762 A, B, C.

a fuller knowledge of the things of God, both from divine oracles and from her own understanding? . . . Who paid such honor to priests? . . . Who opened her house to those who live according to God with a more graceful and bountiful welcome? . . . Whose soul was more sympathetic to those in trouble? Whose hand more liberal to those in want? . . .[1]

The question can also be used as a kind of *paraleipsis* in which the orator exclaims, 'How can I possibly describe such and such a wonderful (or terrible) thing', and then proceeds to describe it in minute detail by a series of questions.[2] The question could also be used as a kind of apostrophe, where the orator addressed a series of questions to an imaginary interlocutor. This was the common technique in the diatribe, which we shall discuss later, but it could also be used as a part of the encomium where the orator, instead of asking the audience 'How can I continue? What shall I say next?', addresses such questions to the man he is praising himself, as though he were present in the room. In his oration on Hero, Gregory uses this technique, addressing Hero with the words: 'How many men have you taught the maxims of the true philosophy? How many have you freed from their errors and impiety? How many have you led to the cause of virtue?'[3] Then, giving full rein to his imaginative powers, Gregory conjures up a vision of a great throng of pious Christians surrounding Hero. Continuing with his hyperbolic questioning of Hero, Gregory says: 'What solace do you find in your sufferings? When did you not cultivate poverty? What companions do you have in your struggles? . . .'

In the oration *In patrem tacentem*, Gregory addresses a similar series of questions to his father. This oration was occasioned by a hailstorm which destroyed the crops of the citizens of Nazianzus. Gregory's father was so affected by the disaster that he could not preach the sermon of consolation to his people and begged his son to do so. Gregory starts the address by protesting his inadequacy to take the place of his father, and then begins the exposition of the theme by way of a series of questions which combine the suggestion of humility with praise of his father, as if appealing to the wisdom of the older man for guidance.[4] After a few preliminary exhortations—

[1] *Or.* 8. 11: *P.G.* 35. 802 A–C.
[2] *Or.* 25. 9: *P.G.* 35. 1218 B, C.
[3] *Or.* 25. 14: *P.G.* 35. 1218 B, C.
[4] *Or.* 16. 5: *P.G.* 35. 940 B ff.

Give a lesson to me in the pastor's art, to this people of obedience. Discourse awhile on our present heavy blow, whether we grasp its meaning or are ignorant of its great portent. . . . Tell us whence come such blows and scourges and what account we can give of them. Is it some disordered and irregular current, some unreason of the universe, as though there were no ruler of the universe? . . . Or are the disturbances and changes of the universe . . . directed by reason and order under the guidance of the reins of Providence? Whence come famines and tornadoes and hailstorms, our present warning blows? Whence come pestilences, diseases, earthquakes, tidal waves, and fearful things in the heavens? And how is the creation, once ordered for the enjoyment of men, . . . changed for the punishment of the ungodly?'

Gregory continues in this vein until, through the pretence of questioning his father, he has laid out the whole groundwork by which he intends to develop his theme. These are only a few examples of rhetorical questions in Gregory. They do not even begin to exhaust the varied ways in which he uses this device, numerous examples of which could be cited from every oration.

The exclamation is also a common Gregorian figure. This figure is used particularly to climax an impressive effect, as though the orator can no longer contain his emotions. Thus in his oration on Caesarius, after developing the *topos* of *apatheia*, in which the funeral orator declares the necessity of philosophic restraint of grief, Gregory bursts out, as if unable to restrain his feelings, in spite of his best efforts: 'Oh, how can I recall those days, without my tears showing that, contrary to my promises, my feelings have overcome my philosophic restraint?'[1] There is also the exclamation of simulated rage and indignation, as when Gregory, recounting the efforts of Julian to win over his brother, exclaims: 'How utter was the derangement and folly which could hope to take for his prey a man like Caesarius, my brother, the son of parents like ours!'[2] In his oration on Gorgonia Gregory uses the exclamation to give a highly coloured exposition of the virtues of the ascetic life:

O untended body, and squalid garments whose only flower is virtue! O soul, clinging to the body, when reduced almost to an immaterial state through lack of food! or rather, when the body had been mortified by force, even before dissolution, that the soul might

---

[1] *Or.* 7. 6: *P.G.* 35. 762 A.   [2] *Or.* 7. 11: *P.G.* 35. 769 A.

attain to freedom and escape the entanglements of the senses! O
nights of vigil and psalmody, and standing which lasts from one day
to another! O David, whose strains never seem tedious to faithful
souls![1]

This exclamatory exposition is continued for some time ('O
tender limbs . . . ! O fountains of tears . . . ! O cry in the night
. . . ! O fervour of spirit . . . ! O nature of woman . . . ! O baptismal purity . . . ! O soul . . . ! O bitter eating! O Eve, mother
of our race and of our sin! O subtle serpent and death, overcome
by her self-discipline! O self-emptying of Christ! . . . Oh, how
am I to count up all her traits, or pass over most of them without injuring those who know them not?'). The same exclamatory exposition is repeated several times in succeeding parts of
this oration. In the passage we have quoted we note the use of
correctio, a figure in which the orator restates an idea in amended
form. The same figure also occurred in the passage quoted on
Caesarius (above, p. 71). This figure is very common in
Gregory and serves the function of *amplificatio*. The orator can
pack even more nuances and variant aspects of the idea into his
exposition in this way.

Apostrophe or direct address is also a frequent figure in
Gregory's orations, making for liveliness and focusing of attention. In his orations he frequently addresses the audience
directly or some person within it or argues with imaginary foes.
This also was a characteristic of the diatribe, which was in-
fluential in the formation of the Christian sermon.[2] In the oration on his father, Gregory addresses the following hyperbolic
speech to Basil, who was present in the congregation:

O man of God and faithful servant and steward of the mysteries of
God and man of desires of the Spirit; for thus Scripture speaks of men
advanced and lofty and superior to visible things. I will call you also
a God to Pharaoh (Exod. 7. 1) and all the Egyptians and hostile
power and pillar and ground of the Church (1 Tim. 7. 15) and will of
God (Isai. 62. 4) and light of the world holding forth the word of life
and prop and resting place of the Spirit. But why should I enumerate
all the titles which your virtue, in its varied forms, has won for and
applied to you?[3]

[1] *Or.* 8. 14: *P.G.* 35. 806 A–D.
[2] See Hubbell, 'Chrysostom and Rhetoric', *C.Ph.* 19 (1924), 261 f.; also Norden,
Antike Kunstprosa 2. 556.
[3] *Or.* 18. 1: *P.G.* 35. 986 A.

In addition to the address to persons present, we also have the imaginary address of absent persons, such as Gregory's apostrophe to the martyrs in *Oration* 35,[1] and his exclamatory address to the Trinity in *Oration* 23, reproducing in Christian terms the pagan *topos* of the address to the gods.

Ὦ Τριὰς ἁγία, καὶ προσκυνητή, καὶ μακρόθυμε!
μακρόθυμος γὰρ ἡ ἐπὶ τοσοῦτον ἀνασχομένη τῶν σὲ τεμνόντων.
Ὦ Τριάς, ἧς ἐγὼ κατηξιώθην, καὶ λάτρης εἶναι, καὶ κῆρυξ
ἐκ πλείονος ἀνυπόκριτος! Ὦ Τριὰς ἡ πᾶσί ποτε
γνωσθησομένη, τοῖς μὲν τῇ ἐλλάμψει, τοῖς δὲ τῇ κολάσει![2]

Closely related to such an address to the gods is the *invocatio*, or solemn invocation of the gods. In *Oration* 43 Gregory uses such an invocation in a way that pointedly imitates the use of the *invocatio* in the forensic speech: 'What in the name of the Trinity itself, if I may introduce into my panegyric somewhat of the forensic style, ought to have been done! . . .'[3]

Another common figure is the *prosopopoeia*, in which speeches are put into the mouths of other persons. Thus in *Oration* 24 Gregory puts an imaginary speech into the mouth of Cyprian exhorting the martyrs,[4] and in *Oration* 15 the mother of the Maccabees is given several long speeches exhorting her sons to heroic death.[5] Personification is another method of creating vivacity. Thus in Gregory's second oration on peace he begins with an address to Peace as if it were a person.[6] In a similar fashion he addresses Pascha in the second oration on Easter.

But, O Pascha, great and holy and purifier of the world—for I will speak to thee as to a living person—O word of God and Light and Life and Wisdom and Might—for I rejoice in all Thy names—O offspring and Expression and Signet of the Great Mind; O Word conceived and Man contemplated, Who bearest all things, binding them by the Word of Thy power, receive this discourse. . . .[7]

One of the high points of sophistic artistry is the combination of these two figures, in which a speech is put into the mouth of an inanimate object or an abstraction. Gregory uses this technique

---

[1] *P.G.* 36. 258 B.
[2] *P.G.* 35. 1165 B; compare with the apostrophe to Artemis in Libanius' oration (translation in Downey's *History of Antioch* 681 ff.).
[3] *P.G.* 36. 568 A.   [4] *P.G.* 35. 1172 B ff.   [5] Ibid. 928 B ff.
[6] Ibid. 1132 A.   [7] *Or.* 45. 30: *P.G.* 36. 264 A, B.

in his letter to Olympias after the revolt of the city of Neo-Caesarea against the governor. Olympias had threatened the city with destruction, and Gregory pleads for mercy, putting the following speech into the mouth of the city:

Imagine then that in my person this city is prostrate before you, that it is articulate, that it is in the garb of mourning, that its head is shaven, as in a drama, and that it is addressing you in these terms: Stretch forth your hand to me as I lie upon the earth, assist my weakness. Do not add your blow to the ravages of time; do not destroy what the Persians left behind. Raising up cities becomes you better than destroying those that are enfeebled. Become a city founder, then, by adding another to those already existing or by protecting one already existing. Do not let it be said that a city was in existence up to your reign, but afterwards was not. Do not hand on the bad reputation to posterity of having received that which was numbered among cities and leaving behind the erstwhile city a desert site known only to mountains, cliffs, and woods.[1]

Other figures which had been developed by forensic orators were *diaporesis*, or the pretended doubt about where to begin or what to say, and *communicatio*, in which the orator begs the audience to help him or pretends to take counsel with the audience. Thus in *Oration 7, On Caesarius*, in the oration on Cyprian, and in the discourse on the martyrs,[2] Gregory expresses doubt about where to begin and what to say. This was particularly useful in the encomium, where the orator pretends that the virtues, marvels, or horrors which he is about to describe are so astounding that he does not know how to start, what to describe, and what to leave out. In *Oration 32, On Moderation in Disputes*, Gregory begins by taking counsel with his audience, like a father, both rebuking and questioning his children. He addresses the audience with a series of questions, asking them how he should begin, what he should say, what is best and most useful to them, what best suited to the occasion.[3] In *Oration 26*, which Gregory preached to his congregation after his return from the country, he addresses the audience as a friend, asking them to tell him all they have been doing in his absence and saying that he, in turn, will tell them what he has done during

---

[1] *Ep.* 141: *P.G.* 37. 240 c ff.
[2] *P.G.* 35. 762 b; *P.G.* 36. 257 a; *P.G.* 35. 1176 c.
[3] *Or.* 32. 2: *P.G.* 36. 176 b.

his solitude.[1] *Communicatio* was also useful for picking up the thread of a speech as well as a figure of the prooimion. Here the orator keeps the prolixity of his address from becoming tiresome by pretending to make a fresh start. In the panegyric this could also be given a hyperbolic turn by pretending that the virtues of the person being praised were so great that the orator was exhausted in trying adequately to describe them all, and he called upon his audience to help him out. Thus, after describing the early career of Athanasius, Gregory makes a fresh start with the words:

Come then to aid me in my panegyric; for I am labouring heavily, and though I desire to pass by point after point, they seize upon me one after the other, and I can find no surpassing excellence in a form which is in all respects well proportioned and beautiful, for each as it occurs to me seems fairer than the rest and so takes by storm my speech. Come then, I pray you, you who have been his admirers and witnesses, divide among yourselves his excellences, contend bravely with one another, men and women alike, young men and maidens, old men and children, priests and people, solitaries and cenobites, men of simple or exact life, contemplatives or pragmatic men. Let one praise him in his fasting and prayers as if he had been disembodied and immaterial; another his unweariness and zeal for vigils and psalmody, another his patronage of the needy, another his dauntlessness towards the powerful, or his condescension towards the lowly. Let the virgins celebrate the friend of the bridegroom [i.e. Christ]; those under the yoke [the married] their restrainer; hermits him who lent wings to their course, cenobites their lawgiver, simple folks their guide, contemplatives the divine, the joyous their bridle, the unfortunate their consolation, the hoary-headed their staff, youths their instructor, the poor their resource, the wealthy their steward. . . . [2]

Another useful figure for the orator was *paraleipsis*, where he recounts some facts or events while declaring his intention to pass them over in silence. This was useful in the panegyric, where the orator would hint at the great virtues of a man by declaring that he must pass over the greater part of them in silence. Thus in the passage following the one quoted above, Gregory declares that he must pass over most of Athanasius' virtues in silence, since they could fill myriad discourses

---

[1] *Or.* 26. 1: *P.G.* 35. 1228 A ff.   [2] *Or.* 21. 10: *P.G.* 35. 1092 c ff.

(having, of course, already enumerated all these virtues in considerable detail), and confine his account only to the most important points.[1] The *paraleipsis* could also be used to continue with an amplification of virtues or marvels while declaring that these things are so great that they cannot possibly all be recounted. Thus in *Oration 32, On Moderation in Disputes*, Gregory gives a long account of the wonders of nature. After an apparently endless list, he begins a new series by saying 'I do not speak at all of such things as . . . ' and then continues with numerous additional details.[2] The *paraleipsis* was also very useful to the Christian orator as a way of hinting at things which his Christian principles forbade him to mention. In following the *topoi* of the panegyric, the Christian encountered many things which were subjects of praise according to pagan standards of values, such as ancestry, wealth, good looks, but which the Christian should not consider praiseworthy. Gregory can bring these matters in paraleiptically by saying something like: 'Well, of course, we Christians have no regard for noble birth, but if we cared about such things, so-and-so's ancestry was among the most illustrious.' Thus in speaking about the ancestry of Basil, Gregory says:

Had I seen him to be proud of his birth, and the rights of birth, or any of those infinitely little objects of those whose eyes are on the ground[3] we would have had to inspect a new catalogue of the Heroes! What details as to his ancestors might I not have laid under contribution! Nor would even history have had any advantage over me, since I claim this advantage, that his celebrity depends, not upon fiction or legend, but upon actual facts attested by many witnesses. On his father's side Pontus offers to me many details, in no wise inferior to its wonders of old time, of which all history and poesy are full; there are many others concerned with this my native land, of illustrious men of Cappadocia renowned for its youthful progeny no less than for its horses (note the Homeric image; i.e. *Od.* 9. 27). Accordingly we match with his father's family that of his mother. What family owns more numerous or more illustrious generals and governors, or court officials, or again, men of wealth, and lofty thrones, and public honours and oratorical renown? If it were permitted to me to mention them, I would make nothing of the Pelopidae, and Cecropidae, the Alcmaeonids, and Aeacidae, and the

---

[1] *Or.* 21. 11: *P.G.* 35. 1093 B, C.   [2] *P.G.* 36. 200.
[3] i.e. the pagans, but the image itself suggests Plato's usage, e.g. *Resp.* 7. 514.

Heracleidae and other most noble families; inasmuch as they, in default of public merit in their houses, betake themselves to the region of uncertainty, claiming demigods and divinities, merely mythical personages, as the glory of their ancestors, whose most vaunted details are incredible, and those which we can believe an infamy.

Gregory then contrasts the merely mythical and obscene stories which pagans tell about their ancestors, by telling an edifying tale of the heroism of Basil's ancestors under persecution.[1]

Guignet, in his chapter on Gregory's techniques of argumentation, shows that Gregory uses many of the methods current in the sophistic schools.[2] One of the most common of these is what we might call the enumerative method, whereby the orator presents a barrage of arguments for a particular position, never choosing among these arguments or correlating them into a consistent pattern, but bowling his audience over by the sheer prolixity of his arguments and the forcefulness of his style. The sophists also tended to argue by way of comparison or metaphor, arguments which often lean on little more than a play on words or an accidental association of two ideas. Thus in *Oration* 16, as a kind of protest of modesty, Gregory pours forth a series of arguments based on rather vague associations and images of the situation at hand and designed to show that a mere youth like himself should not be asked to speak when his father is silent. All of this is merely a *topos*, of course, since Gregory has a lengthy sermon into which he is about to launch himself.

Why, when you have excused the head, do you hasten to the feet? Why do you pass by Aaron and urge forward Eleazar? I cannot allow the fountain to be dammed up while the rivulet runs its course; the sun to be hidden while the star shines forth; hoar hairs to be in retirement while youth lays down the law; wisdom to be silent while inexperience speaks with assurance. A heavy rain is not always more useful than a shower. Nay, indeed, if it be too violent it sweeps away the earth, and increases the proportion of the farmer's loss; while the gentle rain which sinks deep enriches the soil, benefits the tiller, and makes the corn grow into a fine crop. So the fluent speech is not always more profitable than the wise. For the one, though it perhaps gives a slight pleasure, passes away and is dispersed as soon and with as little effect as the air on which it struck,

---

[1] *Or.* 43. 3–8: *P.G.* 36. 500 ff.　　　[2] Guignet, *S. Grégoire* 231–67.

though it charms with its eloquence the greedy ear. But the other sinks into the mind and, opening wide its mouth, fills it with the Spirit, and showing itself nobler than its origin, produces a rich harvest in a few syllables.[1]

The above passage shows another very typical feature of Gregory's style, the rather indiscriminate mixture of literal references and abstractions with Biblical typology and nature metaphors of diverse types.

Gregory also makes frequent use of techniques developed by the judicial pleader. In his apologetic orations he frequently poses as the defendant on trial presenting his defence. In *Oration* 2 in defence of his flight to Pontus Gregory pleads his cause as if he were on trial.[2] In *Oration* 17 he plays the part of the attorney for the defence pleading for mercy from the governor for the people of Nazianzus. There we find the common *topoi* of the defence. Gregory presents his white hairs to the governor, weeps, lifts up the cross of Christ to move the governor to pity.[3] The influence of courtroom techniques is also strong in *Oration* 33 against the Arians, where Gregory answers a lot of mock accusations of himself, all designed to redound to his own credit, and presents the Arians as if they were unruly criminals on trial who must constantly be silenced.

Another very common technique of pleading in Gregory is *dialektikon*, or the question-and-answer method, in which the orator supposes that he is arguing with his adversary. This technique was one commonly used in the diatribe of the Stoic and Cynic popular preachers.[4] Thus in the oration on baptism Gregory enters into a hypothetical argument with a Novatian, although no Novatians were present and indeed the Novatian heresy actually arose a century earlier and was not an immediate threat in Gregory's own locality. Gregory uses this technique of person-to-person argumentation to make vivid the orthodox position on the forgiveness of sins against the tendency to set up excessively puritanical standards of Christian life.[5]

---

[1] *Or.* 16. 1: *P.G.* 35. 936 A, B.

[2] See also *Oration* 42 where Gregory plays the part of the defendant answering charges, and *Or.* 3 where he uses similar courtroom language: 'What will ye? Shall I be judged by you or shall I be your judge? Shall I pass a verdict or receive one? For I hope to be acquitted if I be judged, and if I give sentence, to give it against you justly.'   [3] *P.G.* 35. 976 C ff.

[4] See above, p. 74, n. 2.   [5] *Or.* 39. 19: *P.G.* 36. 358 B, C.

But what say you, O new Pharisee pure in title but not in intention who discharge upon us the sentiments of Novatus, though you share the same infirmities? Will you not give any place to weeping [i.e. repentance]? Will you shed no tear? May you not meet with a judge like yourself? Are you not ashamed of the mercy of Jesus? . . .

In *Oration* 40 we have the same technique of raising an objection of some imaginary interlocutor and then answering it:

But some will say, what shall I gain, when I am preoccupied with baptism and have cut myself off from the pleasures of life, when it was in my power to give the reins to pleasure and then obtain grace? . . . You have delivered me from some trouble, whoever you are who say this, because you have at last with much difficulty told the secret of your delay, and though I cannot applaud your shiftiness, I do applaud your confession. But come forward and listen to the interpretation of the parable [parable on the eleventh hour: Matt. 20. 1] that you may not be injured by Scripture for lack of information.

Gregory then launches into the proper understanding of the parable of the eleventh hour lest anyone use it as an excuse for the delay of baptism until the last moment.[1] In the theological orations where Gregory is arguing with the Arians in Constantinople, particularly the Eunomians, he constantly employs the dialectical method, raising the arguments of his opponents and answering them. Thus in *Oration* 27(8):

And yet, O talkative dialectician, I will ask thee one small question and answer thou me, as He saith to Job, who, through the whirlwind and the cloud, gives divine admonitions. Are there many mansions in God's house, or only one as thee hast heard? Of course you will admit that there are many and not only one. Now are they all to be filled, or only some and others not; so that some will be left empty, and will have been prepared to no purpose? Of course all will be filled, for nothing can be in vain which has been done by God. And can you tell me what you will consider this mansion to be? Is it the rest and glory which is in store there for the Blessed, or something else? No, not anything else. Since then we are agreed upon this point, let us further examine another also. Is there anything that procures these mansions, as I think there is, or is there nothing? Certainly there is. What is it? Is it not that there are several modes of conduct, and various purposes, one leading one way, and another another, according to the proportion of faith, and these we call

[1] *Or.* 40. 20: *P.G.* 36. 284 D–385 A.

Ways? Must we then travel all or some of these Ways? Or the same individual along all of them if that is possible; or, if not, along as many as can be; or else along some of them? . . .

This kind of argumentation continues for some time in this oration, and the same style is found in the succeeding theological orations (*Ors.* 28–32). Here we can see Gregory directly imitating the Socratic *elenchus* in the manner of a Platonic dialogue.

Two other important sophistic techniques found in Gregory are irony and paradox (oxymoron). As Guignet points out,[1] Gregory is particularly skilful in the use of irony, a technique which was congenial to his temperament and natural ironic wit. This is especially true when his use of irony is contrasted with the strained and heavy-handed irony of Libanius. A good example is found in his farewell address to Constantinople, where he ironically begs the pardon of the Byzantine throng because he has tried to conduct himself as a Christian and was not aware that a bishop should behave like a Byzantine noble.

Perhaps we may be reproached with the exquisite character of our table, the splendour of our apparel, the officers who precede us, our haughtiness to those who meet us. I was not aware that we ought to rival the consuls, the governors, the most illustrious generals, who have no opportunity of lavishing their incomes; or that our belly ought to hunger for the goods of the poor, and to expend their necessities on superfluities, and to belch forth over the altars. I did not know that we were supposed to ride on a splendid horse, and to drive in magnificent carriages, and be preceded by a procession and surrounded by applause and have everyone make way for us, as if we were wild beasts, and open out a passage that our approach might be seen from afar. . . . Forgive me this wrong. Elect another who will please the majority and give me my desert, my country, and my God.[2]

Paradox or oxymoron is another figure whose excessive use is a mark of sophistic style. It consists in a combining of opposites in such a way that they become complementary. Typical oxymorons are phrases like this:

ζώνη τῷ ἀκόσμῳ κοσμία[3]

[1] Guignet, *Les Procédés épistolaires de Saint Grégoire de Nazianze comparés à ceux de ses contemporains* (Paris, 1911) 28 ff.
[2] *Or.* 42. 24: *P.G.* 36. 488.   [3] *Or.* 6. 2: *P.G.* 35. 724 A.

or his exclamations on the sufferings of Hero:

ὦ τῆς εὐγενοῦς συμφορᾶς!
ὦ τῶν ἱερῶν σου τραυμάτων![1]

Paradoxical phrase-making such as this abounds in Gregory's writings:

ἡ τῆς ἀνισότητος ἰσότης.[2]

οὐ φέρω ἀφώτιστος εἶναι μετὰ τὸ φώτισμα[3]
ὡς εἰς Θεὸν πιστεῦσαι καὶ ἀνελθεῖν ἄθεον.[4]

An example of the more involved use of oxymoron is found in this exhortation to Christians to stand firm in troubled times:

ἐν καιροῖς τρεπτοῖς ἄτρεπτος μένων περὶ ἀτρέπτου πράγματος.
Μίμησαι τὸν Πιλᾶτον ἐπὶ τὸ κρεῖττον, κακῶς γράφοντα, καλῶς γεγραμμένος.
... δέον εὐμετακινήτους μὲν εἶναι πρὸς τὸ κρεῖττον ἀπὸ τοῦ χείρονος, ἀκινήτους δὲ πρὸς τὸ χεῖρον ἀπὸ τοῦ βελτίονος.[5]

Paradox could also be used for striking ironic effects. In his orations on peace Gregory summons all his sophistic skills to show the irony and paradox of the quarrels within the Church; the paradox of Christians who hate each other in the name of love of God, utter a host of lies in their zeal for truth, and despise each other in the name of charity:

ὅτι διειλόμεθα τὸν Χριστόν,
οἱ λίαν φιλόθεοι καὶ φιλόχριστοι,
καὶ ὑπὲρ τῆς ἀληθείας ἀλλήλων κατεψευσάμεθα,
καὶ διὰ τὴν ἀγάπην μῖσος ἐμελετήσαμεν,
καὶ ὑπὲρ τοῦ ἀκρογωνιαίου διελύθημεν,
καὶ ὑπὲρ τῆς πέτρας ἐσείθημεν.[6]

But the most important use of oxymoron in Gregory is as a means of expressing the paradoxes of Christian theology. Christian thought, built on a series of antitheses, contrasts of the

---

[1] *Or.* 25. 13: *P.G.* 35. 1217 A.   [2] *P.G.* 36. 69 B.
[3] Ibid. 252 B.   [4] Ibid. 252 C.
[5] *Or.* 40. 44: *P.G.* 36. 421 B.
[6] *Or.* 6. 3: *P.G.* 35. 725 A; see also *Or.* 22, *On Peace* (*P.G.* 35. 1134 B) and *Or.* 32, *On Moderation in Disputes* (*P.G.* 36. 117 ff.) for more use of irony and paradox in reference to discordant Christianity.

literal and the spiritual meaning of Scripture, the flesh and the
spirit, the Old Law and the New Law, this world and the next
world, lent itself to the use of paradox as a way of describing its
own life. Gregory describes the ascetic life in such fashion:

> ὁ ἐν πενίᾳ πλοῦτος, ἡ ἐν παροικίᾳ κατάσχεσις,
> ἡ ἐν ἀτιμίᾳ δόξα, ἡ ἐν ἀσθενείᾳ δύναμις,
> ἡ ἐν ἀγαμίᾳ καλλιτεκνία.[1]

The conflicts of flesh and spirit also provided a fertile source of
oxymoron for the Christian orator:

> ὃ καὶ εὐεκτοῦν πολεμεῖ, καὶ ἀνιᾷ πολεμούμενον·
> ὃ καὶ ὡς σύνδουλον ἀγαπῶ, καὶ ὡς ἐχθρὸν ἀποστρέφομαι.
> Ἐχθρός ἐστιν εὐμενής, καὶ φίλος ἐπίβουλος.
> Ὦ τῆς συζυγίας καὶ τῆς ἀλλοτριώσεως!
> Ὁ φοβοῦμαι περιέπω, καὶ ὃ στέργω δέδοικα·
> πρὶν πολεμῆσαι, καταλλάσσομαι·
> καὶ πρὶν εἰρηνεῦσαι, διίσταμαι.[2]

The doctrines of incarnation and salvation also provide Gregory
with many opportunities for oxymoron and metonymy. The
idea of the unlimited eternal Godhead becoming man, becoming an individual bound by space and time, was perhaps one of
the most extraordinary paradoxes to the Greek mind, and
Gregory plays upon this paradox continually:

> ὁ ὢν γίνεται,
> καὶ ὁ ἄκτιστος κτίζεται,
> καὶ ὁ ἀχώρητος χωρεῖται.[3]

The paradox of God becoming man becomes more complex
when it is extended to include the idea that God becomes man
to make man like God:

> καὶ ὁ πλουτίζων πτωχεύει,
> πτωχεύει γὰρ τὴν ἐμὴν σάρκα,
> ἵν' ἐγὼ πλουτήσω τὴν αὐτοῦ θεότητα·

[1] *Or.* 6. 2: *P.G.* 35. 724 B.
[2] *Or.* 14. 6–7: *P.G.* 35. 865 B.
[3] *Or.* 38. 13: *P.G.* 36. 325 C; see also *Or.* 39. 13: *P.G.* 36. 349 A for similar paradoxes on the incarnation.

καὶ ὁ πλήρης κενοῦται·
κενοῦται γὰρ τῆς ἑαυτοῦ δόξης ἐπὶ μικρόν,
ἵν' ἐγὼ τῆς ἐκείνου μεταλάβω πληρώσεως.[1]

In speaking of the birth of Christ in Bethlehem Gregory indulges in some particularly piquant oxymorons combined with metonymy or the use of words on more than one level of meaning:

καὶ γέννησιν σεβάσθητι. Δι' ἣν ἐλύθης τῶν δεσμῶν τῆς γεννήσεως ... καὶ τὴν φάτνην προσκύνησον, δι' ἣν ἄλογος ὤν, ἐτράφης ὑπὸ τοῦ Λόγου.[2]

The mysteries of the Godhead, His immanence and transcendence, also lent themselves to paradoxical modes of expression:

Θεοῦ λαμπρότητα, ὃν ἄβυσσος καλύπτει·
οὐ σκότος ἀποκρυφή, φωτὸς ὄντος·
τοῦ καθαρωτάτου καὶ ἀπροσίτου τοῖς πλείοσιν·
ὃς ἐν τῷ παντὶ τῷδε, καὶ τοῦ παντός ἐστιν ἔξω·
ὃς καλόν ἐστιν ἅπαν, καὶ ἄνω παντὸς καλοῦ·
ὃς νοῦν φωτίζει καὶ διαφεύγει νοῦ τάχος καὶ ὕψος·
ὑποχωρῶν ἀεὶ τοσοῦτον, ὅσον καταλαμβάνεται....[3]

Closely associated with this fondness for the paradoxical are certain *topoi* which were particularly cultivated by late sophistical oratory, such as the child–old man and the world-upside-down. The child–old man *topos* occurs most strikingly in Gregory's autobiography, where he speaks of himself as having the dignity and seriousness of 'hoar hairs' even as a tiny child.[4] In Gregory's oration *On Moderation in Disputes* he describes the order and regularity of nature to prove the existence of God as manifested in His providential design of the universe. Then to point up this order and design, he evokes the contrasting image of the world-upside-down: 'One does not see dolphins in the furrows, nor cattle thrown upon the waters. The sun does not shine during the night; the moon does not illumine the day.'[5] As Curtius points out, these two *topoi*, the child–old man and the world-upside-down, enjoyed remarkable popularity in late

[1] *Or.* 38. 13: *P.G.* 36. 325 c; for similar paradoxes on incarnation and salvation, see *P.G.* 35. 397 c.
[2] *Or.* 38. 17: *P.G.* 36. 329 D–32 A. [3] *Or.* 2. 76: *P.G.* 35. 484 A, B.
[4] *Carm. de vita sua*, l. 95: *P.G.* 37. 1036.
[5] *Or.* 32. 9: *P.G.* 36. 184 c; also see *Or.* 36. 7: *P.G.* 36. 272 B, C, and *Or.* 33. 6: *P.G.* 36. 222 c, for other examples of this motif.

antique literature. One may perhaps see in this a kind of *fin de siècle* psychology whose jaded appetite reaches out to the grotesque, but these motifs enjoyed a long popularity in classical literature, particularly the world-upside-down, which made its first appearance in Archilochus.[1] The taste for such a motif may well come from the Greek sense of order and design itself, and thus the idea of the disordered cosmos appeared so particularly piquant and intriguing.

Imagery

In discussing the use of imagery in Gregory we shall primarily consider the use of simile and metaphor, with some special attention to allegory. A detailed examination of minor tropes, such as synecdoche,[2] and antonomasia (giving the part for the whole, or the epithet of the person instead of his name), while they could be illustrated from Gregory, would serve only to point out that he makes use of sophistic figures, a point that should be sufficiently obvious by this time.[3] Thus this section will concentrate on Gregory's general use of imagery. There will be no attempt sharply to separate simile from metaphor, even though this was the method used by earlier writers on Second Sophistic in the Christian Fathers. However, an examination of the results of these studies, as well as similar results of the study of Gregory's use of images, makes it clear that there is no essential difference in the way he uses simile and metaphor. The same kind of images are used in each, so it is repetitive to consider them separately.

Sophistic use of imagery is characterized by prolixity. Every idea is belaboured with images. The orator will illustrate an idea, not with just one image but with three or four. Images are often elaborated in great detail so that the things compared are not just equated with each other, in a general way, but a strained effort is made to find numerous points of comparison, the skill of the rhetorician being displayed in the ingenious ways he can

---

[1] Curtius, *European Literature*, 94 ff.

[2] See *Or.* 7. 15: *P.G.* 35. 773 C for an example of synecdoche.

[3] Quintilian (8. 6. 1) also considers irony and hyperbole under the category of tropes, but irony seems to fit in more easily with the consideration of oxymoron, and hyperbole is so closely related to panegyric that discussion of it is reserved for the section on epideictic genre.

interconnect the ideas. Thus in *Oration* 36 Gregory pours forth a series of images to represent his efforts to save the Church from calamity; a boat about to sink in a tempest, leading an army to succour a besieged city, the extinguishing of a fire in a house.[1]

Images are often mixed together in a somewhat confusing fashion in an effort to evoke as many aspects of the situation as possible by suggestive symbols. Thus in discoursing on virtue and vice Gregory says:

As I take it, goodness can with difficulty gain a foothold upon human nature, like fire upon green wood, while most men are ready and disposed to join in evil, like stubble; I mean, ready for a spark and a wind, which is easily kindled and consumed from its dryness. For more quickly would any one take part in evil with slight inducement to its full extent, than in good which is fully set before him to a slight degree. For indeed a little wormwood most quickly imparts its bitterness to honey; while not even double the quantity of honey can impart its sweetness to wormwood; and the withdrawal of a small pebble would draw headlong a whole river, though it would be difficult for the strongest dam to restrain or stay its course.[2]

Gregory reflects the sophistic tendency to run to the grotesque in the search for striking and evocative images. For example, in describing the difficulty of the pastor who must rule a congregation composed of persons of many types and temperaments Gregory writes:

If anyone were to undertake to tame and train an animal of many forms and shapes compounded of many animals of various sizes and degrees of tameness and wildness, his principal task, involving a considerable struggle, would be the government of so extraordinary and heterogeneous a nature, since each of the animals of which it is compounded would, according to its nature and habit, be differently affected with joy, pleasure, or dislike by the same words or food or stroking with the hand or whistling or other modes of treatment. And what must the master of such an animal do but show himself manifold and various in his knowledge and apply to each a treatment suitable to it, so as successfully to lead and preserve the beast?[3]

Gregory's fondness for images sometimes creates results which are unintentionally humorous, as when he describes his separation from Basil as the cutting of a body in two or the severance of

[1] *Or.* 36. 6: *P.G.* 36. 273 B.   [2] *Or.* 2. 12: *P.G.* 35. 421 A, B.
[3] *Or.* 2. 44: *P.G.* 35. 452 B, C.

two bullocks who have shared the same manger and the same yoke and protest against the separation amid piteous bellowing after one another.[1] Sometimes Gregory mixes images together in ways which are discordant or inappropriate. In *Oration* 31, for example, he speaks of men who have more truths than they can handle as 'men loaded with food beyond their strength'. This unedifying image he rather inaesthetically mixes together with the Platonic figure 'and presenting eyes as yet too weak to bear it to the sun's light, risk the loss of even that which was within the reach of their powers'.[2] In his first oration on Julian, Gregory, in trying to evoke the image of the rock as symbol of stability, alters the evangelical image of the sower of seed to read 'nevertheless I exclude by proclamation all those who have not been sown upon the solid and immovable rock, but upon the dry and barren ground', oblivious to the fact that the Gospel writer himself speaks of the seed sown upon rock as drying up and blowing away (Matt. 13. 3: compare *Oration* 4. 11: *P.G.* 35. 541 A). Another doubtful mixture of images occurs in his *epitaphios* on Basil:

> He drew up a sketch of pious doctrine and by wrestling with and attacking their opposition he beat off the daring assaults of the heretics; overthrowing in hand-to-hand struggles by word of mouth those who came to close quarters, and striking those at a distance by arrows winged with ink, which is in no wise inferior to inscriptions on tablets. . . .[3]

However, on the whole, Gregory's good taste and sense of appropriateness are sound, especially when compared with the *mauvais goût* characteristic of contemporary sophistry.

Studies of images in sophistic and Christian writers influenced by sophistic have revealed that these writers use images drawn from stock sources. Medicine, the games, nature and pastoral images, sea images, the army, the arts, and technology are all conventional sources of images.[4] In Gregory we find such stock sources of imagery used over and over again, often in very similar fashion. Metaphors and similes drawn from medicine are probably found more often than any other type of image.

[1] *Or.* 43. 24: *P.G.* 36. 529 B.   [2] *Or.* 31. 26: *P.G.* 36. 162 D.
[3] *Or.* 43. 43: *P.G.* 36. 553 A.
[4] See Guignet, *S. Grégoire* 131–87; Méredier, *S. Grégoire de Nysse* 96–138; also Ameringer, *St. John Chrysostom*, chs. 8–9; and Campbell, *Basil the Great* 56–85.

The constant use of medical images may be explained in part by Gregory's own preoccupation with his health, making this kind of figure particularly congenial to him.[1] The guidance of God or the pastor of souls is regularly compared with the physician who heals the body, the treatment for the cure of the soul is compared to medicines or surgery.[2] In *Oration 2*, where Gregory discusses the nature of the priesthood, the image of the pastor as physician of souls is worked out in great detail. Gregory is particularly concerned to show how much more difficult is the work of the physician of souls than that of the physician of the body:

> Place and time and age and season and the like are the subject of the physician's scrutiny; he will prescribe medicines and diet, and guard against things injurious that the desires of the sick may not be a hindrance to his art. Sometimes and in certain cases he will make use of the cautery or the knife or the severer remedies, but none of these, laborious and hard as they may seem, is so difficult as the diagnosis and cure of our habits, passions, lives, wills, and whatever else is within us, by banishing everything from our compound nature that is brutal and fierce, and introducing and establishing in their stead what is gentle and dear to God. . . .[3]

The games, athletic contests, and horse-racing provide another important source of images in Gregory. St. Paul made use of the athlete image as the symbol of spiritual struggle,[4] and this was the classical source of this image for Christians thereafter. However, the use of the athlete as the image of the ascetic, the utilization of athletic vocabulary, and the whole concept of athletic *askēsis* applied to internal combat seem already to have been current in Hellenistic circles in the first century. For example, Philo, undoubtedly borrowing the image from contemporary Hellenism, speaks of Jewish ascetics and contemplatives in this manner:

> The whole of this company ($\theta\iota\alpha\sigma\sigma$) have voluntarily deprived themselves of the possessions of aught in abundance, thinking little of things dear to the flesh. Now athletes are men whose bodies are

---

[1] M. S. Keenan, 'St. Gregory of Nazianzus and Early Byzantine Medicine', *B.H.M.* (1941) 8–30.

[2] The comparison of the physician of souls with the physician of the body was a common image of Plato's (*Politicus* 293 B). For some examples of Gregory's frequent use of this image, see *Or.* 31. 25; *Or.* 6. 10; *Or.* 32. 2 and 28; *Or.* 17. 2 and 7; *Or.* 18. 1; *Or.* 26, 18; *Or.* 43, 20.

[3] *Or.* 2. 18: *P.G.* 35. 428 A, B.   [4] Rom. 12. 1.

well cared for and full of vigour, men who make strong the fort of their body against the soul, whereas the athletes of this discipline, pale, wasted, and, as it were, reduced to skeletons, sacrifice even the muscles of their bodies to the powers of their souls, dissolving, if the truth be told, into one form—that of the soul, and by their minds becoming free from body.[1]

The Christians applied the athlete image to the martyr, and then, when the monk replaced the martyr as the Christian popular hero, to the ascetic. In Gregory we find this ascetic–martyr–athlete typology closely woven together. In the athlete image we see classical culture transmuted and put at the service of a different value system from the system of *aretē* which first produced it. Gregory can constantly enrich this symbol with fresh details from the games themselves. In his oration on Gregory of Nyssa, for example, an oration which was preached on the festival of martyrs, he exhorts his congregation to combat the flesh and struggle for virtue in order to honour the athletes (martyrs). Inspired by their example and in honour of their victory, the Christian should be encouraged to persevere in the *agōn* in order to win the crown of victory in Heaven.[2] In another oration Gregory evokes the wrestling technique used in the games of getting under the opponent in order to throw him as an image of the Christian athlete who humbles himself in order to conquer.[3] The Christian athlete is said to have the whole world for his arena, and displays his prowess as in some cosmic Olympic games.[4] These types of images drawn from the games and many more are scattered throughout Gregory's writings.

Horse-racing also provided types for the Christian ascetic, but here the classical *locus* was found in Plato's image of Reason as the charioteer disciplining the appetitive soul.[5] This Platonic use of the horse-racing image could also be wedded to the Isocratean commonplace about the spur and the curb,[6] as in the following example:

Some are led by doctrine, others trained by example. Some need the spur, others the curb; some are sluggish and hard to rouse to the good and must be stirred up by being smitten by the word. Others are immoderately fervent in spirit, with impulses difficult to restrain,

---

[1] *De Mut. Nom.* 4.
[2] *Or.* 11. 4: *P.G.* 36. 836 c–9 A.
[3] *Or.* 32. 16: *P.G.* 36. 1150 B.
[4] *Or.* 26. 11: *P.G.* 35. 1242 c.
[5] Plato, *Phaedrus* 246.
[6] See Philostratus, *VS* 598.

like thoroughbred colts, who run wide of the turning post and to im-
prove them the word must have a restraining and checking influence.[1]

In the first theological oration we see the horse-racing image
used in a typically Platonic way but mixed with Biblical typology. This mingling of the classical and the Biblical, often in
practically the same breath, is a typical Gregorian technique
and illustrates perhaps better than anything else how these two
sources flow together to form his thought:

Let us not . . . like hot-tempered and hard-mouthed horses,
throwing off our rider Reason, and casting away Reverence that
keeps us within due limits, run far from the turning-point, but let us
philosophize within our proper bounds and not be carried away into
Egypt, nor be swept down into Assyria, nor sing the Lord's song in a
strange land, by which I mean before any kind of audience, strangers
or kindred, hostile or friendly, kindly or the reverse, who watch what
we do with over-great care and would like the spark of what is wrong
with us to become a flame and secretly kindle it and fan it and raise
it to heaven with their breath and make it higher than the Baby-
lonian flame which burnt up everything around it.[2]

The factious spirit of the horse-racing set could also be used as a
striking image of factiousness in the contemporary Church. In
preaching his last farewell to Constantinople Gregory rebukes
the party spirit of the Byzantine Christians:

I cannot bear your horse races and theatres and this rage for
rivalry in expense and party spirit. We unharness and harness ourselves on the other side, we neigh against each other, we almost beat
the air, as they do, and fling the dust towards heaven. . . .[3]

Gregory uses stock images drawn from the workaday world
which are commonplaces for certain ideas, found over and over
again in the same context. The flint striking a spark from the stone
is a stock image for an idea or an intuition struck in the mind.[4]
The iron drawn to the loadstone is the symbol of the forces
which draw men up to God.[5] The imprint of the seal in wax

[1] Or. 2. 30: P.G. 35. 440 A.   [2] Or. 27. 5: P.G. 36. 17 B.
[3] Or. 42. 22: P.G. 36. 484 B.
[4] Or. 19. 3: P.G. 35. 1045 C; Or. 37. 13: P.G. 36. 297 C; Or. 25. 8: P.G. 35. 1209 B.
[5] Or. 36. 1: P.G. 36. 265 A.

is commonly used for the imprint of baptism on the soul or the imprinting of sound doctrine in the soul.[1] Conversely, rust wearing out the iron suggests the negative forces which degrade the soul. In much of Gregory's image-making he moves from the abstract to the concrete, i.e. the realities on the spiritual level take their symbols from the material level, although occasionally, as in the use of the racing factions, he may use an image to move from one set of concrete particulars to another.

The army and warfare also provides stock images. Here the case is similar to the athlete image. Warfare suggested the Christian *agōn*, and here again there was a Pauline precedent for symbolizing the Christian by the warrior.[2] In *Oration 6*, in language similar to St. Paul's, Gregory speaks of the Christian fighting the common enemy, armed with the buckler of faith.[3] The battle which Gregory describes could be the battle against the senses, the ascetic battle,[4] or it could be the battle of the orthodox against the heretic.[5] Jesus Christ is the *imperator* of the army of the faithful who march under His standard.[6]

The sea and voyaging are another rich source of images. We frequently find the image of the Church as a ship and the Christian as voyaging through the troubled seas of life. Relatively speaking, the sea and seafaring plays little part in Biblical symbolism. Boats, the Sea of Galilee, the fish, play a role, but the Jews were not a maritime people, and actual sea-voyaging was not a part of their cultural experience. Therefore sea and ship symbols in Christianity really developed after the Church was transplanted into the Mediterranean world. Even the ark of Noah as the symbol of the Church develops in the Greco-Roman environment. In Gregory's use of sea symbols we are constantly aware that we are in a Mediterranean rather than a Semitic world. The sea is regarded as a hostile element, a symbol of flux, instability, and chaos,[7] of the spiritual dangers that surround the Christian and threaten his soul. The storm and the tempest stand for the trials and tribulations that beset the Church.[8] The Christian standing firm in the midst of trial is

---

[1] *Or.* 40. 45: *P.G.* 36. 441 D; *Or.* 2. 43: *P.G.* 35. 451 A, B.
[2] Ephes. 6. 14.   [3] *Or.* 6. 22: *P.G.* 35. 749 B.
[4] *Or.* 11. 5: *P.G.* 35. 837 B, C.   [5] *Or.* 43. 31: *P.G.* 36. 537 C ff.
[6] *Or.* 24. 3: *P.G.* 35. 1173 A; *Or.* 13. 1: *P.G.* 35. 253 A.
[7] *Or.* 6. 19: *P.G.* 35. 747 A; *Or.* 14. 19: *P.G.* 35. 881 B.
[8] *Or.* 9. 4: *P.G.* 35. 824 B; *Or.* 13. 1: *P.G.* 35. 853 A; *Or.* 25. 7: *P.G.* 35. 1208 A.

the rock unmoved amid the waves that beat upon it.[1] The pastor
of his flock is a helmsman guiding the ship,[2] while the churches
of the heretics are houses of sand that cannot resist the slightest
ripple.[3] St. Peter almost sinking in the tempest is the symbol of
the soul seeking salvation from the Saviour who stands on the
waters.[4] Gregory's own experience of near-shipwreck and death
as a young man, an event that occasioned a conversion experience, made a deep impression on him, and is probably one
of the reasons why these images play such an important part in
his symbol system. In his poem on his life he describes this experience:

Everything became a great blackness; land, sea, air, the sky all
darkened. Thunderclaps resounded amid flashes of lightning and the
sheets quivered as the sails were filled. The mainmast bent; the
rudder had no effect as the blasts tore it forcibly from one's hands.
Mountainous seas swamped the vessel. A confused clamour arose,
cries of the sailors, helmsmen, officers, passengers, all calling with
one voice upon Christ: even the people who formerly knew not God
—fear is an opportune teacher. The most pitiable of all our misfor-
tunes, however, was that the boat was without water. The moment
she began to roll, the cistern which carried the precious treasure of
water was smashed and scattered to the depths. The question then
was whether thirst or the sea or the winds would make an end of us.
But God sent speedy deliverance from it all. Phoenician merchants
suddenly made their appearance. They were in fear themselves, but
when from our entreaties they realized how desperate was our plight,
they made the craft fast by means of stays and manual strength,
for they were very strong. Indeed they rescued us from practically
a shipwrecked state, like fish gasping out of their native element, or
a lamp flickering out when all the oil is gone.

The sea continued angry, however, and we were harassed for
several days. Driven hither and thither we had no notion where we
were sailing, and could see no hope of safety except from God. All
of us feared a common death; but more terrifying to me was the
hidden death. Those murderous waters were keeping me from the
purifying waters which divinize us. That was my lament and my misfortune. For this I kept sending up cries and stretching out my hands,
and my cries overcame the pounding of the waves. Stretched miserable and prone I lay with garments rent. It seems unbelievable, but
it is perfectly true, that all forgot their particular woes and joined

---

[1] *Or.* 24. 14: *P.G.* 35. 1185 C.   [2] *Or.* 42. 20: *P.G.* 35. 481 C.
[3] *Or.* 29. 9: *P.G.* 35. 85 A, B.   [4] *Or.* 17. 5: *P.G.* 35. 972 B, C.

their prayerful entreaties to mine. The way in which they shared my agonies proclaimed them pious fellow-voyagers on a common sea of woe.

However, Thou, my Christ, wert even then a mighty saviour, just as now Thou art my deliverer from the storms of life. There was no shred of solid hope, no island, no mainland, no mountain-top, no beacon light, no guiding stars for sailors; nothing, large or small, that one could see. What was I to do? Was there any way out of the hazards? Despairing of all hope I turned to Thee, my life, my breath, my light, my strength, my salvation. I was fearful and trembling, coaxing and pleading by turns, and I kept trying to weave threads of good into the dark pattern. I reminded Thee of all the miracles of time past when we had experience of Thy mighty hands: of the sea sundered and the passage of Israel; of enemies defeated by hands raised in prayer; of the affliction from leaders of the Egyptians by scourges; of the reduction to servitude of creation; of walls collapsing at the sound of the trumpet and the people's onset. My entreaties were added to all the cries of old. Thine, I said, I have formerly been; Thine I am now. Please accept me for a second time, the possession of Thy honoured servants, the gift of land and sea, dedicated by the prayers of my mother and by this unparalleled crisis. If I escape a double danger I shall live for Thee; if I am abandoned Thou wilt lose a worshipper. At this moment Thy disciple is tossed upon the waves. For my sake dispel slumber, walk to me and let the fear be stilled.

These were my words. The clash of winds abated, the sea grew calm, the ship straight on course—all this the guerdon of my prayer. The whole ship's company went their way praising the great Christ, for they had received a double salvation at the hands of God.[1]

This passage is an excellent example of the *ecphrasis* or the vivid word-picture. The *ecphrasis* was one of the exercises of the *progymnasmata*, and the ability to draw such vivid word-pictures was an essential part of the rhetor's art. Such pictures are scattered throughout Gregory's orations.[2] Every method to heighten emotion and create verisimilitude is employed in the *ecphrasis*. The details are piled up, all the stops are pulled out on the emotional organ; lavish use of typology, imagery, questions, exclamations, apostrophe, and *prosopopoeia* heighten the effect.

[1] *Carm. de vita sua*, ll. 130 ff.: *P.G.* 37. 1038.
[2] See, for example, *Or.* 34. 7 on the arrival of the Egyptian fleet in the harbour of Constantinople, or *Or.* 43. 52 on Valens entering the church. *Or.* 14 *On the Poor* is filled with vivid word-pictures of the plight of the leper, and *Or.* 28. 24–30 is an extended picture of the wonders of nature.

These techniques of verisimilitude drawn out in great detail also characterize the use of metaphor and simile in late Greek rhetoric. The metaphor or simile too may be drawn out into a vivid word-picture. In one of the most notable of Gregory's sea images such a technique is used. In a description drawn from his lonely walks during his retirement in the country after his experiences with Maximus, Gregory uses his contemplation of the sea to symbolize the whole spiritual state of the Church at Constantinople:

I wandered alone by the seaside when the day was far advanced, for I have accustomed myself to disperse my cares by recreations of this sort; for the string will not bear to be always on the stretch, but requires occasionally to be loosened from the bow's end, if the archer would use it again without finding it unserviceable just when he would use it. Thus I wandered, my feet moving mechanically, whilst my eye swept over the expanse of the sea. But this generally gratifying view was not so delightful as when the dark purple-tinted waves rolled gently forth, and sported softly and pleasantly with the shore. But how was it now? 'The sea arose by reason of a great wind that blew': for I willingly use here the words of Scripture.[1] The waves, as they are wont, increased in size as they approached from a distance —for a moment raised themselves to their highest elevation—again sank, and discharged themselves on the beach; or else they rushed back roaring on the neighbouring rocks, dispersing into light and frothy spray. There were now no small number of stones and sea-weed, mussels and light oysters washed up, and, as it were, spat forth, while many were again absorbed in the retiring wave; but the rocks stood unmoved and unshaken, as if not in the least disturbed, except that the waves broke against them. From this prospect I thought I could derive a profitable lesson, and how I might apply it to my state of mind, especially when I felt staggered at some occurrence, as has been recently the case. So I studied this spectacle not superficially and the sight afforded me instruction. Is not (said I to myself) the sea like our life, and like human concerns in general?—for there is there also as much of angry struggle and fluctuating instability. And the storms—are they not the persecutions which originate from those causes, and all the unlooked-for trouble that befalls us? This is what it seems to me David meant when he said 'Save me, O Lord, the waters have come up to my soul. Rescue me from the abyss of the waters. I have come into deep waters and the tempest sweeps over me.' Some of those who are tempted seem to me to be like the

<hr>

[1] John 6. 18.

very light things without spirit which are seen dragged back and forth and have no resistance to adversity. They have no strength or firmness, no resource in an understanding and prudent reason against the blows of fortune which attack them. The others seem like the solid rock, worthy of that rock upon which we stand and which we worship, who exercise their reason in a philosophic manner upon each eventuality and raise themselves above the feebleness of the crowd, bearing with a firm and unmoved heart all the human vicissitudes. They scorn those who are swayed by such things, or they pity them (the first sentiment is a mark of philosophy, the second of philanthropy).[1]

This passage should serve to warn the modern student of ancient rhetoric and literature against a common pitfall. It is too easily assumed that, because an idea is a commonplace, it is *merely* a commonplace, and that when such commonplaces are used they are automatically to be written off as fictional or as not expressing the author's real feelings. The mind-sets of a culture do not merely affect the window-dressings of its ideas; they affect the way the people in that culture think, and finally they condition the way they actually experience things. The idea of the sea as the symbol of the instability of life, and the rock as the unmovable sage, was an absolutely stock *topos* in classical thought of this period, found alike in the pagan and the Christian authors.[2] Gregory uses exactly the same idea here, and yet we can scarcely doubt that the whole scene reflects a recent and meaningful experience.

Pastoral and nature imagery forms one of the most interesting motifs in Gregory's writings, because it is here that we see quite clearly the intermingling of the scriptural and the classical tradition. In both the Old and the New Testaments the sheep or the flock are used as the symbol of God's people, and God or Christ is the good shepherd leading the flock to green pastures. Gregory plays with this image in numerous variations. The flock may be pictured as scattered without a shepherd or place of refuge, plagued by wild beasts, (the heretics) and wandering into precipitous places (false doctrine). It is in this manner that

---

[1] *Or.* 26. 8–9: *P.G.* 35. 1237 B–40 B

[2] See, for example, Basil's *Quod Mundanis* 171 C: 'But the just man like a promontory stood accepting the buffets of the storm and changing into foam the force of the waves.'

he describes the orthodox believers of Constantinople during the period of Arian dominance before he came to lead them:

This flock was, when it was small and poor, as far as appearances went, nay, not even a flock, but a slight trace and relic of a flock, without order or shepherd or bounds, with neither right to pasturage nor the defence of a fold, wandering upon the mountains and in caves and dens of the earth, scattered and dispersed hither and thither as each one could find shelter or pasture, or could gratefully secure its own safety; like that flock which was harassed by lions, dispersed by tempest, or scattered in darkness. . . . We also were thrust out and cast off, and scattered upon the mountain and the hill, from want of a shepherd, and a dreadful storm came upon the Church and fearful beasts assailed her. . . .[1]

The good shepherd, of course, is the orthodox shepherd who does not allow 'the stranger to climb into the fold like a robber and a traitor', or the flock to listen 'to a strange voice when such would take you away by stealth and scatter you from truth on mountains and in deserts and pitfalls and places the Lord does not visit, and would lead you away from the sound faith in the Father, the Son, and the Holy Spirit, the One Power and Godhead, Whose Voice my sheep always heard, . . . but with deceitful and corrupt words would tear them from their true shepherd, from which may we all be kept, shepherd and flock, as from a poisoned and deadly pasture'.[2] The most interesting feature of Gregory's pastoral imagery, however, is his tendency to incorporate classical bucolic imagery into the stock motifs taken from Scripture. In this passage, speaking of the difficulties of the pastor of souls as compared with the ordinary shepherd, he says:

For in their case it is sufficient to render the herd or flock as stout and fat as possible; and with this object the neatherd and shepherd will look for well-watered and rich pastures, and will drive his charge from pasture to pasture, and allow them to rest or recall them, sometimes with his staff, most often with his pipe, and with the exception of occasional struggles with wolves or attention to the sickly, most of his time will be devoted to the oak and the shade and his pipes, while he reclines on the beautiful grass, and beside the cool waters, and shakes down his couch in a breezy spot and ever and anon sings

[1] Or. 42. 2: P.G. 36. 459 A, B.
[2] Or. 1. 7: P.G. 35. 400 C–401 A; see also Or. 6. 9: P.G. 35. 733 A.

a love ditty, with his cup by his side and talks to his bullocks or his flock, the fattest of which supply his banquet or his pay.[1]

Nature imagery plays a very important part in Gregory's writings as a whole, and he was obviously a lover and keen observer of natural beauty. There is little trace in his thought that nature is evil, no matter how negative he may be about the material part of man's nature. Physical nature apart from man and his works is almost always viewed in the light of creation as God's handiwork. Here, in the variegated beauty and magnificent order of nature, God's existence is revealed. As we shall see in Chapter III, Gregory has very little genuine mysticism in his thought in the sense of man's ability to transcend the plane of his own nature and unite with God on His own level. Rather, the primary place where man meets and contemplates God is through nature, or, as Gregory would say, through the 'veil' of creation. In speaking of God, Gregory quite often breaks into a kind of hymn on the wonders of nature. This idea of nature as the manifestation of God as Creator is a frequent theme in Scripture, but in such passages, for example in the Psalms, the emphasis is on God's power and might as seen in the winds, the mighty rivers, the awesome manifestations of divine creative energy. When, on the other hand, Gregory hymns creation, we immediately feel that a Greek mentality has overlaid a Semitic one. Gregory emphasizes the order and design of creation as manifesting the creative rationality of the Deity. He draws from the whole store of Greek natural philosophy, and begins to speak of the four elements, the various species of animals and plants and their habitats, and the movements of the heavenly bodies. In his second theological oration, as a proof of the existence of God, he gives practically an epitome of natural history, describing the wonders of the human body, the various species of animals, fish, insects, plants, rivers, continents, mountains, the sea, and finally, a fitting climax for a Greek contemplation of nature, the movements of the heavens. The following *ecphrasis* of the marvels of the insect world reveals very clearly how imbued Gregory is with the Greek scientific and artistic tradition, even in the midst of spurning it for the greater glory of God:

[1] *Or.* 2. 9: *P.G.* 35. 417 A, B–422 A.

But I would have you marvel at the natural knowledge even of irrational creatures, and if you can, explain its cause. How is it that birds have for nests rocks and trees and roofs and adapt them both for safety and for beauty, and suitably for the comfort of their nurslings? Whence do bees and spiders get their love of work and art, by which the former plan their honeycombs, and join them together by hexagonal and coordinate tubes, and construct the foundation by means of a partition and an alternation of the angles with the straight lines; and this, as is the case, in such dusky hives and dark combs; and the latter weave their intricate webs by such light and almost airy threads stretched in diverse ways, and this from almost invisible beginnings to be at once a precious dwelling and a trap for the weaker creatures with the intent of the enjoyment of food? What Euclid ever imitated these, while pursuing philosophical inquiries with lines that have no real existence, and wearying himself with demonstrations? From what Palamedes came the tactics, and, as the saying is, the movements and configurations of cranes, and the systems of their movement in ranks and their complicated flight? Who were their Phidiae and Zeuxides, and who were the Parrhasii and Aglaophons who knew how to draw and mould excessively beautiful things? What Gnossian chorus of Daedalus, moving in harmony, brought feminine grace to the highest pitch of beauty?[1] What Cretan labyrinth, hard to get through, hard to unravel, as the poets say, and continually crossing itself through the tricks of its construction? I will not speak of the storehouses and storekeepers, and of their treasuring of food in quantities corresponding to the time for which it is wanted and all the other details which we know are told of their marches and leaders and their good order in their works.[2]

Perhaps one of the most charming of Gregory's nature images, however, is his description of springtime in his oration on the martyr Mamas, where the resurrection of nature and the Christian Easter become beautifully intertwined. For all the words that have been written by comparative religionists on the relation of Christian resurrection to pagan mystery religions, nevertheless the historian of religion cannot afford to lose sight of the fact that the Semitic and Biblical idea of resurrection does not arise from the contemplation of the seasonal rhythms of nature, but from an eschatological vision of judgement in the world to come, and it was in this context that the Biblical

---

[1] This alludes to a group made by Daedalus for Ariadne, representing a chorus of youths and maidens moving in rhythm: *Iliad* 18. 592.

[2] *Or.* 28. 25: *P.G.* 36. 60 C–61 A.

Easter was originally understood. Therefore when Gregory sees the motifs of Easter in springtime, he is showing us a creative vision that can arise only when Christianity has been transplanted into the Hellenistic world and now feels sufficiently at home in that world to shrink no longer from using such symbolism:

All things combine and are accumulated for the purpose of doing honour to this festive season; see how beautiful is all that meets the eye! The Queen of the seasons is holding a festive pomp for the Queen of days,[1] and brings as an offering all that is the most costly and beautiful of her stores. The sky is already brighter, the sun already higher in the heavens and more golden; the moon's orbit is already more cheering and the host of stars more bright. The waves are on more friendly terms with the shore, the clouds with the sun, the wind with the air, the earth with the plants, the plants with the eye. The fountains now flow more transparent; the rivers loosed from the bonds of winter run in full stream; the meadow smells sweetly, the plants swell, the grass is being moved, and the young lambs are frisking on the fresh green plains. The ship now issues forth from the haven with loud and holy songs; it is winged with sails; the dolphin swims gaily around her, snuffing up and again blowing forth the water in delight, while it accompanies the course of the mariner. The husbandman now puts his hand to the plough in order, and looks up in prayer to the Giver of fruits; he leads the ploughing-ox under the yoke, and divides the field with regular furrows, full of joyful hope. The shepherds and herdsmen now play their pipes in harmony; they recommence their pastoral songs, and spend the spring amongst trees and rocks. The gardener tends his plants; the fowler prepares his rods and reeds, and looks up to the boughs to spy out their feathered inhabitants. The fisher glances through the deep water, prepares his net, and takes his seat upon the rocks. The busy bee now spreads her wings; she leaves her hive, displays her sagacious instinct, and robs the flowers of their sweetness—let her be to you a pattern of industry and wisdom! Now the bird builds its nest; one is sitting thereon, another glides softly into it, a third flits around, making the wood ring with its note, and flying round the dwellings of men with twittering tongue. All things praise and glorify God with inarticulate voices, for all things thanks I now offer to God, and thus that universal hymn of praise is also ours, even that whose tones of praise I here express. . . . Yes, it is now the spring of the world, the spring of the mind, the spring for the souls of men, the spring for their

---

[1] The queen of the seasons is springtime, while the queen of days is Easter. See Ullmann, *Gregory of Nazianzus* 211, n. 1.

bodies, the visible spring, the invisible spring; even that one which we will participate in There, if Here we are transformed aright, and having been renewed, enter upon a new and spiritual life.[1]

One of the sources of imagery most characteristic of sophistic oratory was the pictorial arts. The *ecphrasis* or description of painting and sculpture was developed into a genre of its own. The *Eikones* of the younger Philostratus and the *Descriptions* of Callistratus remain to give us an idea of this genre of writing. The idea of a detailed description of a work of art, often with a mythological subject, and described in such a fashion that the whole myth is recounted or alluded to and the figures of the work take on life and action quite beyond the bounds of an actual piece of art—this technique first entered the Greek tradition in the description of the shield of Achilles in *Iliad* 18. 475 ff., and thereafter became a stock *topos* of Greek literature.[2] One of the skills of a sophistic orator, therefore, consisted in being able to produce such an animated *ecphrasis* of a work of art, and the sophists frequently describe their rhetorical art as 'painting' or 'depicting', alluding to their descriptive powers.[3]

In Gregory we find much the same kind of allusion. He, too, frequently refers to a discourse as a painting and the rhetor as a painter.[4] He also uses the image of the musician, and describes the orator as playing on his audience like a musical instrument with many strings.[5] Musical and artistic images are also common in the letters, and a letter itself may be referred to as a work of art. In Gregory's letter to his friend Amphilochus, for example, his letters are called 'an excellent plectrum for me, which plays upon the harmonious lyre you have installed in my soul'.[6] In speaking of his growing friendship with Theodosius, Gregory writes: 'I am taking a leaf from the painters' book. They get the general configuration first into a sketch, and then go over it again a second or a third time with their colours to secure perfect accuracy. . . .'[7]

The most remarkable of Gregory's images drawn from the

[1] *Or.* 44. 10–12: *P.G.* 36. 617 C–620 A, B, 621 A.
[2] See A. Fairbanks, *Philostratus, Imagines*, Loeb (Cambridge, 1960), xvii–xix.
[3] Philostratus, *VS* 592.
[4] *Or.* 11. 2: *P.G.* 35. 833 A; *Or.* 24. 2: *P.G.* 35. 1171 B; *Or.* 2. 13: *P.G.* 35. 421 B; *Or.* 43. 1: *P.G.* 36. 493 A.
[5] *Or.* 2. 36: *P.G.* 35. 448 A.   [6] *Ep.* 171: *P.G.* 37. 280 C.
[7] *Ep.* 230: *P.G.* 37. 372 C, D.

plastic arts, however, occurs in his thirty-fifth oration, where he
is describing the evils of the heretics. Searching for an image
sufficiently vivid to do justice to the supposed lewd behaviour of
the heretics, he creates an *ecphrasis* of Dionysus surrounded by
his band of Maenads, obviously drawn from stock pictorial
representations. 'Where can I find an example which will
sufficiently depict all these evils?', Gregory exclaims. 'I have seen
a mural painting which is sufficiently suited to this tale.' He
then exhorts his audience to enter into this picture and share his
indignation as he recounts its divers abominations in great detail. He describes a group of women dancing in a lewd and
insolent manner. The wind makes their hair fly in all directions.
Fury is painted on their faces. They carry lighted torches whose
flames leap with the contortions of their bodies. Their agitation
throws their clothing into disarray. They leap and dance on
the tips of their toes. They demonstrate complete lack of
modesty in all their actions. In the midst of this dance there is
a figure of an effeminate man. In looking at his face, one has
difficulty deciding to what sex he belongs. His gait is languid
and dissolute, he behaves as a drunkard who has lost his sense
of reason. Gregory then describes the satyrs leaping and dancing
around Dionysus. The whole band is described as running
through the town, setting up their Corybant on the holy chair
of the church, profaning the holy places with wine, tearing a priest
to pieces, and filling the town with revelry and confused and
tumultuous cries.[1]

In addition to these types of secular imagery, which can be
traced to the classical tradition and to sophistic rhetoric—
although often transmuted by the Biblical tradition—Gregory
draws a rich store of images from the Bible. It would be beyond
the purpose of this chapter to discuss his use of Biblical imagery
in detail, but several interesting features may be noted here.
First of all, Gregory looks at the Bible in terms which the
modern scholar would call *Heilsgeschichte*. The whole Biblical
tradition is seen as a vast continuous drama illustrating over and
over the same basic pattern of meaning. Consequently he seldom draws an illustration from simply one event in the Bible,
but commonly runs through the whole list of the 'mighty deeds
of God' from Abraham up to Jesus as part of one great design.

---

[1] *Or.* 35. 3–4: *P.G.* 36. 260 B–261 D.

Consequently references or allusions from any part of the Bible
can be compressed together as so many alternative typologies of
the same idea creating what we might call a 'mosaic of Biblical
images'. For example, in speaking of the three names of the
Deity used in the baptismal formula, Gregory creates this remarkable mosaic of images:

I have three stones which I will sling against the Philistines.[1] I have
three inspirations against the Son of Sareptan,[2] with which I will
quicken the slain; I have three floods against the faggots with which
I will consecrate the sacrifice with water, raising the most un-
expected fire,[3] and I will throw down the prophets of shame by the
power of the sacrament.[4]

All the incidents and figures of Scripture become claimed by the
Christian as archetypes of his present existence. So, in speaking
of his own spiritual struggles, Gregory can say:

For my own warfare, however, I am at a loss what course to pursue,
what alliance, what word of wisdom, what grace to devise, with
what panoply to arm myself against the wiles of the wicked one.
What Moses is to conquer him by stretching out his hands upon the
mount, in order that the cross, thus typified and prefigured, may
prevail? What Joshua, as his successor, arrayed alongside the Cap-
tain of the Lord's hosts? What David . . . What Samuel . . . What
Jeremiah, . . . What Noah, Job, or Daniel . . .?[5]

Gregory's typological use of Scripture is based on the principle
that the Old Testament does in a literal or material way what
the New Testament does in a spiritual way. Thus the dramas of
the Old Testament are viewed as a kind of play-acting of the
inner spiritual drama that is revealed and fulfilled in the New
Testament and in the reality of present Christian life. In this
spirit the whole drama of Exodus is taken as a typology of
Easter or baptism, the Christian inner renewal of the soul.[6] So

[1] 1 Sam. 17. 49.   [2] 1 Kings 17. 21.   [3] Ibid. 18. 33.
[4] *Or.* 40. 43: *P.G.* 36. 420 D–421 A.
[5] *Or.* 2. 88–9: *P.G.* 35. 492 B, C.
[6] The use of Egypt as a symbol of the evil world of matter and the escape from
Egypt as an escape from matter was current in Jewish gnosticism, and probably
passed into Christianity from a previous development in hellenized Judaism. For
example, in Manichean literature Mani is said to leave Egypt, meaning that he departs from the world of matter (see J. Doresse, *The Secret Books of the Egyptian
Gnostics* (New York, 1960) 49, n. 120). Egypt is also used in this sense in the Hymn
of the Pearl from the *Acts of Thomas* (see Jonas, *The Gnostic Religion* 116).

in speaking of the plagues which the people of Nazianzus have
felt and the need to see this as a call of God to repentance,
Gregory uses this typology:

There remain also the locusts, the darkness that may be felt, and
the plague which, last in order, was first in suffering and power, the
destruction and death of the first born, and, to escape this, and to
turn aside the destroyer, it were better to sprinkle the doorposts of
our minds, contemplation and action, with the great and saving
token, with the blood of the new covenant, by being crucified and
dying with Christ, that we may both rise and be glorified and reign
with him both now and in His final appearance, and not be broken
and crushed and made to lament, when the grievous destroyer smites
us all too late in this life of darkness, and destroys our first born, the
offspring and results of our life which we have dedicated to God.[1]

In the same fashion the ascent of Moses to Mount Sinai is
typically seen as the ascent of the mind to God in contemplation.[2] So, in describing the difficulties of the contemplative
ascent and showing that even at the highest level of contemplation of the most christianized of philosophers (Gregory's word
for contemplatives) the saint can only reach God through
creation and through appearances, Gregory uses this Sinai-
typology:

I was running to lay hold of God, and thus I went up into the
Mount, and drew aside the curtain of the cloud and entered away
from matter and material things, and as far as I could I withdrew
within myself. And then when I looked up, I scarce saw the back
parts of God (Exod. 33. 23), although I was sheltered by the Rock,
the Word that was made flesh for us. . . .[3]

Not only the Old Testament but the stories of the New Testament also can be taken as figurative dramas of the inner life of
the soul. So in speaking of the meaning of Christmas, which
Gregory was celebrating with his congregation, he says:

At his birth we duly kept the festival, both I, the leader of the
feast, and you, and all that is in the world, and above the world.
With the star we ran, and with the Magi we worshipped, and with

[1] Or. 16. 11: P.G. 35. 948 c.
[2] This use of Moses' ascent of Sinai as the image of the contemplative ascent
came into Christianity from Philo (De Vita Mosis ii. 66 ff.) and received its fullest
exposition in Gregory of Nyssa, De Vita Moysis. See Danielou, Origen 297.
[3] Or. 28. 3: P.G. 36. 29 A, B

the shepherds we were illuminated, and with the angels we glorified him, and with Simeon we took him up in our arms, and with Anna the aged and chaste we made our responsive confession.[1]

It is important to distinguish this kind of typological thinking from allegory. Allegory moves from the concrete to the abstract, from the historical to the timeless and eternal, whereas typology remains on the historical level, using past experiences as types of present experiences, even though it commonly moves from the 'bodily' or what Gregory calls the *sōmatikos* level to the inner level (*pneumatikos*). Thus typology has a kind of dynamic quality, as each present experience gathers up into its self-understanding the experiences of the past, whereas allegory has a static quality, as an event in the past is transformed into a symbol of a timeless or eternal truth. Although there are various examples of pure allegorical thinking in Gregory's writings, such as his interpretation of Jonah and the whale,[2] and his interpretation of the evangelical saying of the three eunuchs,[3] it is fair to say that the allegorical use of Scripture is the exception in Gregory and the typological use is the norm. This is interesting, since Gregory is commonly seen as the child of the Alexandrian school with its allegorical exegesis. Although he is certainly much influenced by this school, and by Origen, whom he studied very closely, it would be well to recognize the degree to which he also makes use of the Antiochene tradition, which always emphasized the historical and typological levels of Scripture.

The Influence of Sophistic Theories on Epideictic and Epistolary Genre

In addition to the use of figures and tropes, Gregory is also deeply imbued with the sophistic distinctions of styles and *topoi* appropriate to different literary genres. Sophistic theorists, such as Menander (Περὶ ἐπιδεικτικῶν: Spengel, *Rhet.* 3, 329–446), distinguished a number of different types of epideictic oratory, such as the *basilikos logos*,[4] the farewell address, the encomium on

---

[1] *Or.* 39. 14: *P.G.* 36. 349 C.
[2] *Or.* 2. 106–9: *P.G.* 35. 505 ff.
[3] *Or.* 37. 20: *P.G.* 36. 305 A–C. For other examples of developed allegorical interpretation, see *Orr.* 37. 1; 38. 9; 39. 15; 40. 9; 40. 12; 40. 46; 45. 1 ff.
[4] i.e. exhortation to a king: see Burgess, op. cit. 111.

a city, the *epitaphios*, and the *paramūthētikos logos*.[1] The encomium or speech in praise of a person was one of the exercises of the *progymnasmata* which every schoolboy practised as a part of his secondary education. The writers of the *progymnasmata* distinguish the stock *topoi* to be followed in the development of the encomium. Although the subdivisions may be developed in greater or lesser detail, the main outlines of the encomium were fixed. The speaker began with the *prooimion*, which has certain stock topics, such as the inability of the speaker to do justice to the subject, and the offering of the speech as a debt of gratitude. The speaker then launched into the main body of the speech, using a series of conventional topics: race, city, family, circumstances of birth, home life and early education, more advanced education; then the man's achievements, whether of body, soul, or fortune, usually picking out certain outstanding events to describe; then the *synkrisis* or the comparison of the man to the great heroes of yesteryear (this topic might be scattered through the previous topics concerned with the various aspects of the man's life), and finally the summing up or peroration.[2] These were the stock topics of all encomia, and the different epideictic genres were modelled upon this outline with appropriate adaptations. For example, the praise of a king often took the form of an exhortation on the duties of an ideal ruler, or the praise of a city could be approached by way of either the praise of its *genos* or people, or the praise of its *praxis* or deeds. Menander distinguished four types of encomia on a person; the encomium of a person living or dead, the *epitaphios* or funeral oration, the monody or plaint, and the *paramūthētikos* or speech of consolation. The encomium used the topics we have described above. The *epitaphios* used these *topoi*, but concluded with a description of the death and burial and a plaint for the dead man. After the plaint, the orator would develop the *paramūthētikos*, or consolation. Certain commonplaces were used to develop the consolation, such as the exhortation to philosophic acceptance in times of adversity, remarks on the transitoriness of life, and the picturing of the departed among the blessed. The consolation

[1] i.e. speech of consolation, esp. at a funeral; see Burgess, op. cit. 111.

[2] For the topics of the encomium, see Baldwin, *Medieval Rhetoric and Poetic* 31. Also Nadeau's translation of Aphthonius, *Speech Monographs* 19 (1952), 264 ff. For a discussion of Menander's rules of epideictic oratory, see Burgess, op. cit. 174–90.

often ended with an apostrophe to the departed and a prayer. In the monody, the plaint became a separate speech, while a *paramūthētikos logos* took the topics of consolation as a separate speech. In the invective, which was also a progymnastic exercise, all the topics of the encomium were used, only now developed to blame the person instead of praising him; he would be said to be the child of low-born parents, a bastard, etc.

Most of Gregory's speeches are occasional orations, *apologiae* for his own actions, festal orations, and doctrinal sermons. He has, however, eight orations of praise and two invectives, and these are our best sources for studying the extent to which he is influenced by sophistic models. He has no complete speech of the type of a praise of a city or a *basilikos logos*, but in some of his speeches he develops topics taken from these models. For example, in *Oration 33* he employs the topics for praise of a city, but in a satiric manner:[1]

> But we, you will go on, have walls and theatres and racecourses and palaces and beautiful porticos and that marvellous work, the underground and overhead river and the splendid and admired column[2] and the crowded market-place and a restless people and a famous senate of highborn men. Why do you not mention the convenience of the site and what I may call the contest between land and sea as to which owns the city and which adorns our royal city with all its good things?[3]

In *Oration 36*, delivered in the presence of Theodosius, Gregory turns to the Emperor and addresses to him a short speech which contains many of the topics of the *basilikos logos*, exhorting him on the proper use of authority.[4]

Of Gregory's eight speeches of praise—the orations on the Maccabees, Athanasius, Cyprian, and Hero, and the orations on his own family and friends, i.e. Caesarius, Gorgonia, his father, and Basil—the first four follow the topics of the

---

[1] *Or.* 33. 6–7: *P.G.* 36. 221 c–4 a. Compare this mock encomium with a real praise of a city, for example Libanius' praise of Antioch: see Downey's translation, *A.Ph.S.* 103 (1959), 652–86.

[2] These references are to the aqueduct built by Valens and the column on which stood a huge statue of Constantine.

[3] Here Gregory makes a sarcastic reference to the stock conceit which a sophistic orator would have used in praising the site of Constantinople. Such a conceit was well known to his audience, so he has only to make a bare reference to it.

[4] *P.G.* 36. 277 c ff.

encomium in a loose way, while the last four follow them with almost slavish fidelity.

The first of these, however, probably should not be seen strictly as an encomium, but rather as belonging to a new Christian genre, the speech on a festival of a martyr which consists largely of a vivid *ecphrasis* of the whole scene of the martyrdom. In this speech we see Gregory's epideictic style at its most frenzied peak of hyperbole. After a series of introductory questions intended to show that the Maccabees can be seen as true Christian martyrs, even though they are pre-Christian, Gregory describes their father, showing that he was the true progenitor of their virtue. The rest of the piece is an *ecphrasis* of the martyrdom itself, in which all the emotions of the scene are recreated in the most violent colours possible. The martyrs themselves are pictured, all of them resolved to die, eager for death; their only fear is that they might not be tortured sufficiently and might lose the crown of martyrdom. A large part of the description is occupied with the emotions and speeches of the mother, who is displayed with such frenetic melodrama that she becomes totally unbelievable. She makes numerous speeches to her children, exhorting them to courage. She shows her sons her maternal breasts and her white hairs, crying to them to respect her old age, not in order to keep their life, but in order to suffer the cruellest torments. She is in a frenzy of anxiety lest the torturers grow weary and her sons lose the crown of martyrdom. She takes the keenest joy in the spectacle. Gregory makes lavish use of exclamation and *prosōpopoiia*, continually exclaiming upon the intrepidity of the mother and sons, constructing long speeches of exhortation of the mother to her sons, the sons exhorting each other, the sons heroically answering the queries of the judge. Much of this reminds the reader of the Christian Acts of the Martyrs, where the martyrs were pictured witnessing to their faith before the cross-examination of the pagan judge,[1] and there is no doubt that this kind of literature formed the background of such scenes in later Christian orators. Finally, after the martyrs have suffered the last extremity, the mother raises her hands in thanksgiving to Heaven, and then rushes herself to the stake without the help of the executioners and jumps

---

[1] See, for example, the courtroom scene in the *Martyrium S. Justini et sociorum*, P.G. 6. 1565 ff.

upon it 'as if it were a nuptial bed', not wishing profane men to place a hand upon her. Gregory then concludes with a series of *synkriseis*[1] showing that the sacrifice of the Maccabees exceeded all the great sacrifices of the Bible, and that they should be taken as an example to all Christians.

Gregory's encomium on Hero takes on a somewhat ironic coloration when we realize that it was preached in praise of Maximus, who Gregory was soon to find was a man somewhat less praiseworthy than he had thought. In any case, it is an interesting piece of Christian sophistry and revolves mostly round the praise of Maximus as the model of the philosopher. The piece has certain of the *topoi* of the *stephanōtikos logos* or the speech upon the presentation of a crown in a public festival. After showing that Maximus, even though he wears the alien habit of a Cynic philosopher, is in every sense a true Christian philosopher, Gregory pictures himself as placing a crown upon his head in some celestial festival. Here the Christian image of the athlete–martyr–ascetic draws upon its pagan sources, and the ascetic as the spiritual athlete is pictured receiving the crown of victory. Gregory constructs his panegyric as if it were a victory tribute. He then makes a series of allegorizing plays upon the *topoi* of the encomium. He speaks of Maximus' *eugeneia*, his noble birth; only, of course, the true *eugeneia* of a philosopher is his virtue, not his ancestry. Then he tells us that Maximus' *polis* is Alexandria, but, of course, the true *polis* of a Christian philosopher is not any earthly city, but the Jerusalem above. Then he notes Maximus' excellent education, in every way worthy of his noble ancestry, and finally his choice of the philosophic life. Gregory then describes Maximus as the model philosopher, scorning the pagan philosophers, whose philosophy is mere gesture and shadow, and manifesting by word and deed that it is in Christianity that the true substance of philosophy is to be found. Maximus is then pictured fighting for the truth, being persecuted and exiled from Alexandria, finally as conducting a general crusade against all the evils and heresies of the times. After summarizing all these heresies, Gregory then gives a summary of orthodox doctrine under the pretence of asking Maximus to teach him theology.

In the two orations on Cyprian and on Athanasius, both

[1] On this term, see above, p. 106 ; also Guignet, *S. Grégoire et la rhétorique* 275.

being models of the powerful churchman in times of upheaval, Gregory follows the *topoi* of the encomium somewhat more closely. In the panegyric on Cyprian, Gregory constructs his *prooimion* around the theme of the ascetic–martyr, and the renunciation of all the pleasures of the flesh. The stage is thus set for picturing Cyprian as the model ascetic whose lifelong struggles with the flesh are climaxed by a martyr's death. Gregory then launches into an account of Cyprian's life and deeds in the conventional order of an encomium. He tells us that Cyprian's homeland is Carthage, and that he was a man of noble birth and highest rank; that he was a senator, and came from a senatorial family. He then hyperbolizes for a while on Cyprian's education. Using a typical sophistic figure, Gregory professes himself undecided as to what he should praise the most: Cyprian's broad expanse of knowledge, or the perfection with which he grasped each branch of knowledge. He then expresses doubt as to which of Cyprian's deeds he should relate, since they are so many and so excellent, and calls upon the audience to help him and to fill in for each other all the many deeds which should be praised. Gregory announces that he, however, will confine himself only to a few of the most important deeds. It soon becomes apparent, however, that what Gregory is to tell are a few of the most interesting details of Cyprian's life rather than what is most important. He first tells us a titillating story of Cyprian's passion for a young virgin and his attempts to seduce her, and recounts how he is finally converted through her tears and prayers. Then after a brief excursus on all of Cyprian's subsequent mortifications, he passes on to the struggles and final martyrdom of Cyprian under the Emperor Decius. In the description of the martyrdom, Gregory indulges in some rather doubtful plays on words, such as his aphorism of Cyprian 'taking off his head, and putting on a crown', and then a little *ecphrasis* of the women of the city discovering the place where the martyr's body was laid, obviously modelled on the empty-tomb story in the Gospels. Gregory then uses the stock *topoi* of the exordium, expostulating upon his inability to do just homage and exhorting his audience to imitate Cyprian's virtue. Finally he concludes with the commonplace that eloquence is the highest gift of praise that can be given to a man, a thought commonly evoked in sophistic oratory, and makes a series of

synkriseis with the prizes for virtue at pagan festivals, showing
that eloquence is the best prize of all. By some sleight of hand
we are made to feel as though eloquence was a uniquely Christian gift, while pagans had only tripods and crowns to offer to
their heroes.

In Gregory's oration on Athanasius this formidable bishop
of Alexandria is also pictured as the model of the ascetic contemplative. Gregory begins with the *sententia* Ἀθανάσιον ἐπαινῶν,
ἀρετὴν ἐπαινέσομαι and then goes on to praise all the Christian
virtues exemplified in Athanasius with many *synkriseis* from the
Old and New Testaments. The *prooimion* concluded, Gregory
then recounts Athanasius' life. First he points to his pious
upbringing, which in every way suited him for his Christian
vocation. He then discourses on his excellent education, indicating that he was thoroughly versed in literature and philosophy as well as Scripture. Then his life in the priesthood and
his accession to the episcopacy are recounted, showing that in
all ways Athanasius conducted himself in a modest and seemly
fashion. Gregory then uses the same technique that he used in
the oration on Cyprian. He declares his inadequacy to praise the
myriad virtues and deeds of the man, and calls upon the audience to help him. Each is to pick one of his virtues and praise it,
so that some justice can be done to the excellence of Athanasius.
For his part, however, Gregory will pass on to what is most important. In this case what is most important turns out to be the
story of Athanasius' expulsion from Alexandria by the Arian
bishop George of Cappadocia. In the process, Gregory gives us
a specimen of his best invective style:

> There was a monster from Cappadocia, born on our furthest
> confines, of low birth and lower mind, whose blood was not perfectly
> free, but mongrel, as we know mules to be; at first, dependent on the
> tables of others, whose price was a barley cake, who had learnt to
> say and do everything according to his stomach, and, at last, after
> sneaking into public life, and filling its lowest offices, such as that of
> contractor for swine's flesh, the soldier's rations, and then having
> proved himself a scoundrel for the sake of greed in this public trust,
> and been stripped to the skin, contrived to escape, and after passing,
> as exiles do, from country to country and city to city, last of all, in an
> evil hour for the Christian community, like one of the plagues of
> Egypt, he reached Alexandria. There, his wanderings being stayed,

he began his villainy. Good for nothing in all other respects, without culture, without fluency in conversation, without even the form and pretence of reverence, his skill in working villainy and confusion was unequalled.[1]

Gregory then goes on to describe Athanasius' sojourn among the hermits of Egypt and his reconciliation of the priesthood and the monastic movement; the Council of Seleucia (A.D. 359) and the temporary triumph of Arianism; then Athanasius' return under the principate of Julian and his triumphal entry into Alexandria, described in conscious imitation of the triumphal entry of Jesus into Jerusalem. Finally, Gregory extols Athanasius' orthodoxy and hails him as the first true trinitarian theologian. Athanasius' pious death and magnificent funeral are then described, and Gregory concludes with a final prayer addressed to Athanasius in Heaven.

Gregory's funeral speech on his own father, the elder Gregory, is interesting for its adaptation of the sophistic topics of the *epitaphios*. Since Basil, then bishop of Caesarea and Gregory's ecclesiastical superior, was present on this occasion, Gregory constructs the *prooimion* around a eulogistic address to Basil, as if exhorting him to give the oration. He then runs through a kind of outline of the funeral oration, showing its main purpose: i.e. to praise the deceased person and hold him up as an example to others, and then to give a consolatory address on the nature of life and death, setting forth the transitoriness of this life and the preference for the life to come. He then rounds out this pretence of asking Basil to speak with these words:

This, with your power of speech and spirit, you will set forth and discuss better than I can sketch it. But in order that, through ignorance of his excellences, your language may not fall very far short of his deserts, I will, from my own knowledge of the departed, briefly draw an outline and preliminary plan of the eulogy to be handed to you, the illustrious artist of such subjects, for the details of the beauty of his virtue to be filled out and transmitted to the ears of all.[2]

Gregory then launches into an oration which could scarcely be described as an outline. Since his father was of lowly birth, and from the pagan sect of the Hypsistarians, Gregory sets aside

[1] *Or.* 21. 16: *P.G.* 35. 1097 C–1100 B.   [2] *Or.* 18. 4: *P.G.* 35. 989 C.

the first topics of country, race, family, and personal magnificence, but, even in doing so, he makes clear his constant aware-
ness of the topics which govern the panegyric.

Leaving to the laws of panegyric the description of his country, his
family, his nobility of figure, his external magnificence and other
subjects of human pride, I will begin with what is of most conse-
quence and closest to ourselves.[1]

Gregory begins with the description of his father's conversion,
or what Christians would regard as his spiritual birth. He paints
a charming picture of his mother as the model Christian wife,
and shows how his father was converted through her tears and
prayers. Just as the sophist surrounded the description of the
birth of a great man with marvels and portents, so Gregory
surrounds his father's conversion and baptism with miraculous
events. His actual conversion corresponded with a dream sent
from Heaven. He was then baptized by the bishop Leontius,
who was on his way to the Council of Nicaea, and this bishop in-
advertently mingled the formula of ordination with that of baptism, giving a portent of the elder Gregory's sacerdotal destiny.
At the moment of baptism a flood of supernatural light illumined his head, and the presence of the Holy Spirit in the administration of the baptism was made manifest. Gregory's
election by God is then compared with that of Moses, Isaiah,
Jeremiah, and Paul.

As we saw in the discussion of the topics of the encomium,
synkrisis, or comparison of the person praised with great heroes
of yore, was a standard feature. Gregory makes constant use of
synkrisis, occasionally comparing the person to pagan heroes,
but continually making comparison with the great heroes of the
Old and New Testaments. The pagan *synkrisis* is quite different
from Christian typology. A Christian might well show that a
great man had followed in the footsteps of Jesus or of Paul, but
in the sophistic *synkrisis* hyperbole was the rule, and the person
praised, no matter how insignificant he might be, was regularly said to rival or surpass the heroes of the past, e.g. Pericles,
Demosthenes, the Atreidai, etc. When in Gregory we constantly
see persons compared with Moses, or Abraham, or John the
Baptist in such a way that they are said to rival or surpass these

[1] *Or.* 18. 5: *P.G.* 35. 968 c.

Biblical heroes, we can discern the influence of sophistic *synkrisis*.

Gregory then recounts the various excellences (*aretai*) of his father. In his zeal he even tries to make his father into an orator in addition to being a model of Christian piety. 'He was more pious than those who possessed rhetorical power, more skilled in rhetoric than those who were upright in mind', but then, thinking better of this, he contents himself with the emendation, 'or rather, while taking second place as an orator, he surpassed all in piety'.[1] He describes his father as a second Noah, keeping the ark of the Church afloat in times of factional strife. Having come to a transitional point in his oration, Gregory uses the same technique that we have noticed in his previous speeches; he professes his inability to go on, the number of his father's excellences being so great, and then he quickly sketches out a limitless panorama of these virtues, using the rhetorical question: 'Who was more anxious than he for the common weal? Who more wise in domestic affairs . . . ? Who was more sympathetic in mind, more bounteous in hand toward the poor . . .?' He still allows himself to dilate rather profusely on these various virtues, however, in spite of his profession of incompetence, and tells us much of his father's magnanimity, humility, simplicity and freedom from guile and resentment, his industry and practical virtues, his ascetic life. Here we find some fairly tasteless turns of phrase, such as his conceit that his father kept the belly in check without ostentation 'that he might be kept down without being puffed up'.[2] After this general picture of his father's virtues, Gregory recounts various 'edifying incidents', many of a semi-miraculous character. He tells how his father was cured as he lay almost upon his deathbed in a remarkable coincidence with the Easter vigil celebrations heralding the Risen Lord. This 'family miracle' leads Gregory on to several more of the same type. He tells how his mother was cured of an illness after a dream in which Gregory fed her blessed loaves. He recounts his parents' vision of his own near-shipwreck at sea, and attributes his salvation to their prayers. Gregory tells us that he too had a corresponding vision, while on the tempest-tossed ship, of his mother dragging the ship to safety, and this vision was seen also by a shipmate.

[1] *Or.* 18. 16.   [2] Ibid. 23.

After these tales Gregory launches into an account of his father's *praxis*, the deeds which are his claim to renown, a topic essential to any encomium. Under this heading Gregory recounts his father's confrontation with the Emperor Julian, who attempted to confiscate Church property, his intervention during the election of Eusebius and again of Basil to the episcopacy of Caesarea, defending the validity of their elections against their enemies. Gregory mentions his own forced ordination, not without disgust, however, as though even the law of encomium that the orator say nothing derogatory of the one praised must be suspended in the case of this still-remembered affront to his freedom. Finally he notes his father's holy death at the age of almost 100.

Having completed the topics of praise, Gregory turns briefly to the topic of consolation and preaches a brief *paramūthētikos* to his mother on his father's death, speaking of the transitory nature of earthly things, the unchangeableness of heavenly things, and the necessity to be detached from the one and to place one's hope in the other.

Gregory's *prooimion* of the funeral speech on his sister Gorgonia is largely concerned with the propriety of praising one's own relatives. It is an artfully constructed piece intended to show both directly and by implication the impossibility of adequately praising Gorgonia's virtues, a stock topic of the introduction. He expresses his fear 'not of outrunning the truth, but, on the contrary, of falling short of it, and lessening her just repute by the extreme inadequacy of my panegyric; for it is a hard task to match her excellences with suitable action and words'. Gregory also makes the frequent claim of the sophistic speaker that he will reject all daintiness and elegance of style and speak in an unadorned manner.

He then goes on to the topics of country and family, bringing these in by way of *paraleipsis*:

The task of praising the country and family of our departed one I leave to another, more scrupulous in adhering to the rules of eulogy; nor will he lack for many fair topics. . . . For my part I will only conform to such rules so far as to allude to our common parents . . . then speedily direct my attention to herself. . . .[1]

[1] *Or.* 8. 3: *P.G.* 35. 792 D–3 A.

Gregory then spends some time praising their parents, Gregory the elder and Nonna, using his oft-repeated *synkrisis* of his parents with Abraham and Sarah.

In the pagan encomium the ancestry of the person was discussed to show that he was a fitting heir to the *aretē* of his forebears.[1] Such a topic belongs to the ethos of an aristocratic culture. Gregory regularly develops this topic of ancestry to show that the person inherited his Christian piety from the piety of his ancestors and the example of his home life. He uses the same device here, showing that Gorgonia was a model Christian daughter because of the piety instilled in her by her parents. He then develops the topic of *polis*, using the same metaphorical transformation of this topic that we saw in the encomium on Hero, and speaking of her *polis* as the Jerusalem above. In the same manner he shows that her nobility consisted, not in birth, but in her sanctity:

> But, if I must treat of her case in a more philosophic and lofty strain, Gorgonia's native land was the Jerusalem above, the object, not of sight, but of contemplation, wherein is our commonwealth, and whereto we are pressing on: whose citizen Christ is, and whose fellow citizens are the assembly of the first born who are written in heaven, and feast around the great Founder in contemplation of His glory, and take part in the endless festival; her nobility consisted in the preservation of the Image and the perfect likeness to the Archetype, which is produced by reason and virtue and pure desire, ever more and more conforming, in things pertaining to God, to those truly initiated into the heavenly mysteries.[2]

In this passage we see how skilfully Gregory weaves the symbolism of the heavenly kingdom into the key ideas of Greek civic life, playing upon the fact that the word *ecclēsia* can mean both 'Church' and the 'civic assembly', speaking of Christ as the 'city Founder', and the faithful as taking part in a 'festival', a word which recalled both the civic festivals and the Christian celebration of the mysteries, commonly referred to as festivals.

Since his sister did not have much in the way of *praxis* to be recounted, the rest of the oration is mostly concerned with picturing her in her married life as the image of the perfect Christian matron; her modesty, decorum, her liberality and hospitality, her asceticism and piety. In both his account of his

---

[1] See Burgess, op. cit. 120 ff.   [2] *Or.* 8. 6: *P.G.* 35. 796 B.

mother and that of his sister Gregory paints an interesting picture of the Christian woman who fulfils equally the duties of the
married state and what Gregory would call the 'virgin' life,
or the ascetic–contemplative life.

Gregory concludes the oration with a little *ecphrasis* of his
sister's pious death, showing how she fell asleep with the words
of the psalm upon her lips, 'I will lay me down in peace and take
my rest' (Ps. 4. 8). Then, as was common at the conclusion of
an *epitaphios*, Gregory addresses the departed and pictures her
among the blessed, asks her prayers for those who remain, and
begs her to accept his panegyric as a fitting tribute to her.

In his *epitaphios* upon Caesarius, Gregory has the material to
follow the laws of encomium in somewhat more detail than was
the case with Gorgonia. He enters the *prooimion* with the commonplace that his eloquence will be a fitting tribute to the departed and a payment of a debt. 'Albeit that language is a dear
and especially proper tribute to one gifted with it, and eulogy to
one who was exceedingly fond of my words—aye, not only a
tribute, but a debt, the most just of all debts.' Then, as if aware
that this use of the sophistic topic of eloquence as the payment
of a debt might sound strange to Christian ears, Gregory feels
constrained to justify it from Scripture: 'Nor is this alien to our
philosophy, for he says "the memory of the just is accompanied
with eulogies" (Prov. 10. 7), and also "let tears fall down over
the dead . . . "' (Eccl. 38. 16).[1]

Gregory then launches into his first topic of praise, the laudation of their common parents, calling his father a second Aaron
or Moses. Here again Gregory develops the topic of ancestry by
translating nobility of birth into the legacy of Christian piety.
This topic he can develop better in the case of his mother than
in that of his father, since she came of a Christian family—'his
mother was consecrated to God by virtue of her descent from a
saintly family, and was possessed of piety as a necessary inheritance, not only for herself, but also for her children' (*Or.* 7. 4:
P.G. 35. 757 D–760 A). Caesarius is thus shown to be the heir of
the *aretē* of his ancestors and the examples of his kinsmen, and
'his early life was such as becomes those really well born and
destined for a good life' (5). Again we see how closely Gregory
is following the pagan patterns in regard to nobility and virtue,

[1] *Or.* 7. 1: *P.G.* 35. 756 B.

but always translating these topics so that they take on a spiritualized significance. Gregory cannot, however, restrain himself from mentioning his brother's good looks, a topic normally developed at this stage of the encomium, but since the attention to *aretai* of the body was not suitable Christian material, he mentions it only by way of *paraleipsis*:

I say little of his qualities evident to all—his beauty, his stature, his manifold gracefulness and harmonious disposition, as shown by the tones of his voice—for it is not my office to laud qualities of this kind, however important they may seem to others.[1]

Gregory next mentions Caesarius' early education in Nazianzus, and then his higher education in Alexandria. In discussing the topic of education the sophistic orator would indicate the quickness of the man's mind and natural abilities as well as his accomplishments. Here Gregory paints a hyperbolic portrait of his brother as a boy of natural genius and encyclopedic learning:

The brilliant in intellect he surpassed in industry, the devoted students, in quickness of perception; nay, rather he outstripped in rapidity those who were rapid, in application those who were laborious, and in both respects those who were distinguished in both. From geometry and astronomy . . . he gathered all that was helpful. . . . In arithmetic and mathematics and in the wonderful art of medicine . . . who is there so ignorant and contentious as to think him inferior to himself, and not be glad to be reckoned next to him and carry off the second prize? This indeed is no unsupported assertion but East and West alike and every place which he afterwards visited are as pillars inscribed with the record of his learning.[2]

After discussing Caesarius' education, Gregory goes on to his *praxis*, and recounts his career as a public physician in Constantinople. Gregory pictures his brother as virtually the most brilliant inhabitant of this brilliant city and the cynosure of all eyes. The Emperor himself is said to have begged Caesarius to adorn their city 'so that to all its other titles to distinction, this further one be added, that it was embellished by having Caesarius as its physician and inhabitant' (8). After having described all Caesarius' honours and distinctions, Gregory makes it clear that his greatest honour lay in being a faithful Christian

[1] *Or.* 7. 5: *P.G.* 35. 760 c, d.   [2] *Or.* 7. 7: *P.G.* 35. 761 c-4 A.

in the midst of this luxurious metropolis. As an example of this he tells how the Emperor Julian tried to win Caesarius over to his cause, but his brother proved incorruptible. The match between the two is envisaged as a gladiatorial contest:

> However, that I may dwell awhile upon this point, and luxuriate in my story as men do who are eyewitnesses at some marvellous event, that noble man, fortified with the sign of Christ, and defending himself with His Mighty Word, entered the lists against the adversary experienced in arms and strong in his skill in argument. In no wise abashed at the sight, nor shrinking at all from his high purpose through flattery, he was an athlete ready in word and deed to meet the rival of equal power. Such then was the arena and so equipped the champion of godliness. The judge, on the one side, was Christ, arming the athlete with His own sufferings; and on the other was a dreadful tyrant, persuasive in his skill in argument and overawing him by the weight of his authority; and as spectators, on either side, both those who were still left on the side of godliness, and those who had been snatched away by him, watching whether the victory inclined to their side or to the other, and more anxious as to which would gain the day than the combatants themselves.[1]

This type of description of a combat with the spectators torn between the two, anxiously inclining, now to one side, now to the other, was a motif developed in Thucydides' description of the siege of Syracuse,[2] and was long a favourite in the sophistic *ecphrasis*. Gregory then recounts the speeches on either side in the manner of a rhetorical debate, showing Caesarius triumphantly tearing apart Julian's impudent sophistries and loudly proclaiming the Christian truth.

Gregory continues with his tale of Caesarius' life after this high point. He tells us of his retirement during the persecution of Valens, his return to public life, and his office as treasurer in Bithynia; then of an earthquake which nearly took his life and engendered a conversion experience whereby he resolved to renounce worldly things and retire to the monastic life. However, disease took his life shortly thereafter, before he could carry out this intention. Gregory then describes the funeral honours, the mourning of all for the passing of this young man. He gives us a *thrēnos* for his dead brother, pictures Caesarius in Heaven, and speaks of his oration as a funeral garland fairer than any pagan

---

[1] *Or.* 7. 12: *P.G.* 35. 769 B.   [2] 7. 71.

prize or honour. Gregory then enters into the *paramūthētikos* and speaks of consolation as a powerful medicine against sorrow, and the orator as a physician. He speaks of the transitoriness of human life, the vanity of worldly things, and the necessity to press on to the life above, where our only safety lies. He pictures the bliss of Caesarius in Heaven, the bliss which awaits all those who remain behind if they are faithful to virtue. He concludes with an exclamatory prayer to God to receive Caesarius and in due time all those present into their eternal resting-place.

If Gregory's oration on Caesarius is notable for its fidelity to sophistic topics, his oration on Basil is surely his *tour de force* of this genre of eloquence. However, since it was preached some time after Basil's death and lacks any *thrēnos* or *paramūthētikos*, we must class it as an encomium rather than an *epitaphios*. Gregory opens the *prooimion* with the commonplaces about eloquence as the discharge of a debt, and his inability to do justice to the topic. These topics are rounded out by the platitude that no matter what happens, whether he does justice to the topic or falls short, in either case all will be well.

For, if the discourse be almost worthy of its subject—eloquence will have given an exhibition of its power. If it fall far short of it, as must be the case when the praises of Basil are being set forth, by an actual demonstration of its incapacity, it will have declared the superiority of the excellence of its subject to all expression in words.[1]

In our previous discussion of *paraleipsis* we have shown Gregory's paraliptical development of the topic of ancestry. After declaring his intention to pass over this topic, as a concern unworthy of the Christian, Gregory gives full vent to a display of Basil's noble forebears, comparing them to the great Greek houses of mythology—the Pelopidae, the Cecropidae, the Alcmaeonids, the Aeacidae, and the Heracleidae—and comparing their noble deeds with the legends of heroes, the myths of Artemis, and the fate of Orion and Actaeon.

After setting forth the nobility of his ancestry, Gregory pictures Basil's parents as models of Christian piety and the blessedness of their home life as a true training-ground of philosophers and saints. He describes Basil's early nurture under the tutelage of his father, comparing his upbringing with the training

---

[1] *Or.* 43. 1: *P.G.* 36. 496 A, B.

of Achilles under the guidance of Chiron. As is usual with Gregory, he draws upon such types of pagan *synkrisis*, but does it in such a way that he simultaneously depreciates the pagan example as a thing of no worth and yet lets the Christian shine in reflected glory by contrast to it:

> Under him [Basil's father] then, as life and reason grew and rose together, our illustrious friend was educated: not boasting of a Thessalian mountain cave, as the workshop of his virtue, nor of some braggart Centaur, the tutor of the heroes of his day: nor was he taught under such tuition to shoot hares, and run down fawns or hunt stags, or excel in war, or in breaking of colts, using the same person as teacher and horse at once: nor nourished on the fabulous marrows of stags and lions, but he was trained in general education and practised in the worship of God, and led on by elementary instruction to his future perfection.[1]

Next Gregory develops at great length the topic of Basil's higher education at Caesarea, Byzantium, and Athens, giving us the full story of their schooldays and friendship together. This was doubtless one of Gregory's fondest memories, and he takes great pleasure in bridging the times of later conflict between himself and Basil and looking back to those 'good old days'. Basil is, of course, pictured as possessing extraordinary natural endowment, quickly mastering all branches of knowledge, and as demonstrating his powers as 'an orator among orators', 'a philosopher among philosophers', even while he was still a boy and had not yet studied in the schools of rhetoric and philosophy. Gregory describes their love for each other in a discourse on friendship that is reminiscent of Plato's *Symposium*; each clung to the other because of the vision of beauty he perceived in the other's soul (19). Gregory describes the marvels of their love and educational prowess by various *synkriseis* with classical wonders; the ring of Gyges, Midas' gold, the arrow of the Hyperborean Abaris[2] or the Argive Pegasus, whose flights through the air were less notable than the rising of Basil's and Gregory's souls to God. Their friendship is seen as renowned throughout Greece; nay, rather throughout the civilized world,

[1] *Or.* 43. 12: *P.G.* 36. 509 B, C.
[2] Gregory seems to be fond of the tale of Abaris (see *Ep.* 2: *P.G.* 37. 24 A), and appears to know a version of this story from some mythological handbook of his time that departs from the usual account: see F. Lefherz, *Studien zu Gregor von Nazianz: Mythologie* (Bonn, 1958).

making the comradeship of Orestes and Pylades or the sons of Molione a mere nothing by comparison. Basil's instant mastery of rhetoric, grammar, philosophy, dialectic, astronomy, geometry, medicine is detailed in many exclamatory phrases, and the wisdom of Minos and Rhadamanthus is seen as a mere trifle by comparison.[1]

After telling of Basil's departure from Athens for his native Cappadocia, Gregory passes on to the *praxis* of his mature life. He tells us that Basil taught rhetoric briefly in Caesarea and then became renowned as the young sacerdotal assistant of the bishop of Caesarea. He recounts the various trials of Basil with this jealous prelate and his temporary retirement to Pontus, his return to aid the Church during the persecution of Valens, and his works of charity, in which he is compared with Joseph, Moses, Elijah, and Christ, and even said to surpass Joseph as an administrator and Moses as a legislator and to be a veritable second Bezaleel, the architect of the divine tabernacle. Basil's great confrontation with Valens is then recounted, in which the heretic Emperor is compared to Xerxes as the epitome of overweening *hybris*. Gregory puts speeches into the mouths of Basil and Valens' prefect, and gives us one of those little vignettes of the Christian confronting the enemy in which he is so skilled— the raging prefect, the intrepid Christian impervious to all threats and tortures, and finally winning the day and leaving even his enemies in open-mouthed admiration. The prefect is pictured reporting this confrontation to the Emperor in these words:

Sire, we have been worsted by the prelate of this church. He is superior to threats, invincible in argument, uninfluenced by persuasion. We must make trial of some more feeble character, and in this case resort to open violence, or submit to the open disregard of our threatenings.[2]

Basil is pictured as on the verge of banishment, but is then saved by the sickness of Valens' son, whom he alone is able miraculously to heal. The child died soon afterwards anyway, but Gregory attributes this to the fact that Valens did not sufficiently trust the orthodox prelate, but called in heterodox ones as well:

---

[1] Gregory does not fail to note at this time the usual Christian theme (taken from Jewish apologetics) that Greek wisdom was originally stolen from the Torah. See below, p. 167 and n. 1.   [2] *Or.* 43. 51: *P.G.* 36. 561 B.

'... had he not blended salt water with fresh, by trusting to the heterodox at the same time that he summoned Basil, the child would have recovered his health and been preserved in his father's arms' (53). Basil receives his full meed of satisfaction when the prefect himself falls ill and calls in Basil in desperation.

Basil is then described taking up the defence of a woman forced into marriage against her will. In a picture inspired by the Gospel story of Jesus before Pilate, Basil is seen answering the charges of the judge, showing himself impervious to threats, calming the riots in the city, finally winning the day. Gregory then recounts Basil's conflicts over episcopal jurisdiction with Anthimus, faltering in his praise over the Sasima incident, the one event for which Gregory still could not forgive his friend.[1]

Gregory then goes on to describe Basil's monastic legislation and to picture him as the perfect ascetic. His hospital in Caesarea is described and compared with the seven wonders of the world; the seven portals of Thebes, the Egyptian city of Thebes, the walls of Babylon, the tomb of Mausolus, the Pyramids, the Colossus of Rhodes, and divers other historic and mythic wonders. Basil is seen as the model of Christian eloquence and the theologian of the new era, surpassing all the work of the past as an instructor in heavenly truths. He is compared to the very sun enlightening the heavens. This laudation concludes with an elaborate section of *synkriseis* where Basil is compared to Adam, Enos, Enoch, Noah, Abraham, Isaac, Jacob, Joseph, Moses, Joshua, Samuel, David, Solomon, Elijah, Elisha, John the Baptist, Peter, Paul, John—Basil rivalled and surpassed them all.

The oration ends with a description of Basil's pious death, his mourning and funeral, and his present life among the blessed. In the final peroration all are exhorted to join in a final hymn of praise, and Gregory addresses Basil in Heaven offering him his oration as a final tribute.

These, then, are Gregory's major encomiastic orations, and they demonstrate both how imbued he was with the *topoi* of this genre of oratory and yet, at the same time, how he continually strove to adapt these *topoi* to the Christian setting.

Gregory is also notable as a letter-writer, and here again he is

---

[1] *Supra*, pp. 34 ff. See S. Giet, 'Sasimes: Une Méprise de S. Basile' (Thèse, Paris, 1941).

scrupulous in observing the laws of this genre, yet he continually transforms the medium by his own personality, so that his letters give us a vivid psychological portrait of the man. Indeed, this was considered one of the virtues of good epistolary writing, that it revealed in a skilful manner the personality of the author. Since Guignet has written in such detail on Gregory's epistolary style, I will only try to summarize the salient points in his work.[1]

The letter was a literary genre much in vogue in this period, as it often is in such neo-Alexandrian periods (e.g. eighteenth-century France). The laws of epistolary style were well known and respected by all literate people, and a person's letters were carefully polished to be little gems of language, in the expectation that they would be passed round and even read out loud to admiring groups of *literati*. Demetrius, in his work *On Style*,[2] outlines the main rules for the letter. It is to be written in a plain style; the long periodic sentence is out of place. It is to have the manner of an actual dialogue, but more studied than usual conversation. There should be frequent parentheses, or breaks in the sentence structure, imitating the manner of actual conversation. The letter should combine the plain and graceful style; it should give little glimpses of the writer's personality, but its length should be kept within due bounds. Elaborate development of ideas is out of place. There should be a certain candour, and a freedom of structure in the letter, although the more formal structure and the more elevated tone are suitable to letters to governments and persons in authority. High-flown philosophy is also unsuitable in the letter. Proverbial wisdom and pithy sayings are the appropriate type of philosophizing.

Nicobulus, Gregory's great-nephew, asked his uncle for some words on good epistolary style, and Gregory complied with a little treatise on this subject which gives us a clear indication of how conscious he was of the demands of style in the letter and in his writings in general. The piece tallies with what Demetrius has told us, and it is interesting enough to be quoted in full.

Writers of letters (as you have asked the question) err either by excess or defect, in that some write at greater length than is fitting while others are much too brief. Either mistake is a failure to achieve the mean, just as, when men shoot at a target, the miss will

---

[1] Guignet, *Grégoire épistolier*, op. cit. *passim*.   [2] pp. 224 ff.

be equally palpable whether one is above or below the mark, though the causes in such cases are precisely the opposite.

The length of a letter is determined by the amount one has to say. When there is not much to say, one ought not to drag it out; when there is, one ought not to be measuring words. Does this mean that physical measurement, the Persian *schoinos*, or juvenile *pecheis*, ought to be applied to one's written wisdom, even though the result be so shapeless as not to be writing at all? Or should one aim at the effect of shadows in the South, or of lines foreshortened by looking straight along them, where the actual length is telescoped and is suggested rather than accurately measured from point to point, where (if I may phrase it more happily), there is simply a likeness of a likeness? Well, one should avoid both extremes and try to achieve the mean. So much for my principle in the matter of brevity.

Concerning the question of clarity, it is an accepted principle that one must eschew wordage as far as possible and tend rather toward the speaking style. In a word the very best letter is the one which commends itself to the ordinary man and to the scholar alike, to the former as something on the popular level, to the latter as something above that level. Then the meaning of a letter ought to be at once quite clear, because a letter which needs to be explained is as irritating as a puzzle that needs to be solved.

The third point about a letter is the charm of its style. This we can achieve if, on the one hand, we avoid complete aridity and gracelessness; I mean, total lack of embellishment or ornament—the 'untrimmed style' as it is called. This comes when there are no pithy sayings, no proverbs, no apophthegms at all, and none of the epigrams and witticisms which give a sweetness to style. On the other hand, we must not appear to make undue use of these adjuncts. Excess is cloying, whereas defect is boorish. They should appear in the same proportions as purple does in embroidery. Thus tropes are permissible occasionally, and they should be in good taste—the figures of *antithesis*, *parisosis*, and *isocolon* may be left to the sophists, or if a slight use is made of them, it should be humorous rather than serious. I may conclude my remarks by repeating a story I heard from one of those clever people. When the birds were trying to decide who should be king, and they all came together to the meeting making the most of their various ornaments, the greatest adornment of the eagle, according to my friend, was the fact that he was unconscious of his magnificence. In letter-writing too it is that sort of unconscious ornament that must be preserved in order that one's style may be as natural as possible.[1]

[1] *Ep.* 51: *P.G.* 37. 106.

As we examine Gregory's letters we see that he is notably faithful to his own rules. One of the significant features of his epistolary style is its variety. We have a gamut of styles; the laconic style written to ascetic friends, particularly when he himself was practising penitential silence (*Epp.* 107–13), the formal and hyperbolic style for petitions and introductions to persons of authority, the bantering style to friends, the grave and serious style written for counsel in matters of morality or church discipline. Gregory consciously varies his style to suit the subject-matter and the recipient, and in his letter seeks the mode of expression suitable to the occasion. Indeed the idea of the *kairos*, or that which is suitable to the occasion, is one of the guiding motifs in his thought and occurs again and again in his letters (e.g. *Ep.* 118). Gregory is a master of irony, the uniting of surface *politesse* with hidden satire, and this penchant comes out in many of his letters, to ecclesiastics particularly. Gregory may take the theme of his letter from Scripture, as in the proverbial saying from Ecclesiastes, 'all things have their season' (*Ep.* 118), or from a line of Hesiod (*Ep.* 195). He may make use of a proverb, such as 'one jackdaw is drawn to another', as an expression of friendship (*Ep.* 224). He frequently tells a tale to illustrate a point, as he did in the letter to Nicobulus quoted above. His most notable use of the parable occurs in his epistle to Celeusius (*Ep.* 114), where he rebukes this young man for his impudence by telling a tale about the swallows and the swans. The swallows fly around and chatter in the dwellings of men, while the swans prefer solitude, and sing noiselessly in remote places. The swallows mock the swans for their quiet and solitude, but the swans know the higher eloquence of silence. The parable, of course, stands for the conflict between the man of the world and the Christian monk, and Gregory concludes with the epigrammatic saying from Pindar that 'when the jackdaws are silent, the swans will sing'.

The most formalized type is the letter of request or petition. It consistently begins with an elaborate introduction designed subtly to praise the recipient of the petition and conciliate his good favour. Only after this encomiastic introduction is over, and almost as if incidentally, does the writer bring in the favour he is asking. Letter 140 to Olympius on behalf of the fugitive soldier Aurelius is a good example of the type:

Again I write you a letter, though I ought to visit you. But it is from you actually that I derive courage, O judge of spiritual things (to mention first things first) and manager of the commonweal, both offices the gift of God. Your piety is rewarded indeed in that everything goes according to your wishes and that you are the only one who finds ready to hand the things that are not vouchsafed to others. Your rule is directed by intelligence and fortitude, intelligence to discover what must be done, fortitude to execute it readily when discovered. But, most of all, the hand that holds the reins is clean. Where is your ill-gotten gold? It doesn't exist: bribery, like a disguised tyrant, was your first exile. Where is enmity? It has been condemned. Where is patronage? Now here (I shall impeach you a little) you do bend a bit, but it is in imitation of the kindness of the Almighty. Aurelius, a soldier of yours, is now asking through me for that very patronage. I call him a foolish fugitive, but a wise suppliant in that he has placed himself under the shelter of my hands, and through mine under yours. Like some royal image he is clinging to my grey hairs and my priesthood, which you have often seen fit to revere. This sacrificing and unbloody hand, then, now leads him to you, a hand that has often written your praise, and that will, I know, continue to do so if the reign is prolonged by God; I am speaking of your reign, of course, and that of Themis, your colleague.[1]

Such letters of petition and patronage point to an interesting mingling of two ideals: first, the Christian ideal of fraternal charity; and secondly, the ancient ideal of patronage in which the aristocrat exercised the duties of liberality and aid to his clients as part of the office of his class. In men like Gregory, who were fully the heirs of both traditions, the two were so interwoven that it would be difficult to say where one ceases and the other begins. In Gregory's many letters of friendship, too, there is as much of the pagan tradition of *amicitia* as there is of the Christian idea of brotherly love. Indeed, it owes perhaps more to the former, for Gregory's letters of friendship seldom express altruistic *agapē*, but have all those marks of conviviality and interested mutuality that characterize the ancient ideal of friendship.[2] Gregory is always eager for return correspondence from

---

[1] *P.G.* 37. 237 B ff.
[2] Cicero's *De Amicitia* is the classical statement of this ideal, a work which was based essentially on Theophrastus' *peri Philias*; see M. A. McNamara, *Friendship in St. Augustine* (Freiburg, 1958) 4 for the bibliography on the sources of *De Amicitia*. A good general exposition is L. Dugas's *L'Amitié antique* (Paris, 1914).

his friends; he is easily hurt by them and anxious that his tokens of love be reciprocated. Most of his letters are informal, and even in the more formal letters written to officials there is the note of intimacy that makes Gregory's letters a vivid record of his personality.

III

GREGORY OF NAZIANZUS AND THE PHILOSOPHIC LIFE[1]

GREGORY OF NAZIANZUS' understanding of the ascetic, contemplative life is an intimate reflection of his own *Lebensideal*. He shares many features of this ideal with his friends and compatriots, Basil the Great and Gregory of Nyssa, but the function of 'philosophy' in his writings can scarcely be understood except in terms of his personal struggle. Gregory's own life was the testing-ground of the values and contradictions of this ideal of life that was drawing man away from the forum into the solitude of the desert. Each of the Cappadocian Fathers put the mark of his own personality on the delineation of this ideal of life, although there is a strong family resemblance between them. Basil was the organizer of monastic life. It was he who laid down the rules for the monastic communities under his tutelage in a strict Biblical language that carefully eschewed the terminology of the philosophic tradition. It was Nyssen who systematized the Cappadocian theoretical structure and unified its theology, angelology, and anthropology round its central vision of man's goal in life. Nyssen was a disciple of both Basil and Nazianzen and built upon their common teachings, and much of what is systematized in Nyssen is found in an inchoate form in Nazianzen. Gregory of Nazianzus never wrote any systematic treatise on asceticism or contemplation. He hymned it in his poems; it fills his letters and his orations. He constantly tried to live by its tenets, but he never wrote an organized account of its principles. His doctrine on the subject must be extracted from bits and pieces scattered through his writings.

[1] There is no work comparable to J. Danielou's work on Gregory of Nyssa that treats the concept of the contemplative life in Gregory of Nazianzus. However, J. Plagnieux has some brief remarks on *katharsis* and contemplation in *S. Grégoire de Nazianze théologien* (Paris, 1951) 81–111.

Gregory's Cosmology and Anthropology

Gregory's cosmology might be described as reformed Origenism. On the one hand, Cappadocian theology removed from its doctrine of the second and third persons of the Godhead any economical functions. *Logos* and *Spiritus* ceased to function as descending levels of emanation from the Father which relate the world to the Father. Rather *Logos* and *Spiritus* both withdraw into a transcendence equal to that of the Father. In the homoousian theology the three persons all exist on the same ontological level and contain the same essence (*ousia*). There is no question of increasing articulation or diversity as the Godhead moves from Father to Son to Spirit. As the Christian Church battled within itself to define the soteriological function of the *Logos*, which was seen as the divine component of the Messiah, it became apparent that this soteriological function might be called in question as long as there was any doubt about the fully divine status of the *Logos*. As a result a theology was constructed to defend the equality of the *Logos* with the Father, but in the process the *Logos* lost its original philosophic function and henceforth the multiplication of hypostases within the Godhead could only be understood as a 'mystery'. This 'mystification' of what was once a comprehensible philosophical theology can only be understood when we realize that it was soteriology, not systematic theology or cosmology, that ruled the development of Christian doctrine.[1]

Origenist anthropology is also modified in Cappadocian thought. The pre-existence of the human soul as part of the spiritual creation is rejected and is replaced by the more conventional scheme of man's creation after the creation of the material world. Yet, in spite of these changes, basic thought structures inherited from Origen persist. In Gregory's oration on the Theophany (Christmas), he makes a thumbnail sketch of his cosmology. In the beginning God existed alone. Although God existed in three persons, these three are not treated as though they constitute any diversity in the Godhead. They do not succeed each other in time, nor is the succession of persons related to the opening drama of creation, i.e. the *Logos* is not to

[1] For the development of Trinitarian theology from Greek *Logos* theology, see H. A. Wolfson, *The Philosophy of the Church Fathers* (Cambridge, 1956) 141–232.

be equated with the intellectual creation or even the pattern for the intellectual creation. The three exist as One, alone and self-contemplative.[1] This idea that the life of God consists in the contemplation of His own nature was a part of the Greek theological tradition stemming from Aristotle and now taken for granted by Christian and pagan thinker alike. Like Plotinus, Gregory attributes the first creation to an 'overflow of Goodness' that occurs in the divine beneficence. This contradicts his statement in the third theological oration where he vehemently contrasts the Christian view which sees creation as flowing from spontaneous love and the Platonic view which sees this 'overflow' as a necessity of God's nature.[2] And yet it is difficult to distinguish between a necessity of God's nature and spontaneous love, if love and beneficence are God's nature, and so Gregory, in this oration, speaks of the creation in much the same manner as Plato:

> But since this movement of self-contemplation alone could not satisfy Goodness, but Good must be poured out and go forth beyond Itself to multiply the objects of its beneficence, for this was essential to the highest Goodness, He first conceived the Heavenly and Angelic Powers.[3]

The angels or heavenly powers in Gregory as in Origen now become the intellectual creation, taking the place of the *Nous* or *Logos* of Greek philosophical thinking which now, paradoxically, has withdrawn into unitary transcendence, although its original philosophic function was to explain the inception of diversity. However, the *Logos* and *Spiritus*, as well as the intellectual creation, the angelic powers, are understood by Christians in the manner in which they had been rethought by Iranian Gnosticism, as personal beings. This meeting of the Platonic Ideas with Iranian angelology had already taken place prior to Origen, and the equation of the angels with the *noēta* was already found in *De principiis*. These angelic powers are described much as Plotinus describes the *Nous*, as an effulgence,

---

[1] *Or.* 38. 8: *P.G.* 36. 320 B; for God's nature as self-contemplative see also *Or.* 40. 5: *P.G.* 36. 364 B.

[2] *Or.* 29. 2: *P.G.* 36. 76 C: 'For we shall not venture to speak of "an overflow of Goodness", as one of the Greek philosophers dared to say, as if it were a bowl overflowing, and this in plain words in his discourse on the first and second causes.' The expression is from Plato's *Timaeus*.

[3] *Or.* 38. 9: *P.G.* 36. 320 C.

a secondary Light circling round the Great Light.[1] Gregory shares the Origenist tradition in being unwilling to conceive of created reality as completely immaterial. The words 'immaterial' and 'invisible' cannot be equated for these thinkers. Created spirit is invisible, but still created and so not substantially the same as God, who alone is totally immaterial. Gregory draws upon the Greek philosophic tradition going back to Heraclitus and suggests the equation of these highest spirits with fire: '. . . whether we are to conceive of them as intelligent spirits or as Fire of an immaterial and disembodied kind, or as some other nature approaching this as near as may be'.[2] We can see from this quotation that Gregory has a semantic problem. He wants to create three levels of reality, God, angelic spiritual beings, and visible material reality, but the Greek philosophic tradition gives him only two levels, the material and the spiritual, the visible and the invisible. Therefore, in contrast to the visible world, the spiritual world is spoken of as 'immaterial and disembodied' (aülon kai asōmaton), but it is also thought to have a kind of matter or substance, a fiery or aerial 'stuff', to differentiate it from the uncreated substance of God. These intermediate levels of 'matter' already played a part in gnostic thinking, and hark back to Aristotle's concept of the fifth essence.[3] Gregory, however, departs from the insight that occurs both in Origen and in Plotinus which found the will of the intellectual being to be the key to its fate. He rather makes the cruder equation of matter with evil and the disembodied state with good, and thus deprives himself of the explanatory principle for the fall of the angels.[4] Immateriality is identified with immutability, and therefore the angels are 'incapable of movement in the direction of evil, and susceptible only to good, as being around God, and illumined with the first rays from God'.[5] But since Biblical tradition contains the fall of the angels, Gregory must revise this statement paradoxically and without any foundation in his cosmological scheme, and state:

[1] Or. 38. 9: P.G. 36. 320 c; compare with Plotinus, Enn. I, v. 6.
[2] Or. 38. 9: P.G. 36. 320 c.
[3] On 'soul substance' and the garments of the soul, see Hans Jonas, The Gnostic Religion 256–66.
[4] See Brooks Otis, 'Cappadocian Thought as a Coherent System', D.O.P. 12 (1958), 94–124.
[5] Or. 38. 9: P.G. 36. 320 c.

. . . but I am obliged to stop short of saying that, and to conceive of them as very difficult to move, because of him who, for his splendour, was called Lucifer, but became and is called Darkness through his pride; and the apostate hosts who are subject to him, creatures of evil by their revolt against good, and our inciters.[1]

After this first creation is completed, Gregory then goes on to describe the creation of the visible universe. The intellectual creation no longer serves as the 'pattern' for the visible creation, as it did in the Greek philosophic tradition. That idea faded when the *noëta* were converted into angels. Rather the visible creation is a second and perfectly gratuitous act on the part of God, unrelated to the first creation. Gregory's concept of the visible creation arises out of two contradictory traditions: the Biblical creationism which regards the universe as good, and gnostic creationism which regards it as a fall and an alienation from God. Both attitudes are exhibited side by side without reconciliation. On the one hand he says:

Then when His first creation was in good order [the fall of the angels is suddenly forgotten], He conceives a second creation, material and visible; and this a system and compound of earth and sky, and all that is in the midst of them—an admirable creation indeed, when we look at the fair form of every part, but yet more worthy of admiration when we consider the harmony and the unison of the whole and how each part fits in with every other, in fair order, and all with the whole, tending to the perfect completion of the world as a unit.[2]

So far Gregory is in perfect harmony with traditional Greek cosmos-piety, and he might almost have gone on and spoken of it as a 'visible god', or at least as an image of the divine reason. But suddenly Gregory adds a few more sentences that reveal an entirely different *Weltanschauung*. This fair cosmos is then described as the utter antithesis of God, and alien to His essence; virtually an evil thing. How God could call into being a reality utterly alien to His essence is left unexplained. Since Gregory has no series of intermediaries to ease the way between unity and diversity, spirit and matter, the confrontation is all the more striking. Gregory's only suggestion to explain this disparity is to pass it off as a bit of virtuosity on the part of God.

[1] *Or.* 38. 9: *P.G.* 36. 321 A.   [2] *Or.* 38. 10: *P.G.* 36. 321 B.

This was to show that He could call into being not only a Nature akin to Himself, but also one altogether alien to Himself. For akin to Deity are those natures which are intellectual and only to be comprehended by the mind; but all of which sense can take cognizance are utterly alien to It; and of these the furthest removed are all those which are entirely destitute of soul and the power of motion.[1]

This second material creation contained no intellectual beings. The two creations, the intellectual creation and the sensible creation, were entirely separate, and both 'remained within their own boundaries'.[2] As a final piece of virtuosity, the Creator–Word now determines to mingle the two creations and to create man.

Nor yet was there any mingling of both, nor any mixture of these opposites, tokens of a greater Wisdom and Generosity in the creation of natures; nor as yet were the whole riches of goodness made known. Now the Creator–Word, determining to exhibit this and to produce a single living being out of both—the visible and the invisible creations, I mean—fashions Man; taking a body from already existing matter and placing in it a breath taken from Himself which the Word knew to be an intelligent soul and the Image of God, as a sort of second world.[2]

Gregory goes on to describe man's nature in dualist terms. He is a 'new angel', a 'mingled worshipper'; he partakes paradoxically of both creations; earth and heaven, visible and intellectual, lowliness and greatness, flesh and spirit. Gregory then describes the fall of the primal parents in paradise, but it is clear that the fall is already anticipated in the creation. Before there is any discussion of the fall, upon the first moment of creation, Gregory describes man's mingled condition as a state of suffering and a training-ground. Already at creation the visible world is alien to his true nature, and he is placed in it as a 'living creature, trained here but moved elsewhere'.[3]

Brooks Otis, in his paper on 'Cappadocian Thought as a Coherent System',[4] suggests that Cappadocian cosmology combines Irenaean and Origenist elements; it sees the first creation both as a state of immaturity destined to grow up to fulfilment through history and as a state of fall which works as a penal and

---

[1] *Or.* 38. 10: *P.G.* 36. 321 B.
[2] *Or.* 38. 11: *P.G.* 36. 321 C.
[3] *Or.* 38. 11: *P.G.* 36. 324 A.
[4] See above, p. 132, n. 4.

pedagogical system. We can see both these elements in Gregory's account. First he describes man's pre-lapsarian state as an immaturity and a training-ground. Man's incarnate state is seen as a trial to him, even before the fall. His flesh is alien to his spirit. This same idea of incarnation as a testing-ground for future disembodied life also occurs in Plato's *Timaeus*, although in the *Phaedrus* he describes the incarnation of man as a fall from a previous disincarnate state.[1] Man's ultimate goal, achieved through this testing-period, is deification. Man realizes through his own free will the image of God placed within him. What was given to him gratuitously, namely a share in the divine nature, he must 'earn', and bring to fulfilment. In this light Gregory interprets the Tree of Knowledge as *theōria*. This fruit was man's legitimate goal when he was ready for it. Gregory interprets man's life in the garden as philosophic ascent; he is given the 'seeds of divine wisdom by God to till the immortal plants', which are the 'divine Conceptions'. The nakedness of man is interpreted as the transparency of his mind to the contemplation of the Ideas. Thus Gregory uses the Garden of Eden mythology to express the Platonic idea that man contemplated the Ideas in some primordial state. Man's sin consisted in precipitously snatching the fruit of *theōria* before he was ready for it. He attempted to rise too high and grasp at the goal of the contemplative life before his spirit was sufficiently mature and thus incurred a fall. This fall is interpreted as a 'setback' in man's *élan* towards deification and *theōria*, rather than as a total perversion of his nature. His task now becomes more difficult, his body grows fleshly and he puts on 'coats of skin' (*dermatinous chitōnas*).[2] Gregory interestingly interprets the Biblical idea that Adam and Eve discovered that they were naked and put on clothes after the fall in terms of the gnostic–Origenist doctrine of 'coats of skin'. By this Gregory means that man's somatic nature grows 'dense' and now offers a great impediment to contemplation; man can no longer contemplate the Ideas transparently as he did before when he was 'naked'. Following Origen, Gregory then interprets history as a pedagogy to bring man back to God

---

[1] *Timaeus* 42 A; *Phaedrus* 248.
[2] *Or.* 38. 12: *P.G.* 36. 324 c. The same concept appears continually in Gregory of Nyssa. In sinning the soul has acquired fleshly 'garments', and in re-ascending to God it removes these garments. See, for example, *P.G.* 44. 1029 B–C.

and to 'cleanse' the image of God within him. For this task God uses the Law, the prophets, diverse natural disasters and benefits to steer man away from evil and turn him to good. Finally, when all this fails, and man obviously needs stronger medicine, the Word of God becomes incarnate. Although this incarnation is spoken of as a paradox and a mystery, Gregory's description of it as a mingling of two natures, flesh and spirit, makes it evident that Greek Christian Christology was modelled on Platonic anthropology. The Cappadocians are careful not to mix Christology and anthropology, and it is clear that they believe there is a difference in kind between the two. Yet a comparison of the terms used for each reveals that their anthropology and their Christology are really founded upon the same philosophic model, the difference being that in man a breath of God's essence is present in the flesh, whereas in Christ the *Logos* Himself is present. If we use *Timaeus* as a predecessor of this kind of thinking, we might say that, whereas the human soul in *Timaeus* was constituted of a secondary mixture of the World Soul, if Plato had had a Christ figure, he would have been an incarnation of the World Soul itself.

The Philosophic Life and the Active Life

The task and the goal of the philosophic life is set for man from the moment of his creation, and it is impeded, but not fundamentally altered, by the fall. The philosophic life is, therefore, the life in which man realizes his inner divine nature. It involves asceticism, particularly since the fall, when man's body has become 'coarsened' and now offers a more severe impediment to his inner spirit. The task of the philosophic life is posed largely in terms of this work of *katharsis*. It is the freeing of the image of God within man from the depressing power of matter and bringing it back to its aboriginal state as a reflection of the divine archetype. As Gregory puts it in one oration:

...the internal warfare within ourselves and in our passions, in which we are engaged night and day against the body of our humilation, either secretly or openly, and against the tide which tosses us and whirls us hither and thither, by the aid of our senses and other sources of pleasure of this life; and against the miry clay in which we have been fixed and against the law of sin which wars against the law of the spirit, and strives to destroy the royal image in us and all the divine emanation which has been bestowed upon us. So that it is difficult for anyone, either by a long course in philosophic training and gradual separation of the noble and enlightened part of the soul from that which is debased and yoked to darkness, or by the mercy of God or by both together, and by constant practice of looking upwards, to overcome the depressing power of matter.[1]

The role of divine grace in this system of thought immediately becomes problematic for the Christian of the Western Augustinian tradition. Indeed, it was this Eastern monastic tradition which saw salvation as a 'long course in philosophic training' which penetrated the West in the following century, and, in the form of Pelagianism and semi-Pelagianism, was answered by the Western formulation of the doctrine of grace. For Gregory of Nazianzus, however, and for the Eastern Christian tradition in general, the problem of nature and grace never arose in the same way as it did in the West. As we see in the above quotation, Gregory can rather casually link salvation as a 'long course of philosophic training' with salvation through the mercy of God in an 'either-or' or 'both-and' formulation. He does not really worry about the exact relationship of the two because, for Gregory, nature and grace, philosophy and mercy are not alternative but co-ordinate terms. The Cappadocians opposed any doctrine of predestination to salvation because, in their minds, it implied the gnostic doctrines of pre-existence and inherently different natures: sarkic, psychical, and pneumatic.[2] The dichotomy of self-salvation and salvation by God did not arise, because they did not divide man's whole self as natural from grace as supernatural, as did the West, but rather considered man's true inner self to be 'grace', to be a gift from God and a part of the divine nature. Therefore man's true self and help from God are essentially in harmony. It is man's alien self, his body and his passions which pull him away from God. Thus Gregory does not fall into the tendency either to attribute all to man, or to attribute a part to man and a part to God, but he can simultaneously say that man's salvation is his own work and also that it is entirely the work of God. In discussing this relationship Gregory uses exactly the same phrases from St. Paul's

[1] Or. 2. 91: P.G. 35. 493 B, C.
[2] Or. 37. 13: P.G. 36. 297 B.

epistles which are considered decisive for the Augustinian interpretation:

even to wish well needs help from God, or rather even to choose what is right is divine and a gift of the mercy of God. For it is necessary both that we be our own masters and also that our salvation should be of God. That is why he said 'not of him who willeth only, nor of him who runneth only, but of God'. . . . Since the will is of God he has attributed the whole to God with reason. 'Except the Lord build the house they labour in vain who build it; except the Lord keep the city, in vain they watch that keep it.' . . . Is then the ruling mind nothing? Nothing the labour? Nothing the reasoning? Nothing the philosophy? Nothing the fasting? Nothing the vigils, the sleeping on the ground, the shedding of floods of tears? Is it for nothing of these, but in accordance with some election by lot, that a Jeremias is sanctified and others are estranged from the womb? I fear lest some monstrous reasoning come in, as of the soul having lived elsewhere and then having been bound to this body, and that it is from that other life that some receive the gift of philosophy and others are condemned. . . .[1]

Gregory then goes on to show that philosophy and grace, *erōs* and *agapē*, are not mutually exclusive, but man's *élan* towards God and God's helping hand to man go together. Man receives in the proportion that he strives, and strives through the power of God that he receives.

This philosophic life combines both *prāxis* and *theōria*. Gregory follows the tradition, going back to Philo,[2] which equated *prāxis* with *katharsis* and with the devotional and ascetical 'practices' which led the philosopher up to the contemplation of God. In *Oration* 14 Gregory speaks of contemplation and action as co-ordinate aspects of the monastic life. Contemplation 'raises us from the earth and leads us back, carrying us to the Holy of Holies and to what is akin with our minds'. Action cleanses the soul, opens it to receive the Lord and to testify to its love through good deeds.[3] In speaking of the monastic life, Gregory can even use the term *to praktikon* in connection with the cenobite life, as contrasted with that of the hermit or solitary whom Gregory sees as living a life entirely of contemplation. The Basilian monastic rules did not create strictly

[1] *Or.* 37. 13: *P.G.* 36. 297 B; also see Rom. 9. 16.
[2] See Butler, *Western Mysticism* 204 and *passim.*
[3] *Or.* 14. 5: *P.G.* 35. 864 A.

cenobite communities, but rather combined some community life with the eremitical principle, so that communities of monks dwelt in the same neighbourhood as cells of hermits, these latter being seen as the more advanced and perfected form of contemplative life. The cenobite life could also be considered 'practical' in that it did communal work and supported itself by the fruits of its labours. Gregory analyses the Basilian achievement in this way:

Moreover, he reconciled most excellently and united the solitary and the community life. These had been in many respects at variance and dissension, while neither of them was in absolute possession of good or evil; the one being more calm and settled, tending to union with God, yet not free from pride, inasmuch as its virtue lies beyond testing or comparison; the other, which is of more practical service, being not free from the tendency to turbulence. He founded cells for ascetics and hermits, but at no great distance from his cenobite communities, and, instead of distinguishing and separating the one from the other, as if by some intervening wall, he brought them together and united them, in order that the contemplative spirit might not be cut off from society, nor the active life be uninfluenced by the contemplative, but that, like sea and land, by an interchange of their several gifts, they might unite in pronouncing the one object, the glory of God.[1]

With Gregory's classical instinct for seeking the mean between extremes, he also broaches the question, in many of his writings, of the relationship between the contemplative life and the *bios praktikos* in the wider sense. What of the priest (who in this period might well be a married man); what of the ordinary layman and woman tending to their worldly affairs? Had they no part in the contemplative life? Were they excluded simply by virtue of being married, or by being busied with *ta pragmata*? Gregory's basic instincts are against the gnostic tendency to divide the Church into first-class and second-class citizens. There were some who had attained greater perfection, while others were less advanced along the road, but the same ideal governed all. Cappadocian thought has no concept equivalent to the 'evangelical counsels' that were developed in Western monasticism, whereby some precepts were given only to a few, to those who chose to live the 'religious' life and embrace the counsels of

[1] *Or.* 43. 62: *P.G.* 36. 577 A, B.

poverty, chastity, and obedience. Gregory believes that the ascetic–contemplative life is the true Christian life and all are required to lead it. The monk, in retiring from the world, has chosen the best and most likely way to lead this life, yet the demand to live the holy life extends to the whole Church.

This leads Gregory to consider the question of how even those who remain within 'the world' might strive for essentially the same ideal, and how the 'virginal' life, a concept so intrinsic to his concept of asceticism, might extend even to those who are married. In both Gregory of Nazianzus and in the more developed treatise, *De Virginitate*, of Gregory of Nyssa, the concepts of chastity and virginity become somewhat spiritualized, so that they cease to be simple equivalents for sexual abstinence. Here again Cappadocian thought is on the horns of a dilemma between gnostic dualism and Biblical creationism, in which the visible creation is 'very good'. Gregory constantly uses phrases that would make us think that, for him, the body *per se* is intrinsically evil, yet when we take these in conjunction with his many other statements which praise the world of nature and especially the fair construction of the human body as the handiwork of God, it becomes apparent that what he intends to say is not that the body and its functions are essentially evil in themselves, but rather that it is the 'fleshly will' that is evil.

Gregory particularly discusses this reconciliation of the married and the 'virginal' life in his funeral oration on his sister Gorgonia:

In regard to the two divisions of life, that is, the married and the unmarried state, the latter being higher and more divine, though more difficult and dangerous, while the former is more humble and more safe, she was able to avoid the disadvantages of each, and to select and combine all that is best in both, namely the elevation of the one and the security of the other, thus becoming modest without pride, blending the excellence of the married with that of the unmarried state, and proving that neither of them absolutely binds us to or separates us from God or the world (so that the one from its own nature must be utterly avoided, and the other altogether praised); but that it is Mind which nobly presides over both wedlock and virginity, and arranges and works upon them as the raw material of virtue under the master-hand of reason.[1]

[1] *Or.* 8. 8: *P.G.* 35. 797 A, B.

From this it becomes apparent that, for Gregory, what is important is the inner substance, not the external state of virginity. Virginity, for him, has become equated with *apatheia* and with the loss of all fleshly will, all subservience to the passions. The unmarried, retired state of life is to be embraced in preference to the married state because it is more conducive to *apatheia*, not because it automatically and necessarily confers it. By the same token, it is possible to attain this ideal within the married state, but with greater difficulty, since the fact of existing in a 'carnal union' and being bound by concerns of children and worldly affairs is seen as an inherent obstacle. This obstacle can be overcome by living in the married state 'as if not';[1] that is, performing the duties of nature, but not allowing one's will and desire to settle there, so that these tasks become concerns and ends in themselves. Thus, Gregory goes on to say of Gorgonia:

> though she had entered upon a carnal union, she was not therefore separated from the spirit, nor, because her husband was her head, did she ignore her first Head; but performing those few ministrations due to the world and nature, according to the will of the law of the flesh, or rather of Him who gave to the flesh these laws, she consecrated herself entirely to God.[2]

Gregory is much more optimistic in his attitude towards the possibility of the holy life for the married woman than for the married man. This is partly because he had before him the example of his mother and sister as well as Basil's female relatives, who dedicated themselves to a life of prayer and ascetic practices within the home. *Hēsychia* or retirement, the life of quiet and non-involvement in worldly affairs (particularly political affairs), these were seen as essential components of the monastic ideal, and since Greek women led a sequestered life in any case, it was easier for them to turn their state of life towards prayer and contemplation than it would be for their husbands.

To Gregory, 'this world' in its most inimical form is the world of economic and political affairs, the world of 'business', devoted to the pursuit of wealth and power. To be involved in such a life is alien to the spirit by nature. In one of his poems Gregory describes the conflicts of the life of 'affairs' with that of contemplation, a description which is the more poignant since

---

[1] Cf. 1 Cor. 7. 29.   [2] *Or.* 8. 8: *P.G.* 35. 797 B, C.

Gregory was himself a landowner all his life, and speaks here from experience:

First to give orders to the servants, what a sink of iniquity! They always hate the alert master and shamelessly vilify a pious one; they can neither be made compliant by bad treatment nor be won over by kindness. Then to watch over the estate, with state burdens always on one's shoulders, and the tax collector's dunning to be endured; for taxes take away the honour of a free man. . . . And to busy oneself in the crowded Forum, amid the hubbub around the seat of judgement with the cares of some ignoble lawsuit . . . where the bad triumph over the good, and the counsels on both sides are venal . . . who could escape in all that from many lies and subterfuges, far from God and in the midst of such men? One must either flee hastily and throw everything to the men of evil or soil one's soul with wrong-doing.[1]

Here Gregory speaks less as a Christian than as an aristocrat of late antique society. He speaks for an aristocracy which had grown discouraged with the world of public business, whose freedom as landed gentry had been stripped from them by an omnivorous bureaucracy, whose dignity as political leaders was reduced to venal bargaining in the seats of power. It was this aristocracy that was turning away from worldly affairs to live a life of *hēsychia* or solitude on their estates, and then, as the estates themselves began to feel the crushing hand of the tax collector, many of them, such as St. Anthony the Hermit, threw over their property altogether to find freedom and peace in the deserts and mountains. Here we touch one of the tap-roots of the turn to the other-worldly in late classical society, a turn from a world which had become too burdensome and too meaning-less to be borne. One can already trace this tendency in the letters of the Younger Pliny, as he deplores the pettiness of public business, the endless round of meaningless social activities, and seeks solitude and cultured ease on his estates.

Yet Gregory could not quite bring himself to condemn the life of business altogether. He himself spent many hours in its service; his brother was a court physician and his parishioners were not all monks. In his orations on his brother Caesarius and on baptism he suggests that even in this alien state the life of

[1] Translated in G. Misch, *A History of Autobiography in Antiquity* (Cambridge, Mass., 1951) 2, 623.

prayer and contemplation is not impossible. Gregory himself was much opposed to Caesarius' continued life in the midst of the Byzantine court, and tried to woo him away to the 'philosophic life'. In his funeral oration on his dead brother the ambiguity is still present, and yet he manages some hopeful words for this way of life:

My brother, who had dedicated to his country the first fruits of his learning, and gained an admiration worthy of his efforts, was afterwards led by the desire of fame, and, as he persuaded me, of being the guardian of the city, to betake himself to court, not indeed according to my wishes or judgement; for I will confess to you that I think it better and grander to be in the lowest rank with God than to win the first place with an earthly king. Nevertheless, I cannot blame him, for inasmuch as philosophy is the greatest, so it is the most difficult of professions, which can be taken in hand by but a few. . . . Yet it is no small thing if one who has chosen the lower form of life, follows after goodness, and sets greater store on God and his own salvation than on earthly lustre; using it as a stage, or a manifold ephemeral mask while playing in the drama of this world, but himself living unto God with that image which he knows that he has received from Him, and must render to Him Who gave it. This was certainly the purpose of Caesarius, we know full well.[1]

Gregory again comes to terms with this question in his oration on baptism. Here he is addressing himself to those who make too simple an equation of Christian baptism with conversion to the celibate monastic life. Many postponed their baptism until their deathbed because of this belief, since they could not or did not wish to surrender their property and their ordinary way of life. Here he makes clear that baptism should preferably be joined with conversion to the ascetic life, but that this need not necessarily be the case:

But if you have to live in the midst of public affairs, and are stained by them, and it would be a terrible thing to waste this mercy, the answer is simple. Flee, if you can, even from the Forum, along with the good company, making yourself the wings of an eagle, or, to speak more suitably, of a dove, for what have you to do with Caesar or the things of Caesar? Until you can rest where there is no sin, and no blackening, and no biting snake in the way to hinder your godly steps. Snatch your soul away from the world; flee from Sodom; flee from the burning; travel on without turning back, lest you should be

[1] *Or.* 7. 7: *P.G.* 35. 761 D ff.

fixed as a pillar of salt.[1] Escape to the mountain lest you be destroyed with the plain. But if you are already bound and constrained by the chain of necessity, reason with yourself thus, or rather let me reason thus with you. It is better both to attain the good and keep the purification. But if it is impossible to do both it is surely better to be a little stained with your public affairs than to fall altogether short of grace; just as I think it better to undergo a slight punishment from father or master than to be put out of doors; and to be a little enlightened than to be left in total darkness. And it is the part of the wise man to choose, as in good things the greater and more perfect, so in evils the lesser and lighter. Wherefore do not dread overmuch the purification. For our success is always judged by comparison with our place in life by our just and merciful Judge; and often one who is in public life and has had small success has had a greater reward than one who in the enjoyment of liberty has not completely succeeded; as I think it is more marvellous for a man to advance a little in fetters, than for one to run who is not carrying any weight, or to be only a little spattered in walking through the mud, than to be perfectly clean when the road is clean.[2]

We can see that Gregory is struggling towards a larger perspective of the Christian life which can cover even those who remain in the world and its activities, yet his guiding criterion of the good life remains the retired life of purification and contemplation, the life which has renounced the world. The world is still regarded as an unalloyed evil and an impediment to the soul drawn to God. Therefore the most he can do is to assume that men will be judged not merely by their accomplishment, but also by their efforts and the impediments against which they must work, like a handicap race. Gregory, consequently, does not arrive at the formula of the 'mixed' life, current in the philosophical schools,[3] because political activity, for him, has no virtue, but is fundamentally evil. The old concept of *politikē aretē*, for him, is completely dead. Activity in the *polis* no longer has any positive value in its own right. Virtue lies solely in the cathartic, contemplative life. The Christian in the forum remains virtuous only to the extent that he lives 'as if not', insulated from any interest or concern for the world of 'affairs' from which he is unable to escape.

This Christian dichotomy between human fulfilment and

[1] Gen. 19. 26.   [2] *Or.* 40. 19: *P.G.* 36. 384 A, B.
[3] See Joly, *Genres de vie* 171.

human created existence in the world came from its implicitly gnostic evaluation of the cosmos and man's place in it. Gnostic man lives in the world as an alien in a foreign land. His only fellowship is with the eschatological community, which stands over against the world, and belongs, in its true nature, to the 'Jerusalem Above'.[1] The Church as the Brotherhood of the Pure stands over against the political community and is seen as the heavenly *polis* which is in the world but not of it. It is the *civitas* of those who have alienated themselves from the world. However, in Gregory's time, the Church had enjoyed two generations as a *religio licita*, and it was gradually ceasing to be a sufficiently convincing symbol of the true eschatological community for those devoted to the cathartic way. The Church was becoming a great imperial, political organization, and to be a bishop meant to be a politician and to be engaged in the constant strife between see and see, between orthodox and heterodox, between Church and Empire, with all the endless conniving that this entailed. Consequently those devoted to the monastic ideal began to flee from priestly and episcopal roles in much the same way as they fled from political life generally and for the same reasons.[2] Activity within the Church and for the Church began to fall into the category of the 'life of affairs'. Gregory and the monastic movement generally tended to place themselves over against the regular hierarchy and to see ministerial roles in the Church in much the same way as Plato in the *Theaetetus* had viewed activity in the *polis*. Now it was to the monastic community that one looked for the true or inner eschatological Brotherhood of the Pure.

This conflict between the monastic and the sacerdotal life is perhaps the central drama of Gregory's own life. In his poem on his life he tells us how, as a young man newly returned from Athens, he tried to resolve this conflict. Torn between his own desire for retirement and his father's wish that he be his sacerdotal assistant, Gregory thought out a scheme of the 'mixed' life for himself. He would assist his father and yet continue in a retired existence on the family estates, without actual ties or commitments, thus preserving the precious 'freedom' so essential to

---

[1] On this theme in gnostic thought, see Hans Jonas, *The Gnostic Religion* 264.
[2] See Owen Chadwick, *John Cassian: A Study in Primitive Monasticism* (Cambridge, 1950) 67.

the ascetic ideal.[1] Yet this compromise did not work, and all his life Gregory struggled between his own desire for retirement and the demands laid upon him by the Church. He fiercely resented his enforced ordinations by his father and by Basil, and never ceased to regard this as a 'tyranny' and a despoiling of his freedom. Only once in his life did he voluntarily take on episcopal duties, and in this role he laboured as an illegal incumbent in the episcopal see and resigned as soon as the orthodox returned to power. In the last ten years of his life he finally returned to much the same compromise he had come to in his youth (if, indeed, this was the compromise of his youth and not a projection of his old age). Then he spent the declining years of his life in retirement on his estates, engaged in religious and literary pursuits, yet with a keen interest and a helping hand for the affairs of the Church or for young people who appealed to his wisdom and guidance. This was his own personal synthesis, the kind of 'mixed' life that suited his own temperament, and yet the larger conflict, the conflict between retirement to the monastery and active service to the Church, remained unresolved, and Gregory spent most of his life wavering indecisively between the two. Before we proceed to condemn him for this and tag him a 'holy ditherer', we should realize the philosophical underpinnings of this conflict. Gregory's 'dither' was just the existential living out of the irresolvable dilemma into which contemporary religious philosophy had cast mankind.

Asceticism and Contemplation

The actual structure of Gregory's concept of the philosophic life follows much the same pattern that is found in Origen and his predecessors in ascetic spirituality. The first and most essential aspect of this life is *katharsis*, the separation of the soul from the body and the attainment of *apatheia*. For the Christian monk, this life is lived primarily as one of purification and mortification. The illuminative and unitive aspects of spiritual ascent are only glimpsed here; they await fulfilment elsewhere.

The Cappadocian interpretation of *katharsis* is governed largely by monastic practices which Basil learned in his travels in Syria and Egypt and from his tutelage under Eustathius of

[1] *Carm. de vita sua*, ll. 270 ff.: *P.G.* 37. 1043.

Sebaste, Basil's master in the ascetic life, who had established monasteries after the Egyptian pattern in Pontus, Roman Armenia, and Paphlagonia.[1] Although Basil and Gregory modified the rigours of the Syriac and Egyptian types of asceticism, and rejected extreme and spectacular practices, in keeping with their innate classical sense of moderation, still the idea remained that, through asceticism, the monk is able partially to free himself from the conditions of corporal existence, to exist without food, sleep, or sex. He becomes angelic in the literal sense, disembodied, or 'as if' disembodied, and steps beyond the physical conditions of common life.[2] In this 'as if' disembodied state he anticipates the angelic state, the state of existence as pure spirit. Chastity becomes important not only as a means of freeing the soul from the reins of passion, but also as a symbol of the 'single' life. To be enmeshed in duality is the beginning of diversification and alienation. It is the principle of matter and the soul's fall into matter. By rejecting marriage, the ascetic rejects duality and returns to the single nature which is thereby the immutable and divine nature. In virginity the ascetic finds his most basic symbol of his withdrawal from Becoming, from the world of change and generation, and returns to the world of immutable being:

A great thing is virginity and celibacy and being ranked with the angels and with the single nature. . . . Christ . . . enacted the law of virginity to lead us away from this life and cut short the power of the world, or rather, to transmit one world to another, the present to the future.[3]

This Egyptian idea of asceticism has a great hold over Cappadocian thought. In spite of their tendency towards the more moderate path, the Cappadocians still look to the Egyptians as the models and the adepts of this way of life. In Basil's letters we read of his observation of these ascetics and his great admiration for them:

I was amazed at their attention at prayers, their victory over sleep, being overcome by no physical necessity, always preserving lofty and

[1] Basil, 'Introduction to the Ascetical Life', *Ascetical Works*, M. Wagner (New York, 1950), 9–10.
[2] For a discussion of some of these ideas, see H. Musurillo, 'The Problem of Ascetical Fasting in the Greek Patristic Writers', *Traditio* 12 (1956), 1–64.
[3] *Or.* 43. 62: *P.G.* 36. 576 c, d.

unconquered the resolution of their soul, in hunger and in thirst, in cold and nakedness, not paying any attention to the body or consenting to waste any thought upon it, but as if living in flesh not one's own, they dwell among those on earth, and have their citizenship in heaven. I admired these things and considered the life of these men blessed because they showed by their works that they bear around in their body the dying of Jesus. And I prayed that I also, as far as was possible, might become a zealous follower of these men.[1]

To stand through the night chanting the psalter, to fast, sleep on the ground, to regulate and mortify every sense, to keep silences, these were the ways that the ascetic 'subdued his dust'[2] and 'turned inward the view of beauty, from the visible to the invisible, by wasting away the external and withdrawing fuel from the flame'.[3] The gift of tears was important in Eastern monasticism as the symbol of *metanoia*, the repentance for sin and the conversion of the mind to God, and the ascetic is often described as praying through the night with tears gushing down his cheeks. In this manner Gregory describes his sister's ascetic devotions:

Nor did she, while subduing her dust by fasting, leave to another the medicine of hard lying [i.e., lying on the ground], nor, while she found this of spiritual service, was she less restrained in sleep than anyone else; nor, while regulating her life on this point, as if freed from the body, did she lie on the ground while others were passing the night erect, as the most mortified men struggle to do. Nay in this respect she was seen to surpass not only women, but the most devoted of men, by her intelligent chanting of the psalter, her converse with and unfolding and apposite recollection of the Divine oracles, her bending of her knees which had grown hard and almost taken root to the ground, her tears to cleanse her stains with contrite heart and spirit of lowliness, her prayer rising heavenward, her mind in rapture, freed from wandering. . . .[4]

Gregory then breaks into raptures over his sister's ascetic prowess:

O untended body and squalid garments, whose only flower is virtue! O soul, clinging to the body, when reduced to almost an immaterial state through lack of food; or rather when the body has been mortified through force, even before dissolution, that the soul might

[1] *Ep.* 223.   [2] *Or.* 8. 13: *P.G.* 35. 804 c.
[3] *Or.* 43. 62: *P.G.* 36. 577 A.   [4] *Or.* 8. 13: *P.G.* 35. 804 c.

attain to freedom, and escape the entanglements of the senses! O nights of vigil, and psalmody and standing which lasts from one day to another! O David, whose strains never seem tedious to faithful souls! O tender limbs, flung upon the earth and, contrary to nature, grown hard! O fountains of tears, sowing in affliction that they might reap in joy! O cry in the night, piercing the clouds and reaching unto Him that dwelleth in the heavens! O fervour of spirit, waxing bold in prayerful longings against the dogs of night and frost and rain and thunders and hail and darkness![1]

We can see from these passages that the ascetic's struggle is couched primarily in terms of philosophic dualism, the struggle against man's physical body, and his 'fleshly' will, all that binds his soul to the earth. The daemonological aspect, so prominent in non-hellenized Christian asceticism, is largely absent in Gregory, although it is suggested in phrases like 'against the dogs of night'.

Gregory speaks of this cathartic life in language which is heavily influenced by Plato. In more than one place he speaks of the purpose of the philosophic life as one of 'providing the soul with wings, to rescue it from the world and give it to God'.[2] *Katharsis* is fundamentally a withdrawal from the sense world, withdrawal from the visible to the invisible, from the flux of appearance to pure being:

For nothing seemed to me so desirable as to close the doors of my senses and, escaping from the flesh and the world, collected within myself, having no further connection than was absolutely necessary with human affairs, and speaking to myself and God, to live superior to visible things, ever preserving in myself the divine impression pure and unmixed with the erring tokens of this lower world, and both being, and constantly growing more and more to be, a real unspotted mirror of God and divine things, as light is added to light, and what was still dark grew clearer, enjoying already by hope the blessings of the world to come, roaming about with the angels, even now being above the earth by having forsaken it, and stationed on high by the Spirit.[3]

Gregory's understanding of *theōria* is both noetic and ecstatic. He describes it as a purification of the mind which is achieved by withdrawal from the visible to the invisible world, from the

---

[1] *Or.* 8. 14: *P.G.* 35. 805 A, B.   [2] *Or.* 2. 22: *P.G.* 35. 432 B.
[3] *Or.* 2. 7: *P.G.* 35. 413 C–416 A.

sensible to the intelligible (the intelligible now being understood as God and His angels). Man's encasement in matter
offers a great obstacle to this withdrawal to the noetic world,
and, in this passage, where Gregory uses Plato's image of the
ascent from the cave, we read:

> Who is it that is as yet surrounded by the gloom here below, and
> by the grossness of the flesh can purely gaze with his whole mind
> upon that whole Mind, and amid unstable and visible things hold
> intercourse with the stable and invisible? For hardly may one of
> those who have been specially purged, behold here even the image of
> the Good, as men see sun in water.[1]

The final goal is an ecstatic one, one in which the separation of
the created and the uncreated mind is overcome and man's
human 'mirror' is merged in the Mind of God:

> The mind should retire into itself and recall its powers from
> sensible things in order to hold pure communion with God and be
> clearly illumined by the flashing rays of the Spirit, with no admixture
> or disturbance of the divine light by anything earthly or clouded
> until we come to the source of the effulgence which we enjoy here
> and regret and desire alike are stayed, when our mirrors pass away
> in the light of truth.[2]

Gregory, like Origen, views the spiritual life as one of continuing ascent, but for Gregory God's ineffability so rules his
thought that he tends to think of this ascent as unending, and
having no fixed terminus. Man does indeed progress to contemplation of God in this life, but compared to the full nature of God
this *theōria* 'is but a small effluence, and as it were a small effulgence from the Great Light'.[3] As long as man is in the body he is
hindered by corporeal nature itself. Not merely sin, but the mere
fact of spatio-temporal existence makes it impossible for him to
encompass with his mind a reality that transcends these limits.
Man cannot know God as He is in Himself, or even as He is
comprehended by the angels, but only as He appears under the
images of the spatio-temporal world. Mingling Platonic and
Biblical images, Gregory speaks of this as 'the back parts of
God,[4] which He leaves behind Him as tokens of himself like the
shadow and reflection of the sun in the water, which show the

---

[1] *Or.* 2. 74: *P.G.* 35. 481 B.   [2] *Or.* 12. 4: *P.G.* 35. 848 B.
[3] *Or.* 28. 17: *P.G.* 36. 48 C.   [4] Exod. 33. 23.

sun to our weak eyes, because we cannot look at the sun himself, for his unmixed light is too strong for our power of perception'.[1]

Once man is rid of the body and 'the thick covering of
flesh', then he may more fully comprehend God. Here Gregory
at one moment seems to hold out the possibility that in the next
life man may fully know God:

What God is in nature and essence no man ever yet has discovered
or can discover. Whether it will ever be discovered is a question
which he who will may examine and decide. In my opinion it will be
discovered when that within us which is godlike and divine, I mean
our mind and reason, shall be mingled with its Like, and the image
shall have ascended to the Archetype, of which it has now the
desire.[2]

However, when Gregory contemplates the ineffability of God's
nature and His transcendence even of angelic nature, he
supposes that created being can only increasingly intuit, but
never fully encompass, the mysteries of God's nature, and even
the highest angels perhaps do not know Him fully. Gregory
quotes Plato for his conviction of the ineffability of the divine
nature:

It is difficult to conceive God, but to define Him is an impossibility,
as one of the Greek teachers of Divinity[3] taught, not unskilfully, as it
appears to me; . . . But in my opinion it is impossible to express Him,
and yet more impossible to conceive Him . . . even for those who are
highly exalted and love God, and in like manner every created
nature; seeing that the darkness of this world and the thick covering
of flesh is an obstacle to full understanding of the truth. I do not
know whether it is the same with the higher natures and the purer
Intelligences which because of their nearness to God, and because
they are illumined with all his Light, may possibly see, if not the
whole, at least more distinctly than we do; some perhaps more, some
less than others, in proportion to their rank.[4]

Gregory is primarily influenced by the Platonic tradition,
for which release from the body is itself the condition of the
soul's return to its true home, yet he is still governed by the
Jewish tradition of futuristic eschatology. The attempt to
reconcile these two schemes of after-life—the one which sees the

[1] Or. 28. 3: P.G. 36. 29 B.   [2] Or. 28. 17: P.G. 36. 48 c.
[3] Plato, Tim. 28 c.   [4] Or. 28. 4: P.G. 36. 29 c, 32 A.

true home as 'above', in the timeless, transcendent spheres of
the cosmos, and the other which sees the true home as a future
kingdom to be initiated through cosmic catastrophe—had
already begun in Jewish apocalyptic literature, and yet the combination of these two antithetical typologies inevitably produced a hybrid eschatology. In the one case, release from the
body alone made possible the soul's eternal bliss; in the other,
the life principle was equated with the body itself, which was
resuscitated on the last day. From the time of the inter-
Testamental literature, Jewish thinkers began to combine the
two by postulating an intermediate period. The soul on release
from the body would anticipate its final reward or suffering, but
the full realization of its final state would await the last day,
when the body would be resurrected and re-joined to the soul.[1]
This hybrid eschatology is still preserved in Gregory, although
it is so spiritualized and platonized as to be almost an appen-
dage or afterthought.

I believe the words of the wise that every fair and God-beloved
soul, when, set free from the bonds of the body, it departs hence, at
once enjoys a sense and perception of the blessings which await it,
inasmuch as that which darkened it has been purged away or laid
aside—I know not how else to term it—and feels a wondrous pleasure
and exultation, and goes rejoicing to meet its Lord, having escaped
as it were from the grievous poison of life here, and shaken off the
fetters which bound it and held down the wings of the mind, and so
enters on the enjoyment of the bliss laid up for it, of which it has even
now some perception. Then a little later it receives its kindred flesh,
which once shared in its pursuit of things above, from the earth which
both gave and has been entrusted with it, and, in some way known to
God who knit them together and dissolved them, enters upon the
inheritance of the glory there.[2]

This necessity of bringing in the resurrection of the body can
be only an embarrassment to platonized thought, since the
body, even in its immortal pre-fallen state in the garden of
Eden, is regularly viewed as a hindrance to the soul. In terms of
logical consistency it is impossible to reconcile a view which

[1] See, for example, 1 Enoch 21. 2 and 21. 9–11: 2 Baruch 30. 1–4. For a treatment of the development of Jewish eschatology, see R. H. Charles, *Hebrew, Jewish
and Christian Eschatology* (London, 1913).
[2] *Or.* 7. 21: *P.G.* 35. 781 B, C.

regards the highest state of existence as incorporeal and a view that man's full self is psycho-physical and so man's fulfilment in the hereafter demands a psycho-physical entity. In terms of Gregory's philosophic principles this re-joining of the flesh to the soul can add nothing to its fulfilment and indeed logically should hinder it, but Gregory accepts the bodily resurrection as a part of the tradition, and tries to bridge the gap by using the Origenist concept of a 'spirit matter'.[1] Gregory suggests that the soul's ascent has an effect on the body, and, through its spiritual wrestlings, the body also becomes spiritualized and capable of re-joining the soul in its beatitude. Thus the soul, in some sense, 'saves' the body, just as God has saved the soul. Gregory thus gives two reasons for man's incarnation; i.e. the placing of man's true self or soul in this body alien to its nature. The one is that it may, through struggling with the body, be provided with a testing-ground whereby it can truly 'earn' its beatitude and not merely be given it as a gratuitous gift, and the second is that, thereby, it may 'save' the body in which it is incarnated:

Perhaps there are other reasons for this [the binding of soul to body] which only God, who bound them together, and those who are instructed by God in such mysteries can know, but as far as I and men like myself can perceive, there are two: one, that it [the soul] may inherit the glory from above by means of struggle and wrestling with things below, being tried as gold in the fire by things here, and gain the objects of our hope as a prize of virtue, and not merely as the gift of God. This indeed was the will of the supreme Goodness, to make the good even our own, not only because sown in our own nature, but because cultivated by our own choice. . . . The second reason is that it may draw to itself and raise to heaven the lower nature, by gradually freeing it from its grossness, in order that the

---

[1] This idea of spirit–matter has a long history behind it, but its immediate line of descent for Gregory is through the apocalyptic tradition which regularly saw the bodies of the resurrected as 'transfigured'; see, for example, III Baruch 1, 2. It then finds its place in Paul's belief in the 'spiritual body' of the resurrected (1 Cor. 15. 44). Gnosticism also had its teachings of 'aerial' and 'pneumatic' bodies, and Origen, in turn, reworked this whole tradition as a principle of his cosmology. It is his concept of the body which grows 'coarser' or more spiritual as it turns from or turns to God that is the immediate background of Gregory's concept of the trans-figured body. On concepts of the resurrection and their historical background, see H. [Chadwick, 'Origen, Celsus and the Resurrection of the Body', *J.Th.S.* 48 (1947), 34–9; also see G. Florowsky, 'Eschatology in the Patristic Age', *S.P.* ii. 236–50.

soul may be to the body what God is to the soul, itself leading on the matter that ministers to it, and uniting it as its fellow servant to God.[1]

In another oration Gregory uses the language of the *Phaedrus* to speak of the upward flight of the soul, and yet invokes an idea, incomprehensible in Platonic terms, that this upward flight, instead of merely forsaking the body, may rather draw the body with it:

> For even if our dust contracts somewhat of wickedness and the earthly tabernacle presseth down the upward flight of the soul which at least was created to fly upwards, yet let the image be cleansed from filth and raise aloft the flesh, its yoke-fellow, lifting it on wings of reason.[2]

The source of this idea is Origen's doctrine of the descending and ascending scale of matter. As we indicated, Origen believes that the soul was first created as a kind of invisible spiritual substance, which became increasingly 'gross' as the soul turned from God and fell further and further from His presence. Gregory invokes the same idea to cover the resurrection of the dead and the ultimate salvation of the body, believing that the reverse process takes place as man cleanses his 'image' and his soul re-ascends to God. Finally, after death, when man is fully reunited with God, he will be re-joined by his body, the companion of his struggles for virtue on earth, but now spiritualized by these struggles and fit to join the soul in its celestial beatitude. However, since Gregory has eliminated the aetiology of this spirit body and placed man's incarnation on earth in the garden of Eden, these Origenist concepts of the scale of matter survive in his thought only in a truncated and unsystematic form.

Gregory's understanding of the philosophic or ascetic–contemplative life shows a clear continuity with the teachings of Greek philosophy as it developed from Plato and was adapted from middle Platonism by Origen. Origen tried to adapt Platonic thought to Christianity, and the Cappadocians made a further effort to purify the Christian concept of 'philosophy' of those Greek elements incompatible with contemporary orthodoxy which Origen had accepted. Yet the adaptation is not

---

[1] *Or*. 2. 17: *P.G.* 35. 425 c.   [2] *Or*. 16. 15: *P.G.* 35. 953 c.

fully successful. Biblical thought derives from such a completely different cosmology, anthropology, and eschatology from that found in Platonism that the attempt to combine the two always results in a hybrid construction. There are several points in the system where the gears do not quite mesh, and the explanation for this lies in the fact that Cappadocian thought rests on the conflation of two world views whose presuppositions are not fully compatible.

IV

CONSCIOUS ATTITUDES TOWARDS RHETORIC AND PHILOSOPHY IN THE WRITINGS OF GREGORY OF NAZIANZUS

Gregory's Attitude towards Literature and Rhetoric[1]

THE previous discussion of Gregory's style should have made it abundantly evident that in his use of stylistic devices, the structure of his language, the motifs which govern much of his thought, and the rules by which he develops an idea Gregory was thoroughly imbued with contemporary sophistic culture. Rhetoric in the ancient world was simultaneously a science, an art, an ideal of life, and the pillar of classical education and culture. To speak of Gregory as rhetor is essentially to say that he was very much the product of this whole system. Rhetoric formed his education, moulded his literary style, and gave him the oratorical tools to fight his enemies, praise his friends, and enhance his daily correspondence. Yet Gregory's conscious attitude towards sophistic and towards classical culture in general can only be described as equivocal at best. Much of the time he sounds as if Christians should have nothing to do with pagan culture or the niceties of sophistic eloquence. How can this conscious attitude be reconciled with the obvious fact that he took over so much of sophistic culture? In terms of content his writings achieved in a high degree the synthesis of Christianity with classical culture, and yet there seems to be little development of a corresponding theoretical rationale for this synthesis. Are we to say that he was unconscious that he was making such a synthesis? This may be

---

[1] Guignet has an excellent chapter on this topic: *S. Grégoire de Nazianze et la rhétorique* 43–70. For a general treatment of the problem in the Fathers, see G. L. Ellspermann, *The Attitude of the Early Christian Writers toward Pagan Literature and Learning* (Washington, 1949).

a partial explanation. No one, particularly at such a transitional point, is quite aware of the full implications of his own intellectual formation or the forces that are playing upon him and governing the choices that are open to him. And yet when we read a piece of stylistic analysis such as his literary letter to Nicobulus, we can scarcely suppose that Gregory was really unaware of his use of the pagan tradition of literary criticism. Are we to say that he was merely inconsistent or perhaps even somewhat dishonest in that he took over so much of Greek culture and yet was too small-minded to be able openly to avow its worth and grant its validity? This too may be a partial explanation—though it is too narrow—and leads on to a broader consideration of the whole problem of Christianity *vis-à-vis* classical culture.

Christianity, at about the end of the first century A.D., completed its great leap from a Jewish to a Hellenistic milieu. By this time it had given up its Jewish identity almost completely, except for taking with it the Jewish Scriptures, which, however, it now interpreted in terms of the Gospel. Except for some Syrian Christians, its language, both for liturgy and for preaching, was Greek. The Hellenistic world into which the Church had moved, however, was viewed as hostile to itself and to true religion and ultimately as hostile to God. It was 'pagan' in the derogatory sense of the term. The eschatological orientation of Christianity led it to see the world as sunk in vice, the domain of the Devil, and soon to be swept away by God's avenging hand and replaced by the Kingdom of God, where the nobodies of this world would be enthroned as saints. All that belonged to the present world order (and this meant for them the Roman Empire), the religion, the philosophy, the culture of the Hellenistic world were therefore viewed as 'secular', and belonging to the order of this world hostile to God and soon to be rushed into the abyss. The Greek too might have spoken of the transitoriness of things, but in quite different accents from the Christian. The Greek might view himself, his own life, his own circumstances as temporary and fleeting, but the cosmos, the world order, the cultural order, these were permanent. The Christian, however, looked within and saw his own soul as permanent, but the cosmos and the socio-political order as passing. Consequently Christianity looked upon the pagan world and the whole contemporary world order as a thing to be refuted, a thing destined for destruction.

However, the Christian Church also wished to convert this pagan world, and to do this it had to speak its language. It would never succeed in impressing the highest representatives of this world unless it could, to some extent, rival its cultural skills—its eloquence and its philosophy. So, in spite of its fundamental stance against pagan culture, and the polemics against its religion, literature, and culture which fill second- and third-century apologetic literature, Christianity began more and more to present itself as a superior 'philosophy', and even a superior 'eloquence', and to argue with paganism in terms of pagan values. Although, in one way, Christianity continued to glory in its *'alogia'*,[1] its culturelessness, as evidence of its truthfulness and lack of artifice, on the other hand it soon recognized that this pagan world which it wished to win held nothing in greater contempt than this very *'alogia'*, this barbarism and boorishness, this lack of cultivation. So Christianity, by the time it had become a *religio licita* in the fourth century, was in a basic dilemma. It still considered the pagan world to be the work of the devil, and yet, unless it was to remain an illiterate proletarian religion, it could do nothing else but adopt the culture of this world, since it was the only culture that it knew.

The tension between these two polarities is nowhere better illustrated than in the writings of Gregory of Nazianzus. On the one hand, there are many passages in Gregory which stand fully in the anti-cultural tradition. Greek literature is commonly viewed as mere fiction and indecency, and the Greeks themselves as interested only in form and style with no respect for truth. In this line of thought Gregory, of course, takes over a whole line of argument stemming from Plato which viewed rhetoric as mere 'opinion' and specious argumentation as contrasted with philosophy, which represented genuine dedication to truth. In a typical passage from one of his sermons Gregory contrasts the complete veracity of Scripture with the literature of the Greeks:

Let us not suppose these events [the events of Scripture] to have been recorded without purpose, nor that they are a mere assemblage of

---

[1] See below, p. 164, for Julian's use of this term for Christians.

words and deeds gathered together for the pastime of those who listen to them, as a kind of bait for the ears, for the sole purpose of giving pleasure. Let us leave such jesting to the legends and the Greeks, who think but little of truth and enchant ear and mind by the charm of their fictions and the daintiness of their style.[1]

Gregory often extols the plain uncultured language of Christianity, which speaks with evangelical simplicity and scorns all pretence of ornament and style:

The first wisdom is to despise that wisdom which consists of language and figures of speech and spurious and unnecessary embellishments. Be it mine to speak five words with understanding in the church, rather than ten thousand with a tongue (1 Cor. 14. 19), and with the unmeaning voice of a trumpet, which does not rouse my soldiers to spiritual combat. This is the wisdom which I praise, which I welcome. By this the ignoble have won renown and the despised have attained the highest honours. By this a crew of fishermen have taken the whole world in the meshes of the gospel-net.[2]

Sophistry is commonly seen as the father of lies and the source of all heresy, and the heretics themselves are constantly referred to as 'sophists'. In his discourse against the Eunomians he pictures them as mere sophists and dialecticians, and begins his oration with the words 'I am to speak against persons who pride themselves on their eloquence' (27. 1). In discussing the theological squabblings of the Arians, Gregory cries out, 'Oh cease, ye sophists of vain talk that falls immediately to the ground' (34. 10).[3] Gregory even calls the devil himself a sophist, full of beguiling words and subtle argumentation.[4] He often inveighs against that phenomenon of his day, the sophistical Christian preacher whose sermons turned into oratorical displays, who hungered after the plaudits of the crowd, and whose congregation cheered, murmured, and clapped at his brilliant turns of phrase and scribbled down his speech in shorthand. All the present factiousness and decline in the Church can be attributed to this invasion of rhetoric into the Christian community:

In the palmy days of the Church, when all was well, the present elaborate, far-fetched, and artificial treatment of theology had not

---

[1] Or. 2. 104: P.G. 35. 504 B.   [2] Or. 16. 2: P.G. 35. 936 c.
[3] For other examples of this use of the words 'sophist' and 'sophistry' see Or. 22. 12: P.G. 35. 1145 A; Or. 27. 1: P.G. 36. 12 A; and Or. 32. 26: P.G. 36. 204 B.
[4] Or. 40. 10: P.G. 36. 372 A.

made its way into the schools of divinity, but playing with pebbles which deceive the eye by the quickness of their changes, or dancing before an audience with varied and effeminate contortions [referring to the mannerisms of sophistic declamation] was looked upon as all one with speaking or hearing of God in a way unusual and frivolous. But since the Sextuses and Pyrrhos, and the antithetic style, like a dire and malignant disease, have infected our churches, and babbling is reputed culture, as the book of Acts says of the Athenians, we spend our time in nothing else but either to tell or to hear something new (Acts 17. 21). Oh what Jeremiah will bewail our confusion and blind madness? He alone could utter lamentations befitting our misfortune![1]

In spite of the fact that both he and Basil taught rhetoric briefly, Gregory considers the rhetorician's art incompatible with a serious Christian vocation. When Gregory of Nyssa turned to the teaching of rhetoric, Gregory rebuked him as though he had become an actor or a gladiator:

Whatever possessed you, or what violence have you wrought yourself, to cast aside the sacred and wholesome books which you used to read to the people, you the wisest of men? Surely it shames you to hear it? You have stored them over smoke, as one stores the rudder and spade in winter; and you have turned your hand to the bitter and unwholesome literature, choosing the name of rhetor rather than Christian. Now the latter title is much more precious to me, and thank God for that. Now you, excellent man, must see that you are not to continue in this situation indefinitely. You must return to sobriety and your true character. You must justify yourself before the faithful, before God, and before the altar and the mysteries from which you have drawn apart.

Now you will please not make me a subtle and oratorical sort of answer, thus 'what, you mean that in being a rhetor I was not behaving in a Christian fashion? That in dealing with young men I was an unbeliever?' And perhaps you will call God to witness. My dear fellow, even if I do concede you something, I contend that your Christian behaviour fell short of the proper measure. What about the scandal given to others by your present behaviour, others who are naturally given to evil? What grounds [are not] given for unpleasant suspicions and rumours about yourself? False suspicions, of course, but where is the necessity for them? A man's life is not his own concern exclusively; his neighbour matters too. It is not enough to convince oneself; one must convince others. Suppose you were a public

[1] *Or.* 21. 12: *P.G.* 35. 1093 c ff.

boxer, giving and taking head blows, ducking and writhing shame-
fully in the theatre, would you have said you were doing wisely for
your soul? No, such sentiments would not suggest a wise man, but an
empty-headed fool.[1]

However, even in the midst of scorning and condemning
rhetoric, Gregory often reveals his own inability to escape from
it. In the *prooimion* of *On the divinity of the Son* he sets up his
argument against the Eunomians in the conventional manner
established by rhetoric, and, in the midst of this, suddenly
polemicizes against the rules which he himself intends to
follow:

And since every discourse is of a two-fold nature, the one part
establishing one's own position, and the other overthrowing one's
opponent's position, let us first state our own position, and then try
to controvert that of our opponents—and both as briefly as
possible, so that our arguments may be taken in at a glance (like
those of the elementary exercises which they have devised to deceive
simple or foolish persons), and that our thoughts may not be
scattered by reason of the length of the discourse like water which is
not contained in a channel but flows to waste over open land.[2]

In his autobiographical poem, Gregory makes clear his own
youthful struggle between the life of the rhetorician and the life
of the Christian contemplative. His fellow students and instruc-
tors begged him to stay on at Athens to teach, and he clearly
prolonged his stay there to an inordinate degree, but finally
wrenched himself away with the intention of giving up all such
ambitions for the life of philosophic retirement. So it would
seem that, in Gregory's mind, the life of philosophy entailed the
sacrifice of the life of letters.

They [his fellows at the school of Athens] held on to me tightly,
insisting that they would not let me go for any reason. It was not
right that venerable Athens should lose me, to whom they were prepared by vote to concede the primacy of learning. They finally prevailed upon me, for only an oak tree could withstand such laments
and entreaties. Not fully, however, for my native land was beckoning, that country which, in orthodoxy, surpasses practically all under
the sun.[3] To live the philosophic life there seemed a noble ideal. . . .

---

[1] *Ep.* 11: *P.G.* 37. 42.　　　　　　　　　　[2] *Or.* 29. 1: *P.G.* 36. 73 A.
[3] Gregory frequently extols his homeland for its uncompromising orthodoxy,
overlooking the fact that some of the leaders of Arianism were Cappadocians

Accordingly for another little time I lingered on at Athens, and then, almost by stealth, I slipped away.

When I arrived home, to satisfy some people who kept importuning me, I gave a display of eloquence [literally, 'I danced']. It was, so to speak, a debt I owed. Because personally I place no value upon vapid applause or upon those stupid and intricate conceits which are the delight of sophists when a crowd of youth confronts them. The first step in my concept of the philosophic life had long been this: to sacrifice to God, as well as everything else, the labour of letters too, like people who abandon their property to be grazed by sheep or cast treasure that they have amassed to the bottom of the sea.[1]

And yet, although he had resolved to relinquish the role of the rhetor, he could never quite allow himself to relinquish the claim to eloquence. In one oration he tells his audience that he has given up everything else, honours, riches, comforts; the one treasure that he keeps is eloquence.[2] Although he often renounces sophism when writing to Christians, in letters to pagans and to sophists he makes it clear that he is as skilled in this art as they, although he has given it up for higher things. In one interesting letter to the pagan Candidianus he speaks almost wistfully of his lost rhetorical career:

Indeed had my career as a literary man not been brought to a premature close (I can perceive this now), had I not decided with more speed than wisdom, as somebody put it, to give up panegyrics and to give up being a pundit in public, my voice might well have drowned Etruscan trumpets (I make the remark undeterred by Pindar's stone of Momus).[3] But, of course, I have determined to be silent in these untoward times.[4]

A cultivated Christian like Gregory was caught between two value systems, belonging to both and yet feeling that the two were fundamentally incompatible. This is perhaps why he more than anyone else was outraged at the decrees of the emperor

(such as George, Arian bishop of Alexandria, and Euzoius, Arian bishop of Caesarea, who was an old schoolmate of Gregory of Nazianzus—Jerome, *De Vir. Ill.* 113).
[1] *Carm. de vita sua: P.G.* 37. 1047.   [2] *Or.* 6. 5: *P.G.* 35. 728 A, B.
[3] The Etruscans were supposed to be the inventors of the trumpet. For the reference to Pindar, see *Olymp.* 8. 73: μὴ βαλέτω με λίθῳ τραχεῖ φθόνος. Gregory apparently substitutes Μῶμος for φθόνος, Momus being the Greek personification for carping criticism.
[4] *Ep.* 10: *P.G.* 37. 37 A ff.

Julian closing the schools to Christians. Having been a Christian himself, Julian knew well the Christians' weak point, and
he hit them, no doubt with careful forethought, where he knew
it would hurt them most. This affront by the Julian educational
edicts was all the more aggravating because he could truthfully
say that in cutting the Christians off from classical culture he
was only taking them at their word. Since the Christians scorned
the classical heritage, why should they have any share in it?
Julian was also not far from the mark when he declared that
Greek culture and Greek religion were intrinsically related, and
that no one could teach or interpret this heritage who did not
believe in the gods. As we have seen, the canon of literature
taught in the schools leaned heavily on Homer and the poets, all
of whom were full of the gods, and a Christian rhetor like Prohaeresius would still teach the same body of literature. Julian,
of course, fully realized the great power that the Christians
gained by borrowing the tools of Greek rhetoric and dialectic,
and by his educational edicts he apparently intended to push the
Christians back into the cultureless ghetto from which they had
come and, by depriving them of the skills of persuasive language,
prevent them from communicating effectively with the secular
world.

   No one could have been more outraged at these edicts than
Gregory of Nazianzus. On his return to Cappadocia soon after
Julian's demise he preached two invectives which are perhaps
as vindictive a pair of diatribes as have ever flowed from the pen
of an intelligent man. His rebuttal of Julian's educational policy
plays a prominent part in these works.

   But I must carry back my words to the subject of words[1] for I
cannot help returning to this point, and must endeavour to the best
of my ability to advocate their cause; for though there are many and
weighty reasons why that person deserves to be detested, yet in no
case will he be shown to have acted more illegally than this: and let
everyone share in my indignation who takes pleasure in words, and
is addicted to this pursuit—of which number I will not deny that I
am one: all other things I have left to those who like them; riches,
nobility, glory, power, which are of the lower world, and give de-
lights like fleeting dreams. Words alone I cleave to, and I do not

   [1] The passage contains many puns on the various meanings of *logoi*, such as
literature, words, discourse, reason, etc., impossible to preserve in translation.

begrudge the toils by land and sea that have supplied me with them. May mine be the possession of words, and his too, whoever loves me, which possession I embraced and still embrace, first of all after the things which be first of all—I mean Religion and the Hope beyond the visible world—so that if, according to Pindar, 'what is one's own weighs heavily', speech in their defence is incumbent upon me; and it is especially just for me, perhaps more than anyone else, to express my gratitude to words for words, by word of mouth.[1]

Gregory goes on to describe Julian's edicts and his justification of his educational policy: 'Ours [says he] are the words and the speaking of Greek, whose right it is to worship the gods; yours are the want of words (*alogia*), and clownishness and nothing beyond the faith in your own doctrine' (4. 102). Gregory sets about refuting this charge that the Greek language and its literature and culture belong to the Hellene, the worshipper of the old gods. His development of this important theme, however, is rather disappointing. He contents himself with a rather elaborate exposition of the argument that a language, just like any other cultural product, does not just belong to those who created it, but belongs to all who share in it. But he makes no attempt to go deeper and construct a philosophical rationale for the Christian use of classical culture.

And yet, although Gregory never develops at length an unequivocal justification for Christian acculturation in the classical milieu, or lays out principles for the Christian study of the classics, as Basil had done in his address to Christian youth,[2] it can be said that he approaches such a rationale when the various hints on this subject in his writings are gathered together, and, if he had written such a treatise, his principles on the subject would probably have been essentially the same as those of Basil. He makes it quite clear in his oration on Basil that he has no use for Christians who are simply anti-culture, and who consider their boorishness a virtue in itself:

I take it as admitted by men of sense, that the first of our advantages is education; and not only this our more noble form of it, which disregards rhetorical ornaments and glory and holds to

---

[1] *Or.* 4. 100: *P.G.* 35. 633 c–6 a.
[2] See E. Maloney's edition, *St. Basil the Great to Students on Greek Literature* (London, 1901).

salvation, and beauty in the objects of contemplation; but even that external culture which many Christians ill-judgingly abhor, as treacherous and dangerous and keeping us afar from God. For as we ought not to neglect the heavens and earth and air and all such things because some have wrongly seized upon them and honour God's works instead of God, but should reap what advantage we can from them for our life and enjoyment, while we avoid their dangers; not raising creation, as foolish men do, in revolt against the Creator, but from the works of nature apprehending the Worker, and, as the divine apostle says, bringing into captivity every thought to Christ; and again as we know that neither fire nor food nor iron nor any other of the elements is of itself most useful or most harmful except according to the will of those who use it; and as we have compounded healthful drugs from certain of the reptiles; so from secular literature we have received principles of inquiry and speculation, while we have rejected their idolatry, terror, and pit of destruction. . . . We must not then dishonour education because some men are pleased to do so, but rather suppose such men to be boorish and uneducated, desiring all men to be such as they themselves are, in order to hide themselves in the general, and escape the detection of their want of culture.[1]

In Gregory's *Carmina ad Seleucum* he lays down principles for the study of the classics, recommending that the Christian student read the poets, historians, orators, and pagan philosophers for their style, and concludes with a verse summing up the proper attitude to be taken toward such studies: καὶ τὰς ἀκάνθας φεῦγε, καὶ ῥόδον δρέπου.[2] The Christian is, therefore, to cull from classical studies all that is useful for the exposition of Christian standards, and shun the rest; an interesting moral criterion for literary studies which is not incompatible with Plato's educational principles in the *Republic*. Sophistry and literature are condemned only when they are taken as ends in themselves; to accept the standards of rhetoric on their own terms is to remain always a schoolboy, declaiming in the schoolroom; the Christian must study these things, but then pass on to theology and

[1] *Or.* 43. 11: *P.G.* 36. 508 B–9 A.
[2] l. 61: *P.G.* 37. 1581; cf. Basil's address on Greek literature, Maloney's edition, 4. 8–9, where the same phrase is found. Gregory here may be echoing Basil's treatise. A similar phrase is found in Gregory's *Carm. de vita sua*, l. 472: *P.G.* 37. 1062. For one of Gregory's most eloquent arguments in favour of the study of Greek letters, see his poem *Nicobuli filii ad patrem*, where he presents the elder Nicobulus with a petition on behalf of his son's desire to study rhetoric abroad.

the philosophic life. In a letter to a young Christian, Ablabius, who aspired to the career of a sophist, Gregory writes:

> I understand that you have become a devotee of the sophist's art. It seems an admirable thing to you to speak pompously, to have a lofty look, a high and mighty step, to let your imagination whisk off to Marathon and Salamis and such-like wonder-spots of yours; to think of nothing but people like Miltiades, Cynageirus, Callimachus, Telemachus; to have everything à la mode, sophistically as shaped as possible to your leanings. Provided, of course, you still take account of virtue with all this, my friendship is yours, and your good repute is in no jeopardy. But if you are gone over completely to this sophistic business, and have forgotten my friendship and the discussions we often had together about the nature of the good, I had better say nothing else unkind. What I have said is enough perhaps. Realise that, while you may amuse yourself for a short time with such juvenile pursuits, when you come to your senses you will realize how very ridiculous you have been. But more anon.[1]

Rhetoric must be plucked from its native value system and transferred into the Christian value system. There it will no longer be used as an art for art's sake, but will be a tool and handmaiden of doctrine and moral teaching. Christian eloquence is eloquence not merely to give pleasure but for the greater glory of God. Gregory is fond of speaking of *logos* as the most fitting offering to God. As he warms to his oration against Julian, for example, he speaks of his *prooimion* as 'kindling the bloodless offering of words' (4. 2). He frequently plays on the word *logos* as meaning both a discourse and the divine *Logos* and invokes the thought that nothing could be a more fitting tribute to the *Logos* than *logos*, as in the opening of his festal oration on Pentecost: 'Let us reason a little about the festival, that we may keep it spiritually, for different persons have different ways of keeping Festival, but to the worshipper of the Word a discourse seems best.'[2] To offer your eloquence to God and use your eloquence to honour God and serve Him, this is the proper approach to Christian rhetoric. Gregory perhaps could not fully admit the extent to which the structure of his style and mind were the product of the sophistic education, and was undoubtedly not fully aware of the extent of this influence himself, since this was the only culture that he knew. Yet he was

[1] *Ep.* 233: *P.G.* 37. 376 B.   [2] *Or.* 41. 1: *P.G.* 36. 428 A–9 A.

working towards a positive doctrine of Christianity *vis-à-vis* culture, and believed that the Christian cannot shun culture, but must gather its fruits and put them at the disposal of the Gospel.

Christianity and Greek Philosophy

In analysing Gregory's conscious attitude towards Greek philosophy one finds the same anomaly that was found in his attitude towards rhetoric. Never does he acknowledge any direct dependence of Christian ideas on their classical forebears. Seldom does he even have a good word for Greek philosophy, and even then it is frequently modified by polemical qualifications. His overriding attitude is one of hostility and contempt. However, in this respect, as in his attitude towards Greek literature, Gregory is the heir of the Christian apologetic tradition, which had linked up pagan religion and pagan philosophy as simply different aspects of blasphemy and folly. This is particularly piquant, since the Christian apologists, in their polemic against mythology, borrowed heavily from philosophy, which itself had a long tradition of polemic against the anthropomorphism and 'indecency' of mythology, and yet this debt to philosophy for its critique is seldom acknowledged. Yet Greek philosophic language was the only language available in which to speak of ethical and theological ideas, and the Christians inevitably adopted it as the basis for their own theological development. In so doing they could scarcely fail to recognize the affinity between their own ideas and those of the Greek philosophical tradition. The Christian apologists explained this similarity by asserting that the Greek thinkers had borrowed their ideas from Moses, and therefore any truth that was contained in Greek philosophy actually belonged to the Christians in any case. This idea was borrowed from Jewish apologetics, and appeared in Josephus' defence of Jewish antiquity against the Greeks.[1]

Clement of Alexandria follows the standard Christian apologetic tradition in his *Exhortation to the Greeks*, although he was himself a Christian humanist and as much influenced by Greek philosophy as any Christian Father of his time. First he dilates on the indecency and profanity of the Greek mysteries. In his

---

[1] *Contra Apionem* 2, 168.

polemic against Greek religion, Clement employs the argument
that pagan divinities were originally mortal men who were
taken to be gods, a type of rebuttal of Greek religion which he
took from the Greeks themselves, this line of argument having originated in Euhemerus' work Ἱερὰ ἀναγραφή.[1] Clement
then shows Greek philosophy to be essentially idolatry and the
worship of the elements and the created world. Some of the
Greek philosophers, especially Plato, came closer to the truth of
the transcendent God, but such truth as he was able to grasp
was actually borrowed from the Hebrews.[2]

This inability to accord independent worth to the non-
Christian or non-Mosaic traditions is in part defensive but also
in part doctrinal. Christianity in this period did not make the
distinction, which was to be defined in the Latin scholastic
tradition, between faith and reason: matters known through
revelation and matters known through natural philosophy.
Rather, all truth about God, all higher insight, was thought to
be revealed, to be inspired by God through the *Logos*. Since the
Logos was the means of God's revelation to the Jews, and finally
became man's saviour through its incarnation in Jesus, all true
theological knowledge was restricted to the Biblical revelation.
Clement indeed hints at an expansion of this concept, using the
doctrine that the *Logos* was also the principle of creation, and
that therefore there is a kind of universal revelation which comes
through nature and which can be shared by non-Christian
thinkers. But these hints of a teaching of natural revelation remained very qualified in his thought. In any case man could
only derive very indistinct understanding of the truth through
this universal revelation, and its clarification and full exposition
were to be found in the Old Testament and finally in their cul-
minating form in Christianity and in the person of Jesus Christ,
the *Logos* incarnate. Therefore Christianity, through its apologetic tradition, had imbued itself with the belief that all truth
was to be found in its own teachings. Any truths found in other
religions or philosophies were merely primitive reflections of
what was to be found in fulfilled form in itself, and such truth
was probably only developed in these traditions through

---

[1] The fragments of this work are to be found in F. Jacoby, *F. Gr. H.* i, A, no. 63,
pp. 300–13; cf. Cicero, *De Natura Deorum* i. 119.
[2] Clement, *Protrepticus* iv. 60 e.

CHRISTIANITY AND GREEK PHILOSOPHY 169

contact with the Mosaic teachings. This situation is further compounded by the fact that Philo Judaeus had already interpreted the Mosaic teachings in terms of eclectic Platonic–Stoic philosophy, and the Christians, inheriting his teachings, then presumed that Platonic philosophy was just a dim reflection of what was to be found in its full form in the 'deeper' meaning of Scripture. Consequently, the way was already prepared for the synthesis of Christianity and Platonism from the first centuries of the existence of the Christian Church, without Christianity ever having to acknowledge any dependence on Greek philosophic thought and indeed dogmatically assuming the opposite, that it was Greek philosophy that was indebted to itself for any glimmerings of truth which it might possess. Therefore, when Christians began to value the words 'philosophy' and 'philosopher', it was a foregone conclusion that they would speak about the Christian as the 'true philosopher',[1] and Christianity as the 'true philosophy', by contrast with which Greek philosophy was 'false philosophy' and a mere shadow and debased mimicry of Christian truth.

In his orations Gregory typically assumes a scornful attitude towards Greek philosophy. In his first theological oration, for example, he exhorts the Eunomians to divert their passion for disputation to refuting the errors of the Greeks, instead of rending the fabric of Christian theology:

You may find many other honourable subjects for discussion. To these turn this disease of yours with some advantage. Attack the silence of Pythagoras and the Orphic beans and the novel brag about 'the Master said'.[2] Attack the Ideas of Plato and the transmigrations and courses of our souls and the reminiscences and the unlovely loves of the soul for lovely bodies. Attack the atheism of Epicurus and his atoms, and his unphilosophic pleasure; or Aristotle's petty Providence, and his artful system and his discourses about the mortality of the soul, and the humanism of his doctrine. Attack the superciliousness of the Stoa or the greed and vulgarity of the Cynic. Attack the 'Void and the Full' (what nonsense!), and all the details about the gods and the sacrifices and the idols and demons, whether beneficent

---

[1] This designation is first found in Justin Martyr, *Dial.* 8.
[2] The disciples of Pythagoras kept a five-year silence during their novitiate, and abstained from beans because they were the receptacle of souls during their transmigrations. When asked for the source of their doctrines, they would reply, 'the Master said' (αὐτὸς ἔφα).

or malignant, and all the tricks that people play with divinations, evoking of gods or of souls, and the power of the stars.[1]

The same style of polemic occurs in various other orations, for example in *Oration 32*, where Greek philosophy is put down as mere useless disputation, to be compared with the plagues of Egypt.[2] When Gregory does compare Christianity to Greek philosophy, it is usually to the disadvantage of the latter, or at least to show that what truth Greek philosophy does have was largely vitiated by its error. In his oration on Basil, for example, Gregory describes him as the true Cynic philosopher, with his single coat and well-worn cloak, with all the virtues of disdain for the conventions of the world and its material goods, but unsullied by the arrogance and ostentation of the pagan Cynic:

> Such being his mind and such his life, he had no need of an altar and of vainglory, nor of such a public announcement as 'Crates sets Crates the Theban free'. For his aim was ever to be, not to seem, most excellent. Nor did he dwell in a tub and in the midst of the market-place and so by luxuriating in publicity turn his poverty to riches; but was poor and unkempt, yet without ostentation, and taking cheerfully the casting overboard of all that he ever had, sailed lightly over the sea of life.[3]

In the same manner, Gregory quotes Plato for the teaching of the ineffability of the divine nature, but immediately goes on to show that this was a mere cloak for pride in Plato's case, whereby he would make himself appear the wiser for knowing what is beyond the reach of ordinary minds:

> It is difficult to conceive God but to define Him in words is an impossibility, as one of the Greek teachers of divinity taught, not unskilfully, as it appears to me; with the intention that he might be thought to have apprehended Him, in that he says it is a hard thing to do, and yet may escape being convicted of ignorance because of the impossibility of giving expression to the apprehension.[4]

Only a student of Greek rhetoric could pack so many devious motivations into a single sentence!

Only occasionally does Gregory cite Greek philosophy in a positive way without some disapproving qualification. In

---

[1] *Or.* 27. 8: *P.G.* 36. 19 c.

[2] *Or.* 32. 25: *P.G.* 36. 201 c. See also *Or.* 4. 43 and 73 and *Or.* 14. 28: *P.G.* 35. 895 c.

[3] *Or.* 43. 60: *P.G.* 36. 576 A.   [4] *Or.* 28. 4: *P.G.* 36. 29 c.

Oration 43, for example, he refers to the doctrine that every virtue has its corresponding vice, only a hairs-breadth away. 'For indeed this philosophic axiom is excellent which says that the vices are settled close to the virtues and are, in some sense, their next door neighbours.'[1] In another case Gregory compares his own contempt for worldly conventions and goods to that of the laughing philosopher Democritus, coupling the reference with another from Scripture:

That which is pleasant to others causes pain to me, and I am pleased by what is painful to others. So that I should not be surprised if I were even imprisoned as a disagreeable man, and thought by most men to be out of my senses, as is said to have been the case with one of the Greek philosophers, whose temperance exposed him to the charge of madness, because he laughed at everything, since he saw that the objects of the eager pursuit of the majority were ridiculous. Or even to be thought full of new wine, as were in later days the disciples of Christ. . . .[2]

Perhaps the most interesting assimilation of Christianity and Cynic philosophy occurs in *Oration* 25. This oration on Hero, spoken in praise of the Cynic philosopher Maximus, shows the striking analogies which existed between the wandering Christian monk and his pagan Cynic counterpart. In this oration Gregory consciously praises Maximus, who in every way assumed the garb and manner of the Cynic philosopher, as the 'true Cynic'. Here we see that Christian monasticism is not only 'true philosophy', but the Christian monk is also the 'true Cynic', the true wandering ascetic, contemptuous of conventions, scorning worldly goods, exercising his precious 'free speech' (*parrhēsia*) without regard for the power and privileges of the world. Referring to Maximus' Cynic cloak and staff, Gregory ingeniously assimilates this garb to the white robes of the angels:

. . . best and most perfect of philosophers . . . one who follows our Faith in an alien garb, nay, perhaps not in an alien garb, if the wearing of bright and shining robes is the mark of angels, as it is so depicted. . . . This man is a Cynic, not through shamelessness, but through freedom of speech, not through gluttony, but through the simplicity of

---

[1] *Or*. 43. 64: *P.G.* 36. 581 B (see notes in Migne version for the source of this reference).
[2] *Or*. 42. 22: *P.G.* 36. 484 C. The Biblical reference is to Acts 2. 4.

his daily life . . . a Dog who greets virtue not with barking but with hearkening,[1] who fawns on what is friendly because it is good, who snarls at what is alien because it is bad.[2]

Gregory reconciles Maximus' obvious profession of Cynicism with this transmutation into the type of the true Christian monk, but suggests that Maximus donned the Cynic robe and beard precisely to rebuke the insolence of pagan philosophy. Maximus, as the Christian and the true philosopher, refutes the false philosophy of the pagans by showing them up on their own ground, by showing them how they should live if they really understand the meaning of the philosophy which they possess in mere caricature:

... with the habit and exterior of the philosophers, he gives himself to follow the truth and raise himself by the sublimity of our [Christian] maxims. He scorns the schools of the Peripatetics, the Academy, the Porch, the atoms and the voluptuousness of the Epicurean. He detests the impiety of the Cynic and the scorn which they have for the Divine, but he adopts their frugality, like the dog who barks against the real dogs.[3]

By such turns and plays on words Gregory manages to claim for Christianity the whole substance of Greek philosophy, while relegating to these philosophers themselves only the empty shell and the outward gesture of that which the Christian alone can understand and exemplify.

This may be said to be Gregory's basic attitude towards Greek philosophy. Even in some of his more favourable statements about it, we find the same standard of thought applied. In one interesting letter to Philagrius, his friend and companion in intellectual pursuits, Gregory analyses the worth of the various Greek philosophers. In their orations the Fathers often took a more polemical line towards things pagan than in their letters. The orations, after all, were delivered in church, and thus represented more of the 'official' attitude on these subjects, while in the letters Gregory, Basil, and other Christian Fathers often reveal more genial attitudes towards classical studies in accordance with their own obvious interest in and pursuit of

---

[1] οὐδὲ τὴν ὑλακήν, ἀλλὰ τὴν φυλακήν . . . , one of Gregory's more unfortunate puns.

[2] *Or.* 25. 2: *P.G.* 35. 1200 A, B.   [3] *Or.* 25. 6: *P.G.* 35. 1205 A.

these subjects. In this letter Gregory shows extensive knowledge of the Greek philosophic tradition, and it is apparent that he has first-hand acquaintance with the philosophers to whom he refers:

Now as a man like yourself whose trained mind has traversed all knowledge, our own and pagan lore as well, who is learned in both fields and a trainer of others, has no doubt compounded from it all some palliative for human vicissitudes, may I, with your permission, enter the field of philosophy in your company? Aristotle, it seems to me is pusillanimous when he presumes to define happiness for us, though up to a point he is right. He asserts that it is 'The energy of the soul directed towards virtuous activity' and adds 'in a full life'— this qualification being very wise, in view of the fickle and mutable character of our nature. He continues with less dignity, and adds something quite unworthy, when he requires 'external well-being' as well; as if happiness were not within the competence of the man who happens to be poor or diseased, ill-born or in exile. On the other hand, I admire the manliness and magnanimity of the Stoics, who assert that external things cannot interfere with man's happiness and that the good man is happy even when burning in the bull of Phalaris.

Consequently I am, of course, an admirer of our own Christian heroes who have faced danger for some noble purpose, or endured misfortune manfully. But I am also an admirer of those pagans who resemble them, like that famous Anaxarchus, Epictetus, or Socrates, to mention only a few. Anaxarchus, when, at the tyrant's bidding, his hands were being crushed in the mortar, told the torturers that they might crush the 'sack which held Anaxarchus', meaning of course, our miserable covering of flesh. For him, the real Anaxarchus, the soul of the philosopher, could not be crushed. In the same way we Christians speak about the 'outer' and the 'inner' man.

Epictetus had a strained and twisted limb; but he went on being a philosopher as if his body were that of another man, and it seemed that the limb could have been shattered in pieces before he would give a sign of pain. Then Socrates, as you know, when condemned to death by the Athenians, for the period of his imprisonment, kept discoursing to his disciples about that other prison, as it were, of the body; and he refused to escape though he might have done so. And when the hemlock was brought to him, he received it very readily, just as if it were a loving-cup rather than a draught of death. I should have mentioned our own Job in company with these men. . . .[1]

---

[1] *Ep.* 32: *P.G.* 37. 69 c ff.

These are the words of a student and lover of the Greek philosophical tradition, the words of a man who even in old age continues to peruse the works of the classical masters, and yet we would be wrong if we were to suppose that Gregory either acknowledges or is aware of any dependence of Christianity on these traditions. On the contrary, his confidence on the subject, as he discourses in the quiet of his study, derives from his perfectly assured assumption that Christianity is the archetype and true form of this ascetic philosophic life which he praises, and if the Greeks may be found to show some of the same characteristics, then they may be commended for being 'not far from our philosophy'.

Conclusion

Thus Christianity, in the persons of men like Gregory of Nazianzus, both appropriated and renewed the traditional conflict between philosophy and rhetoric. On the one hand, the philosophic tradition that was most relevant to this conflict was so naturalized into Christianity that it could be confidently identified with the Christian tradition itself. On the other hand, Christianity inherited philosophy's traditional ambivalence towards rhetoric, both appropriating its tools and polemicizing against its moral premises.

In the last analysis, the answer of the Christian 'philosopher' to the problem of rhetoric and literary culture in general was strikingly similar to that of Plato. Both advocated plucking literature from its native value system and transferring it to the value system of philosophy. Both would envisage a *paideia* in which literature, 'purged' of its indecency, could be used to buttress morality and introduce the student to the higher life. This position, as long as it is stated in vague and hortatory terms, appears exemplary. But as soon as the philosopher or the Christian tries to translate this theory into specific, practical terms, he immediately becomes involved in censorship. It is perhaps not accidental that Plato, in attempting to state his concept of the philosophic *polis* in practical terms in the *Laws*, produced a world which is rather too close to that of the inquisition and the *index expurgatorius* for comfort. A true integration of philosophy and culture which neither turns philosophy into rhetoric nor turns literature into sterile piety is a problem which neither Greek nor Christian can be said to have satisfactorily solved. In so far as it is solved at all, it is solved best on the personal, existential level, as was the case with Gregory of Nazianzus. That is, it is solved best, not by absolute criteria and formulas about the relationship between the two, but rather by the individual experience of relating the two, out of which a rich and genuinely viable synthesis arises for a specific individual.

APPENDIX I

References and Allusions to Classical Literature in Gregory of Nazianzus' Letters and Orations[1]

Poets

Homer: 35. 597 A; 35. 641 B; 36. 61 A; 36. 152 A; 36. 497 C; 36. 517 D; 36. 525 B; 37. 25 B; 37. 28 C; 37. 44 C; 37. 65 C; 37. 108 C; 37. 136 A, B; 35. 716 A, B; 35. 916 C; 35. 925 A; 35. 931 B; 37. 264 A; 37. 276 B; 37. 283 B; 37. 309 A; 37. 312 B; 37. 373 A; 37. 384 A; 37. 542; 37. 568; 36. 520 A.
Hesiod: 35. 993 A.
Theognis: 37. 45 B.
Anacreon: 37. 384 D.
Pindar: 35. 636 B; 35. 1016 C; 36. 521 B; 37. 36 B; 37. 37 A; 37. 40 A; 37. 211 B; 37. 284 A; 37. 337 B.
Aeschylus: 37. 64 B (*Prometheus* 5. 449).
Euripides: 35. 673 C (*Orestes*); 35. 715 C (*Orestes*); 36. 337 C (*Iph. in Tauris*); 37. 41 B (*Phoen.*); 37. 48 C (*Orestes*); 37. 336 A (*Phoen.*).
Aristophanes: 35. 408 B.
Callimachus: 37. 377 D.
Theocritus: 35. 408 B.

Orators and Prose Writers

Herodotus: 36. 553 D; 37. 32 A.
Hippocrates: 35. 436 B.
Lysias: 37. 296 A.
Demosthenes: 35. 557 C; 35. 953 B; 37. 312 A.
Dionysius of Halicarnassus: 37. 296 A.

Philosophers

Pythagoras of Samos: 37. 324 C.
Heraclitus: 35. 597 A.
Zeno of Elea: 35. 596 B.
Anaxagoras: 35. 597 A; 36. 521 C.
Empedocles: 35. 581 B; 38. 46 A.
Socrates: 37. 72 A.
Antisthenes: 35. 596 B; 35. 1208 B.

[1] This list is by no means definitive, but contains the references by names, direct quotations, and the clear allusions, most of which are noted in the footnotes in the Migne text. Philological analysis would reveal many more verbal allusions, but this list gives an idea of the general scope of Gregory's use of classical literature.

Plato: 35. 396 A (*Ti.*); 35. 568 B; 35. 649 B; 35. 1205 B (*Resp.* 2nd book);
36. 24 B; 36. 29 C (*Ti.* 28 E); 36. 40 B (*Ti.* 10); 36. 69 A; 36. 76 C; 36.
128 A (*Cra.* 397C); 36. 189 C (*Ti.*); 37. 60 B (*Resp.* 5. 473 D); 37. 68 C (*Phd.*
67 C); 37. 68 C (*Cra.*); 37. 140 C (*Phd.* 81 A); 37. 292 A.
Aristotle: 35. 597 A; 36. 24 C; 36. 36 A; 36. 581 B; 37. 69 C (*Eth. Nic.* 2); 37.
377 A.
Anaxarchus of Abdera: 35. 592 A; 37. 72 A.
Xenocrates: 35. 596 A.
Diogenes the Cynic: 35. 396 A; 36. 573 C; 37. 69 B; 37. 171 A.
Epicurus: 35. 568 B; 35. 596 A; 36. 24 B; 36. 36 A.
Crates the Cynic: 35. 596 A; 35. 1208 B; 36. 573 D–6 A.
Aristaeus the Cyrenaic: 38. 47 A.
Empedotimus the Pythagorean: 38. 47 A.
Pyrrho of Elis: 35. 1096 A.
Cleanthes: 35. 592 A.
Chrysippus: 35. 1205 B.
Epictetus: 35. 592 A; 37. 72 A.
Sextus Empiricus: 35. 1096 A.
Pythagoreans: 35. 592 B; 35. 1205 A; 36. 24 B; 36. 492 C.
Cynics: 35. 1205 B; 36. 24 B.
Stoics: 35. 1205 A; 36. 24 B; 37. 72 A.
Peripatetics, Academics, Epicureans: 35. 1205 A.

APPENDIX II

Chronology of the Writings of Gregory of Nazianzus[1]

Orations

1. On Easter and on his Delay. 362, Easter.
2. Apology for his Flight. 362, shortly after Easter.
3. To Those who had Invited Him and not come to Receive Him. 362, shortly after Easter.
15. In Praise of the Maccabees. 362.
4–5. Invectives Against Julian. End of 363 or in 364.
6. On Peace I. 364.
14. On Love of the Poor. *c.* 365.
7. Funeral Oration on his Brother, Caesarius. End of 368 or beginning of 369.
8. Funeral Oration on his Sister, Gorgonia. Shortly after the preceding oration.
10. On Himself, after his Return from Flight. Before Easter and before his ordination, 372.
9. Apology to his Father. 372, before Easter, but after his ordination.
11. To Gregory of Nyssa. 372, shortly after *Oration* 9.
12. To His Father, when he had entrusted to him the Church at Nazianzus. 372, shortly after *Oration* 11.
16. On His Father's Silence, because of the Plague of Hail. 372, during the autumn.
13. On the Consecration of Eulalius. 372.
17. To the Citizens of Nazianzus. 373 or beginning of 374.
18. On the Death of his Father. Spring 374.
19. To Julian, Tribune of the Treasury. Advent 374.

Orations Preached in Constantinople

22. On Peace II. Summer 379.
32. On Moderation in Disputes. Summer 379.
33. Against the Arians and on Himself. Summer 379.

[1] Adapted from P. Gallay's chronology, which follows the dating established in his book, *La Vie de S. Grégoire de Nazianze* (Paris, 1943) 252–3.

21. On the Great Athanasius. 2 May 379.
25. On Hero. During 379.
41. On Pentecost. 9 June 379.
34. On the Arrival of the Egyptians. 2 or 4 Oct. 379.
38. Theophany. 25 Dec. 379.
39. On the Holy Lights. 6 Jan. 380.
40. On Holy Baptism. 7 Jan. 380.
26. On Himself. 380, between 28 Feb. and 14 July.
24. In Praise of Cyprian. Same time as *Oration* 26.
23. On Peace III. Same time as *Oration* 26.
27–31. Five Theological Orations. Summer or autumn 380.
20. On the Dogma and Institution of the Bishops. Late summer or autumn, after *Orations* 27–31.
36. On the Martyrs and Against the Arians. Shortly after 27 Nov. 380.
37. On Matthew 19. 1. End of 380 or beginning of 381, but before 10 Jan.
42. Last Farewell. June or July 381, but before 9 July.

Orations Preached After Final Return to Cappadocia

43. In Praise of Basil. August or September, 381, in Caesarea.
45. Easter II. 9 April 383.
44. The New Lord. 1st Sunday before Easter 383, perhaps 16 April.

Letters

1–2. 361	50. 372	93–94. 382
3. 359	51–55. 384–90	95. 2nd half 381
4–6. 361	57. 372–5	96. 382
7–8. 362	58–60. 372–3	98. 381–3
9. 362/363	61. 372–5	100. 2nd half 381
10. 363	62. 373/374	101. summer 382
11. 362–72	63–66. 374	102. 386
12–19. 365	67–69. 374–5	103–6. 382
20. end 368	70–71. 375?	107–19. 384–90
21–24. 369	72–74. 375	120. *c.* Easter 383
25–27. 370–3	75. 378?	125–6. after 3 Sept. 383
29–30. end 369	76. early 379	131–8. 382
37–39. *c.* 369	77–78. after Easter 379	139–51. 383
40. *c.* June 370	79. 379	152. end 383
41–43. June–Sept. 370	80. 1st half 380	153–7. end 383
44. Sept. 370	81–86. 380	162–3. 383
45–46. after Sept. 370	87–88. mid 381	164–7. 383/384
47. 371/372	89–90. 2nd half 381	168–70. 383
48–49. *c.* Easter 372	91–92. end 382	171. end 382

172. Easter 383	193–4. 384/385	227. end 382?
173. end 383	195–201. 384–90	231. 384–90.
174–80. 384–90	202. 387	233–5. 384–90
181. 383	203–11. 384–90	239–42. 384–90
182–5. end 383	213–23. 384–90	
186–92. 384–90	225–6. 384–90	

Some letters cannot be dated, even approximately, and have been omitted from this list: i.e. 28, 31–36, 56, 97, 99, 121–4, 127–30, 158–61, 212, 224, 228–30, 232, 236–8.

Selected Poetry

Poemata de Seipso II, i. 11 (*Carmen de vita sua*). early 382.

Poemata de Seipso II, i. 12–72. 382–90.

Poemata quae spectant ad Alios II, ii. 4–7. 384–90.

BIBLIOGRAPHY

Modern Works on Gregory of Nazianzus

ALTANER, B., *Patrology*, Graef, H. trans. New York, 1960, 345–50.

BENOÎT, A., *S. Grégoire de Nazianze, sa vie, ses œuvres, et son époque*. 2nd ed. Paris, 1885, 2 vols.

CONROTTE, E. J., 'Isocrate et S. Grégoire de Nazianze; le Panégyrique d'Évagoras et l'éloge funèbre de S. Basile', *Musée Belge* (1897) 236–40.

DEVOS, P., 'S. Grégoire de Nazianze et Hellade de Césarée en Cappadoce', *Analecta Bollandiana* 79 (1961), 91–101.

FLEURY, E., *S. Grégoire de Nazianze et son temps*. Paris, 1930.

FREELAND, J., 'St. Gregory Nazianzen from his Letters', *Dublin Review* 13 (1902), 333–54.

GALLAY, P., *Langue et style de S. Grégoire de Nazianze dans sa correspondance*. Paris, 1943.

—— *La Vie de S. Grégoire de Nazianze*. Lyon, 1943.

—— *Les Manuscrits des lettres de S. Grégoire de Nazianze*. Paris, 1957.

GIET, S., 'Sasimes; Une méprise de S. Basile?' Thèse: Paris, 1941.

GRENIER, A., *La Vie et les poésies de S. Grégoire de Nazianze*. Clermont–Ferrand, 1858.

GUIGNET, M., *Les Procédés épistolaires de S. Grégoire de Nazianze comparés à ceux de ses contemporains*. Paris, 1911.

—— *S. Grégoire de Nazianze et la rhétorique*. Paris, 1911.

HAUSER-MEURY, Marie-Madeleine, *Prosopographie zu den Schriften Gregors von Nazianzen*. Bonn, 1960.

HENRY, ROSE DE LIMA, *The Late Greek Optative and its Use in the Writings of Gregory Nazianzen*. Washington, 1943.

KEENAN, M. E., 'St. Gregory of Nazianzus and Early Greek Medicine', *Bulletin of the History of Medicine* 9 (1941), 8–30.

LECLERCQ, H., 'Grégoire de Nazianze', *D.A.L.* 6 (1925), 1667–711; 'Nazianze', *D.A.L.* 12 (1935), 1054–65.

LEFHERZ, F., *Studien zu Gregor von Nazianz: Mythologie, Überlieferung, Scholiasten*. Bonn, 1958.

LERCHER, J., *Die Persönlichkeit des heiliges Gregorius von Nazianz und seine Stellung zur klassischen Bildung*. Diss. Innsbruck, 1949.

MEEHAN, D., 'Editions of St. Gregory of Nazianzus', *I.T.Q.* 3 (1951), 203–19.

MISCH, G., *A History of Autobiography in Antiquity*. London, 1950, vol. 2, 600–24.

MONTANT, L., *Revue critique de quelques questions historiques se rapportants à S. Grégoire de Nazianze et à son siècle. J.T.S.* 28 (1927), 411–15.

PINAULT, H., 'Le Platonisme de S. Grégoire de Nazianze: Essai sur les relations du Christianisme et de l'Hellénisme dans son œuvre théologique.' Thèse: la Roche-sur-Yon, 1925.

PLAGNIEUX, J., *S. Grégoire de Nazianze Théologien: Études de science religieuse*. Paris, 1952.

QUASTEN, J., *Patrology*. Westminster, 1960, vol. 3, 236–54.

RIEPL, R., 'Des Heiligen Gregor von Nazianz Urteil über die klassischen Studien und seine Berechtigung dazu', *Progr. d. Obergymn.* 4. Linz, 1859.

RUGE, W., 'Nazianzos', *P.W.K.* 16 (1935), 2099–101.

STRUNK, O., *Gregory of Nazianzus and the Proper Hymns for Easter: Late Classical and Medieval Studies in Honor of A. M. Friend*, ed. K. Weitzmann, Princeton, 1955, 82–7.

ULLMANN, C., *Gregorius von Nazianz der Theologe: Ein Beitrag zur Kirchen- und Dogmengeschichte des vierten Jahrhunderts*. 2nd ed. Gotha, 1867, trans. C. V. Cox, 1851.

WAGNER, M., *Rufinus the Translator: A Study of his Theory and Practice as Illustrated by his Version of the Apologetica of St. Gregory of Nazianzus*. Washington, 1945.

WEISS, M., *Die grossen Kappadozier: Basilius, Gregor von Nazianz und Gregor von Nyssa als Exegeten*. Braunsberg, 1872.

INDEX

INDEX

Breinigsville, PA USA
27 January 2010
231480BV00004B/4/P